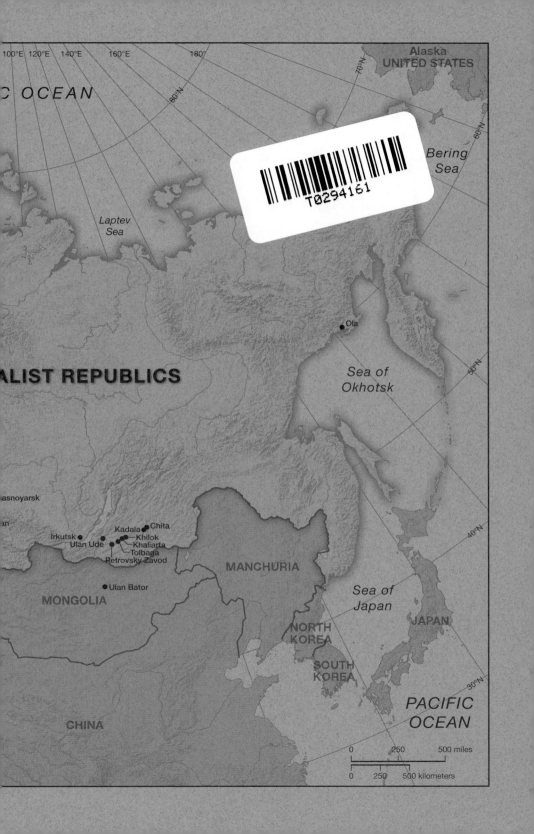

Women of the Gulag

Women of the Gulag

Portraits of Five Remarkable Lives

Paul R. Gregory

HOOVER INSTITUTION PRESS
Stanford University . Stanford, California

www.hoover.org

Hoover Institution Press Publication No. 631

Hoover Institution at Leland Stanford Junior University,
Stanford, California 94305-6010

First printing 2013
19 18 17 16 15   7 6 5 4 3 2

Manufactured in the United States of America

The paper used in this publication meets the minimum Requirements of the American National Standard for Information Sciences—Permanence of Paper for Printed Library Materials, ANSI/NISO Z39.48-1992.♾

Library of Congress Cataloging-in-Publication Data
Gregory, Paul R., author.
   Women of the Gulag / Paul R. Gregory.
      pages cm. — (Hoover Institution Press Publication ; No. 631)
   Includes bibliographical references and index.
   ISBN 978-0-8179-1574-2 (cloth : alk. paper) —
   ISBN 978-0-8179-1576-6 (ebook)
   1. Women political prisoners—Soviet Union—Biography. 2. Gulag NKVD. 3. Political persecution—Soviet Union. 4. Concentration camps—Soviet Union. 5. Prisons—Soviet Union. 6. Forced labor—Soviet Union. 7. Soviet Union—History—1925-1953. I. Title. II. Series: Hoover Institution Press publication ; 631.
DK268.A1G724 2013
365'.45092520947—dc23   2012045817

Contents

Preface

Women of the Gulag is my third book on political repression under Soviet socialism. My first, *Terror by Quota: State Security from Lenin to Stalin* (Yale University Press, 2009), analyzed how Lenin, Stalin, and their successors used the political police in a systematic way to repress the citizenry. But the faces of the victims became lost in the horrendous statistics and the incredible numbers of human tragedies. My second book was *Politics, Murder, and Love in Stalin's Kremlin: The Story of Nikolai Bukharin and Anna Larina* (Hoover Institution Press, 2010). In it, I used Stalin's most prominent victims—Bukharin and his wife, Anna—to give human faces to his top political rivals.

Women of the Gulag is based on an often overlooked point: most of Stalin's victims were quite ordinary people. Only a tiny percentage belonged to the political elite, like Bukharin. *Women of the Gulag* tells the stories of ordinary women and reveals how adversity can make ordinary people do extraordinary things.

To truly understand Stalin's terror and its impact on Russian society and history, we must see the faces of the victims up close. We must follow a peasant girl growing up while confined to a "special settlement" tucked away in the remote Urals. We must observe the life of an engineer's wife and family in Eastern Siberia as ordinary rail accidents somehow become acts of sabotage. We must sit with the teenage sister-in-law of a high party official in a Sukhumi mansion as the secret police close in on family and friends.

Not all the stories of *Women of the Gulag* are of ordinary women and their families coping with tragedy. Under Stalin, the dividing line between victim and executioner was razor-thin. More than a third of the leading executioners were executed themselves. We see repressors turned into the repressed as we visit the luxurious villas, dinner parties, literary salons, and vacation resorts of the wives of Stalin's executioners, and we see their horror as they grow increasingly aware that they are about to cross that line.

Women of the Gulag tells the stories of five women and their families. By "Gulag" I mean more than the barbed wire, camps, and prisons which the term usually conjures up. Instead, the Gulag refers to a state of mind—to the knowledge that anyone and everyone could be shot, jailed, or exiled as the victim of mass insanity and hysteria originating from somewhere above. In this topsy-turvy world, a wrong word or association becomes a crime against the state punishable by the "highest measure of social defense," execution. Neighbors and friends are potential informants. A false move at work becomes deliberate sabotage. The camp system into which "enemies of the people" poured was simply the end stage of the world of the Gulag, reserved for enemies who escaped the anonymous execution pits.

The opening of the Soviet archives in the 1990s made possible a new scholarly literature that is completing our understanding of the Gulag. This literature instructs us on the size and scope of the Gulag, as in Oleg Khlevniuk's *The History of the Gulag: From Collectivization to the Great Terror* (Yale University Press, 2004) and Anne Applebaum's *Gulag: A History* (Doubleday, 2003). Its human costs are explored by Norman Naimark in *Stalin's Genocides* (Princeton University Press, 2011) and its use as an economic institution is the subject of essays in *The Economics of Forced Labor* (Hoover Institution Press, 2003), which I edited with Valery Lazarev. Jörg Baberowski describes how Stalin and his henchmen used political repression to serve their ends in *Verbrannte Erde: Stalins Herrschaft der Gewalt*

(C. H. Beck, 2012) while Stephen Cohen delves into the impact on civilian society in *The Victims Return: Survivors of the Gulag After Stalin* (PublishingWorks, 2010).

I use these archives to visit Stalin's office, apartment, and dacha as he and his henchmen set terror in motion. We watch as they sit and draft decrees in the antiseptic bureaucratic language, such as "first category enemies of the people," that condemns hundreds of thousands to prison or death. We use the archives to follow these Kremlin orders as they filter down to Stalin's loyal executioners, among them the husbands of two of our women of the Gulag.

How political repression struck these unsuspecting women and their families can only be captured by first-hand accounts. Tragic experiences motivate those affected to write memoirs. During the Soviet period, these personalized accounts were hidden away or strictly confined to the family. Then organizations like Memorial and the Sakharov Museum rose up as valiant representatives of victims of political repression and as repositories of their memories. Their shelves and digital archives contain thousands of memoirs, taped interviews, and photographs. Many determined memoirists self-published their works; other memoirs are available in handwritten notebooks or crudely typed pages. Increasingly, victim accounts are being digitized by dedicated human rights advocates. They range from works of high literary value to a few paragraphs scribbled by an irate son or daughter seeking justice. These writers are united by the conviction that their stories must be told, even to a troubled society that prefers to put this shameful historical episode behind it.

Women of the Gulag joins a growing body of literature that personalizes the Gulag experience. Some authors have used diaries and family records to paint a picture of Soviet life during the worst years of Stalin's reign. Examples include: Veronique Garros, Natalia Korenevskaya, and Thomas Lahusen, *Intimacy and Terror: Soviet Diaries of the 1930's* (The New Press, 1995); Jochen Hellbeck, *Revolution On My Mind: Writing a Diary Under Stalin* (Harvard University Press, 2006); Karl Schlögel, *Moscow, 1937* (Polity Press, 2012); Anne

Applebaum, *Gulag Voices: An Anthology* (Yale University Press, 2011); and Orlando Figes, *The Whisperers: Private Life in Stalin's Russia* (Metropolitan Books, 2007).

My account distinguishes itself in four regards. First, I limit myself to only five stories so that we can become intimately acquainted with these women as their tragedies unfold. Their trials and tribulations become shared experiences. Second, I include the wives of two villains, half innocent, half guilty, as they come to grips with their Faustian bargains. They know their husbands are murderers, but they enjoy the benefits and privileges their spouses' macabre profession bestows on them. Third, I interweave decisions taken at the highest levels with the stories of those suffering the consequences. As the Kremlin and the regions bargain for execution quotas, I tell the stories of the wives and families of those who become statistics counted toward fulfillment of the quotas. Fourth, this is a story about women.

Most belles-lettres on the Gulag, starting with the classic accounts of Alexander Solzhenitsyn and Varlam Shalamov, explore primarily the travails of the men. Women are natural subjects because only in the rarest of cases did male victims of Stalinist repression outlive the Soviet system to tell their stories truthfully. Able-bodied male Gulag inmates were sent off to fight in suicidal labor battalions and expired at the front in World War II or did not live long after their release. Of the Stalin generation, women had a ten-year-longer life expectancy than men.

Second, women were often repressed, not for anything they had done or were supposed to have done, but for the supposed sins of their husbands. Once in the Gulag, they were subjected to particular kinds of sexual enslavement and violence that the men did not have to endure. However, women's experiences as forced laborers—brutal hours, harsh cold, poor shelter, insufficient nourishment—were very much like the men's. The Gulag was an equal-opportunity institution.

Third, the dynamics of women's survival, family ties, and transition to "normal" life were unlike those of the men. Women returned to estranged sons and daughters raised in state orphanages, by foster parents, or—in fortunate cases—by relatives. Their children, who had been taught to regard their parents as enemies, had suffered discrimination and hardship as children of enemies of the people. The women's return usually came after a decade or so of absence. They returned, to the embarrassment of their daughters, as hardened and rough women bearing little resemblance to the Mamas those daughters remembered.

As I wrote these intimate accounts of these five women, I began to feel a personal kinship with them. My curiosity piqued, Natalia Reshetova and I began a detective search to see if they or their children were still alive. We knew this was unlikely given that these events occurred in the mid- to late 1930s. To our amazement, two of my primary characters are still alive, albeit in poor health and of extremely advanced age. They still live in the same locations where the action takes place. Two adult children, old enough to bear witness to their mothers' repression, were found.

You can imagine my excitement and emotion when, after many attempts, I spoke by telephone with the now eighty-six-year-old woman whose condemned father entrusted her younger sisters to her care at the age of eleven and a half, as he spoke to her through a cellar window from his prison in a Urals town in 1938.

Armed with this information, I teamed up with Marianna Yarovskaya, a talented young Russian filmmaker trained in Hollywood, to tell the story of *Women of the Gulag* as a documentary film. As I write these words, Marianna is in Russia filming what will become a feature-length documentary. We are working with a sense of urgency. The story must be told before it is too late.

These contacts with our subjects and their children, nieces, nephews, and even great-grandchildren provided valuable new information for this book. Through telephone conversations, e-mails, and filmed interviews, we were able to fill in a number of missing elements in our stories. We wish to thank Adile Abbas-ogly, Fekla Andreeva, and their family members who generously assisted us in our efforts. We wish particularly to thank Leila (now

living in Sukhumi), daughter of Adile; Ekaterina (Katya) Karpova
(Kamensk-Uralsky) and Klavdia Poderina (Ekaterinburg), sisters
of Fekla; Olga Ignatkina and Natalia Belova (Saint Petersburg),
daughter and granddaughter of Maria Ignatkina; Yury Dorfman
(Chita), great-grandson of Maria Ignatkina; Agnessa (Agulya)
Korovicheva (Saint Petersburg), adopted daughter of Agnessa
Mironova-Korol; Professor Josef Feigenberg (Jerusalem), nephew of
Evgenia Ezhova; Alexander Taraday (Kharkov), great-great-nephew
of Evgenia Ezhova; and Memed Dzhikhashvili, Sariya Lakoba's
nephew (Batumi).

Women of the Gulag does not require any special knowledge of
Russian history. I have limited the number of names and places, and
I identify recurring characters with memorable nicknames wherever
possible. We transliterate Russian names and places with a simplified
system that will not satisfy purists, but we use standard translitera-
tion in the list of Sources for specialists.

I wish to thank the Hoover Institution of Stanford University
and its director, John Raisian, for supporting this project and for
fostering its magnificent Hoover Institution Library and Archives.
I used a number of its collections for the chapters that take place in
the Kremlin and in district offices of the political police. I wish to
thank the many professionals of the library and archives for their
assistance, especially Linda Bernard, Carol Leadenham, and Lora
Soroka, without whom this work would not have been possible.
I benefited from the wisdom and advice of colleagues at Stanford and the Hoover Institution, such as Stanford historians Amir
Weiner and Norman Naimark and Hoover Fellow and Oxford his-
torian Robert Service. My unsung heroes are the many lay readers
who volunteered to read earlier versions of the book. Although I
received enthusiastic encouragement from them, they also pointed
out where I was striking false notes. For this valuable service, I am
indebted to them.

This book also would not have been possible without the excep-
tional and dedicated assistance of Dr. Natalia Reshetova, who uncovered, organized, and remembered so many of the details that capture

the sights, sounds, and smells of Russia of the 1930s. Natalia spent many late nights tracking down our *Women of the Gulag* survivors.

A final debt of gratitude goes to Jeff Jones, Jennifer Presley, and Barbara Arellano of the Hoover Institution Press. As usual, Jennifer Navarrette designed the compelling cover, which captures the essence of this book. Barbara Egbert navigated the manuscript with insight and skill through the editorial process, from which it emerged much improved.

CHAPTER ONE

Terror's Human Face

A remark often attributed to Stalin is, "A single death is a tragedy, a million deaths is a statistic."

This is the story of five such tragedies. They are stories about women because, as in so many cases, it was the wives and daughters who survived to tell what happened.

These five women put a human face on the terror of Stalin's purges and the Gulag in the Soviet Union of the 1930s. They show how the impersonal orders emanating from the Kremlin office of "the Master" brought tragedy to their lives. They cover the gamut of victims. Two are wives and daughters in ordinary families unable to comprehend why such misfortune has overtaken them. A third is a young bride living in the household of a high party official. The last two are wives of the Master's executioners. These stories are based on their memoirs—some written by themselves, others by close friends or by their children.

Together, they put a human face on what author Robert Conquest termed *The Great Terror*.

AGNESSA

Agnessa Argipopulo was born in 1903 in the small town of Maikop, in far southern Russia, near the Black Sea port city of Novorossiysk. She and her older sister, Lena, exemplified the mixed heritage of the people of the Russian "South": a blend of Greek, Russian, and Mongol blood which made them the acknowledged beauties of Maikop. The Red and White armies traded control of the town during the Russian Revolution. While the sisters were both still in their teens, Lena married a White Guard officer . . . Agnessa a Red. But Agnessa's fate was settled when she left her first husband for a rising star in the NKVD, the Soviet secret police force that carried out Stalin's purges in the 1930s.

MARIA

Maria Senotrusova was born in 1904 in the isolated village of Tolbaga, in Eastern Siberia. This former czarist dumping ground for exiles and revolutionaries was opening up to the world thanks to the Trans-Siberian Railway. When a spur line was built to nearby coal deposits, Maria joined the local work force and met her future husband, the engineer in charge of the work. They married and raised three children in a hard-working, well-educated family that exemplified everything the USSR wanted and needed in the New Soviet People who would build the socialist paradise. But Stalin's purge destroyed their lives as it did the lives of hundreds of thousands of other innocents.

EVGENIA

Evgenia Feigenberg, born in 1904, had no intention of remaining in her hometown of Gomel, Belorussia, close to Poland and Ukraine but far from the European capitals where she was sure she belonged. Nor did she intend to follow the normal life course for the daughter of a rabbi: an early marriage and many children. Her first marriage took her to Odessa. She left her husband for a better catch, who took her to Moscow and to the Soviet Embassy in London. But it was her third partner who took her with him as he climbed ruthlessly to the highest levels of Soviet power—only to doom them both to destruction when Stalin tired of his purges and looked for a scapegoat for the Great Terror.

ADILE

Adile Abbas-ogly, born in 1920, was only fifteen when she was literally swept away by a handsome older man who was a member of the Lakoba clan, the leading family in Sukhumi, in the Abkhazian portion of the Soviet Union. Adile's father was Persian, and her family, while Muslim, celebrated the Christian holidays. Her choice of a husband appeared inspired: his brother-in-law was Nestor Lakoba, the head of the powerful Lakoba clan and a close associate and personal friend of Stalin. Nestor had led the Bolshevik takeover of the region and appeared solidly in charge. But Lavrenty Beria, his rival for power, set out to destroy the Lakobas and everyone associated with them.

FEKLA

Fekla Andreeva was born in 1926 in Suvory Village in the Ural Mountains. Her pleasant childhood ended early in 1930 when Stalin ordered the "dekulakization" of the Soviet countryside. Her family's relative prosperity—they owned a small farm and some livestock and could afford to hire help to bring in the harvest each year—put them into a group which Stalin wanted "liquidated as a class." Stripped of all belongings, the family was eventually sent to a nearby settlement, where they and other kulaks built crude barracks and worked in mines and fields on starvation rations. Fekla and her sisters went to school where they strived to be good Soviet citizens and learned to revere Stalin. But far worse was yet to come at the hands of "the Master."

CHAPTER TWO

Stalin

Struggles and Successes

Who was this man of diminutive stature but outsized ambition who had clawed, bullied, and assassinated his way to the pinnacle of power in the new nation of the Union of Soviet Socialist Republics?

Joseph Stalin was born Iosif Vissarionovich Dzhugashvili in 1879 in the mountains of Georgia, in the Caucasus region of the Russian Empire. An early convert to the Bolshevik cause, he assumed the name Stalin, "man of steel." He took on a series of low-level leadership positions under Vladimir Lenin after the Russian Revolution, quietly finding ways to gain power. When Lenin, the "Old Man," died in 1924, few of the Old Guard expected Stalin to come out on top in the power struggle that followed. However, the man who would become "the Master" had a game plan and would do anything to win.

Lenin suffered a series of strokes beginning in May 1922 that eventually left him mute and bedridden. Until then, the Old Man had handled details like medical care, leaves abroad, and housing—for example, Lenin gave Stalin a bigger Kremlin apartment. After the Old Man's incapacitation, the Master made sure he decided such things. The others could not be bothered. Only Stalin realized the power it gave him.

As the Old Man's health deteriorated, Stalin chose his doctors and nurses and procured his medications. The Master's own wife, Nadezhda Allilueva, served at Lenin's sickbed in the Kremlin.

The most nerve-racking part of the power struggle was waiting for the Old Man to die. Lenin's crone of a wife, Nadezhda Krupskaya, kept issuing optimistic reports from the sanatorium outside Moscow. He'll return to work any day, she insisted. The Master knew that his political career would be over if Lenin regained his health. In his political testament, the Old Man had advised the party to fire Stalin. As general secretary, Stalin had accumulated too much power and had the audacity to insult the Old Man's wife. Fortunately, the vain Lenin was an even-handed critic with ample insults for the others. Only Lenin could do the job right, it seems.

The Old Man did not return. The Master shrugged off rumors that he poisoned Lenin, but he kept the idea to use against his rivals.

As soon as the Old Man had drawn his last breath on January 21, 1924, the Master sprang into action. He assumed control of the funeral arrangements. The others jockeyed to be at the front of the bier. The Master inconspicuously brought up the rear—an almost invisible pallbearer.

It helped that Stalin's colleagues underestimated him. As far as they were concerned, he sat at his desk and pushed papers. While they made speeches and argued, he quietly placed his people in key positions. His fellow Bolsheviks scarcely noticed that they turned to him for cars, amenities, and even envelopes of extra household cash. The Master supervised—and eavesdropped on—the special Kremlin phone lines.

Stalin dealt easily with his rivals for power. The posturing peacock Leon Trotsky waited in vain to be anointed as a reward for his civil-war heroics. The Master joined the naïve Nikolai Bukharin to get rid of Trotsky. Together they charged Trotsky with "splitting the party" in order to drive Trotsky and his allies into exile in Kazakhstan in 1928. Trotsky was expelled from the country in 1929 but kept up his polemics from abroad until his assassination in Mexico in 1940.

BUKHARIN, THE PARTY'S FAVORITE, proved just as easy to defeat. The Master's allies soon dominated the party's Central Committee.

They booed Bukharin as he spoke out against Stalin's programs in 1928. Feigning regret, the Master bowed to the party's demand that Bukharin be removed. As the Master liked to say in such situations, "Friendship is friendship but duty is duty."

When the Bolsheviks grabbed power in 1917, they ruled out capital punishment for themselves. They feared the bloodbath of the French revolution. Thus constrained, the Master could not yet kill his political rivals, but he could liquidate other enemies. Socialist industry could not prosper until loyal Soviet "specialists" replaced the rotten carryovers from the old regime. The hapless technicians confessed to heinous crimes in open court to save their families. Spectators and journalists left believing in real trials with real villains. The Master shot or imprisoned thousands of these engineers and other skilled workers.

Liquidating the hundreds of thousands of kulak households represented a more ambitious undertaking. In January 1930, the Master assigned each region numerical targets for arrests, shootings, and deportations of kulaks, defined as the more prosperous peasant farmers who owned their own land and who tended to oppose collectivization. Ukraine, in particular, would long remember the Master's lackey, Lazar Kaganovich's, reign of terror. The poor and middle-class peasants provided surprisingly little help—they feared they would be next. But in their place, members of the militia and the secret police force known as the Cheka, plus 25,000 activists, took care of the kulaks and anyone else opposed to Soviet power.

As mass starvation followed the "successful" dekulakization, the Master forbade mention of the word "famine." If we do not speak of famine, he indicated, it does not exist. Such semantics proved little comfort to the six million or more who died in South Russia, Ukraine, and Kazakhstan.

Meanwhile, life in the Kremlin fell into its own routine.

Much like the French court, the Bolshevik monarchs lived together in the Senate House and nearby buildings on the Kremlin grounds. They worked together in the Kremlin or on the Old Square up the hill. Their children played in the alleyways, exploring their nooks and crannies. Armed guards, perched on rooftops, shouted down their advice to the boys and girls playing games below. Cars of every make dropped off officials; mothers strolled with baby buggies. Their children cleaned the floor and washed dishes in the "Red Star" kindergarten alongside the offspring of the staff, but the children understood who was who.

The Master had socialized more in the years before he became "the Master." He liked to appear unannounced at the doors of fellow Kremlin residents, as silent as a cat waiting to pounce. On occasion, he joined Kaganovich, "the Cobbler" for a game of chess. He was less likely to drop in on his most valued deputy, Vyacheslav Molotov, or "Lead Butt," as he was called behind his back. Lead Butt and his wife valued their privacy. Stalin exchanged greetings in Georgian in the courtyard with industry czar Grigory Ordzhonikidze, or "Sergo," as everyone called him.

Back then, Anastas Mikoyan, "the Armenian," ambled across the courtyard, hoping to be invited for dinner. He needed rest from his five energetic boys. The Armenian, like the other Bolshevik elite, had one apartment for his large family. Only the Old Man's spinster sister had a place to herself. "Klim" (Kliment Voroshilov) lived with his Jewish wife in one of the largest apartments in Corpus No. 12. Childless, they adopted three children. The Cobbler, Lead Butt, Sergo, Klim, and the Armenian constituted Stalin's inner circle. They were a strange lot to lead the first socialist state: a Georgian (Ordzhonikidze), an Armenian (Mikoyan), a Jew (Kaganovich), and two Russians (Molotov and Voroshilov). The Cobbler did not mind doing dirty work. No one denied Sergo's commitment and organizational talents, but did he always have to let his temper explode? Only Lead Butt stood up to him. The Armenian took on any job, no matter how disagreeable, without complaining. The dullard Klim was perfect to oversee the military and attack the Master's enemies.

His Kremlin colleagues led happier family lives than the Master. Stalin's first wife, Katya, died of typhus a decade before the Great October Revolution of 1917. They met when her Svanidze family sheltered him from the czarist police. Katya gave him his first son,

Yakov. He loved her unconditionally, and with her died most of his feelings of warmth for humanity. The Master regarded his in-laws as family. His sisters-in-law occupied the neighboring dacha and he included them in his social gatherings.

Stalin's second marriage ended in tragedy as well. Nadezhda gave him a son, Vasily, and a daughter, Svetlana. But in November 1932, following an argument with Stalin at a public event, she rushed back to their Kremlin apartment where, stung by his public humiliation, she fired the fatal bullet. Afterward, the Master traded apartments. He could not live where his Nadezhda had died. At least, Nadezhda could no longer share intimate details with her friends. Stalin did not blame himself. She betrayed him like all the other suicides. They "spat" on the party, he said. But he sobbed at her funeral. His little son, Vasily, comforted him: "Do not cry, Papa."

After Nadezhda's death, Stalin's colleagues wanted him to remarry. They lined up candidates, but the Master remained single. Presumably, he contented himself with dalliances in artistic circles arranged by his chief bodyguard. After all, the Master loved ballet and watched his favorite performances many times over. And he had his "secret wife" in the Near Dacha (so-called because it was nearer to Moscow than his other dachas) in the Moscow suburb of Kuntsevo. She earned that nickname after the staff spied her leaving his bedroom in the early hours.

The Master's two sons gave him no comfort. Yakov, the elder, wed a twice-married ballerina—yet another sign of weakness, in Stalin's eyes. Earlier, when Stalin disapproved of Yakov's first choice for a wife, Yakov tried to commit suicide, but failed. The boy couldn't even shoot straight when he tried to kill himself! His younger son, Vasily, had always been wild and rambunctious. The Master knew Vasily would amount to nothing, just like his older brother who committed suicide in a German POW camp. (Vasily would die a drunk in exile in 1962.) Little Svetlana scarcely saw her busy father. But she was the only one dear to him. He playfully called her his "master." Only she could touch the chords on the iron strings of his heart.

By the mid-1930s, Stalin was ready to consolidate his power. Whether the Master ordered it or not, the assassination of Leningrad party boss Sergei Kirov on December 1, 1934, gave him his chance to kill off the party elite.

The Master rushed with his retinue to the scene. He personally interrogated the assassin and Kirov's bodyguards the next day. A rash of mysterious accidents and suicides of eyewitnesses followed. Stalin ordered his kowtowing NKVD head, Genrikh Yagoda, to find Kirov's assassins among his political enemies, but Yagoda dithered until the Master decided he was not up to the job. The Master needed a loyal executioner who asked no questions and did as he was told.

The Cobbler had discovered Nikolai Ezhov a decade earlier, working as a functionary in the Central Committee on Old Square. Ezhov's immediate boss at the time, Ivan Moskvin, saw promise in this lackluster, dwarfish man dressed in a cheap suit with a collar fastening on the side: "If you give him an assignment, there is no need to check, but you must watch him. He does not know when to stop." The sinister cruelty in this diminutive and quiet man caught the Master's eye. He recognized indiscriminate and uncontrolled appetites when he saw them. He could use Ezhov's "black marks"— his alcoholism, his attraction to men, and his chasing after every skirt in sight—when the time came.

Ezhov did not disappoint as head of the Master's NKVD: he ecstatically tortured prisoners, his shirt covered with their blood. He shot the woman who had treated him as a son in Moscow. He gave the order to shoot a comrade, whose last words were, "I see in your eyes that you feel sorry for me." Ezhov's comrade was wrong.

Ezhov used torture and falsifications to pin Kirov's murder on sixteen Old Bolsheviks who had been Lenin's deputies and Trotsky's allies. They confessed in open court after he promised them their lives. Of course, the Master could not intervene when the court handed down their death sentences on August 24, 1936. They were shot the next day. When Ezhov went after their wives and sons, such matters were outside the Master's personal control.

The executions of the sixteen Old Bolsheviks opened unlimited horizons for Stalin. He could kill any and all of the Old Bolsheviks, including those who knew him when he was a teenage thug called Soso in Tbilisi's back alleys.

It was against this backdrop that Agnessa, Maria, Evgenia, Adile, and Fekla went about their lives. Small wonder if they felt they were too insignificant or too far away to be deeply affected by the scheming of Stalin and his inner circle in the Kremlin.

CHAPTER THREE

Agnessa
Elite NKVD Wife

Maikop to Rostov-on-Don, South Russia (1922–1931)

The Maikop men considered the Argiropulo sisters—Lena and Agnessa—the prettiest girls in town. The older sister, Lena, a natural blonde, was considered the more beautiful of the two. With her around, Agnessa came in second. Lena ran to Mother in tears when the other girls accused her of dyeing her hair. Mama explained that her tormentors envied Lena's golden tresses. Agnessa's hair, however, exploded into a crown of light brown curls. Lena delighted in teasing her younger sister. Agnessa's legs, she sniped, resembled bombs. Agnessa starved her entire life as a result of Lena's biting words. Still, as Agnessa filled out, she discovered that her voluptuous figure appealed to men.

Maikop, in the Russian South halfway between Sukhumi and the port city of Novorossiysk, counted 22,000 residents at the time of the 1917–22 civil war. The Bolsheviks' Red Army occupied Maikop first. The opposing White Army drove them out, but then fled two years later as the Red cavalry approached. Lena and Agnessa saw more than their share of dead bodies and hangings after each change of power. In the course of this see-saw struggle, Maikop filled with handsome officers, both Red and White. They naturally took notice of the Argipopulo sisters.

Lena and Agnessa got their looks from their father, whose parents fled to Russia to escape Turkish repression. Papa longed for his

Agnessa Argiropulo, 1919.

native Greece, but when he tried to return, the Greek authorities denied landing rights to a ship they feared was full of Bolsheviks. They quarantined Papa and his fellow travelers. Fever broke out, and Papa died.

Lena and Agnessa reveled in the social whirl of "White-guardist" Maikop—especially Lena. Young officers offered her rides in their coaches and boasted about their noble lineage. When Lena married one of them, her local suitors complained to Agnessa: "Why could she not wait for us?" Lena lived with her officer-husband until the return of the Reds in March 1920. He remained behind on a promise of amnesty, but the Reds expelled him anyway. Lena accompanied him to the station, where he cried on the platform. Lena returned home, celebrating her freedom. Her husband died of typhus, and the widowed Lena married again, but unhappily. She gave birth to a boy, Borya, before she divorced her second husband. The beautiful Lena lived the rest of her life in Agnessa's shadow.

Agnessa's adventure began on a hot summer day in 1922. Her school friend, Lilia, rushed in and breathlessly announced that she had seen the cultured officers of the Bashkir brigade strolling in the city park. Agnessa hastily donned her white dress, stockings, and black patent-leather shoes. The two girls took their places on a park bench. Lo and behold, three officers, dressed in splendid Cherkassian uniforms, approached. The middle one, tall and upright, caught Agnessa's eye. She thought to herself, "If I marry, I'd want only him."

A sudden gust carried off Agnessa's blue silk headscarf, and she ran to fetch it before it fell in the river. Lilia whispered in reproach, "Why did you do that? They were all running to rescue your scarf." Agnessa deliberately allowed the next gust to carry away her scarf, to be rescued by her favorite officer.

Ivan Zarnitsky was smitten by this eighteen-year-old girl, with deep brown eyes, full lips, and Shirley Temple curls. Ten years her senior, Ivan belonged to the Cheka secret police, the unsheathed sword of the Bolshevik revolution. Ivan's boyish looks, thin face, and soft chin did not convey the resoluteness of a ferocious Chekist officer, but Agnessa knew she wanted him. Dances, stolen kisses, long strolls, and deep conversations followed. In the local movie theater, Ivan romantically brought her hand to his lips, as Agnessa joked, "What strong teeth you have!" Ivan behaved like a gentleman, parting at her door with the order, "It is time for you to sleep." As Ivan's company prepared to ship out, he assured Agnessa that he would come for her. His long letters ceased after a while. As the mailman approached the expectant Agnessa, he would woefully announce, "Nothing for you today." At long last, a letter arrived. Ivan had been sick in a hospital for three months. He promised to come for her on August 16.

On the designated day, Agnessa watched arriving trains from dawn to dusk. No Ivan. Lena teased the disconsolate Agnessa: "Where is your bridegroom, Mrs. Zarnitsky?" After dispatching a bitter letter accusing Ivan of betrayal, Agnessa received a second letter. Ivan had been promoted to head the Northern Caucasus border troops. His adjutant would fetch her on October 20. Again, no one came. Disheartened, Agnessa and her mother left for errands. They returned to find a message that Agnessa should leave with her officer escort the next day. But Mama refused to let Agnessa leave without a proper trousseau and decreed that Agnessa would join Ivan in a month's time. Agnessa, Lena, and Mama furiously packed household items and clothing in trunks, including Agnessa's most valuable possession, a Persian rug given by an older (and unwanted) admirer.

On November 20, 1922, Agnessa, with Lena as a chaperone, departed for her new life in Rostov-on-Don as the wife of a Chekist officer. They had to stay overnight in Armavir for the next day's train to Rostov. Chekists on white horses asking for the "bride of Ivan Zarnitsky" rescued the forlorn Agnessa and Lena from the platform where they waited with their luggage. Agnessa and Lena slept in a comfortable house. The next day, passengers on the Rostov train knew to make room when they saw the two women's Chekist escort. Agnessa for the first time felt what it was like to be the "first lady." In Rostov-on-Don, Agnessa primly informed Ivan that she and Lena planned to live elsewhere until they were married. He had to hurry. The Russian Orthodox Church allowed no marriages during Lent.

Ivan's housemates took charge of the wedding feast. After heavy eating, drinking, singing, and dancing, Ivan and Agnessa retreated to their bedroom. Ivan gave Valerian drops to Agnessa to calm her fears of performing her marital duties. The tranquilizer put Agnessa into a deep sleep. She awoke the next morning to find Ivan sleeping on the couch. The refreshed Agnessa seductively invited him into bed. Although Ivan "had not read the Kama Sutra" (as Agnessa would later state), he did just fine. The newlyweds did not leave the bedroom until their housemate knocked to ask, "Are you still alive?" Agnessa donned her black dress with a high golden collar to conceal the love marks on her throat.

As Agnessa and Ivan settled into married life in Rostov—a bustling administrative center—Ivan put on weight. He struggled into his uniform, tugging and pulling until he buttoned the last button and declared, "Victory at last." Ivan's nosy new deputy, Mikhail Frinovsky, uncovered his boss's deep secret: Ivan was the son of a priest. With a round pancake face and small, cruel eyes, Frinovsky started to boss his boss around. He even demanded that Ivan give him the antique inkwell on his desk.

When Ivan was out of town, Frinovsky conveniently began appearing at their apartment. Agnessa's rebuffs convinced Frinovsky he could not have Agnessa. But he could grab Ivan's position. Frinovsky suggested that an educated man like Ivan would be better served managing the local shoe factory. Ivan took the hint and left the Chekists in 1925. He and Agnessa rented a modest apartment, Ivan took to counting their expenses down to the last kopek, and Frinovsky assumed Ivan's position.

Agnessa had first seen the man she came to call her "Mirosha" a year earlier, in 1924, when he spoke at the Red Army anniversary celebration. This tall man with gray eyes and amazing eyelashes, dressed in a splendid uniform with a sword at his side, captivated her immediately. Mirosha was a genuine "operational officer" of the Cheka. Ivan and his pedestrian border guards paled by comparison.

Shortly after she heard Mirosha's speech, Agnessa was ordered by Ivan to attend a series of lectures for Chekist wives. If she did not go, he said, he would be compromised. Agnessa arrived the next Tuesday punctually at 5:00 p.m. along with the other wives. She was thrilled that the instructor was this magnificent man. He smiled and introduced himself tersely as "Mironov." The other women could not take their eyes off him as he lectured on "the need to defend our revolution with all our might."

Mironov eventually reciprocated Agnessa's admiration. One day after the lesson, Mironov caught up to her and engaged her in conversation. They strolled together as he improvised poems. On this note, they began the "underground phase" of their romance. They met at the river bank under a cottonwood tree, which shed its seeds on the ground like spiny globes. Their conversations became so intense they did not notice the cold winter weather.

During these strolls, Agnessa learned that Sergei Mironov's Jewish grandmother owned a dairy shop on Kiev's fashionable Kreshchatik Avenue. She had wrangled admission for her grandson to the gymnasium and to the Kiev Commercial Academy without him having to earn the gold medal usually required of Jewish students. Such an education placed Mirosha among the best educated of the Chekist leaders. He also told her, with tears welling in his eyes, that his first love, Marusya, had poisoned herself after he rejected her. Agnessa could see that this tragedy affected Mirosha deeply. Despite his considerable appeal to the opposite sex, Mirosha treated women with respect. He was not one to play with their affections. Mirosha did not hide that he had a wife, Gusta, who lived elsewhere, waiting on the sidelines for his return.

Mirosha had served with distinction in the Red cavalry. As a Jew, he considered the Bolshevik revolution "his revolution," one that opened doors otherwise shut. He fought on the Polish front, became a Chekist, and was awarded the Cheka's highest medal. Mirosha truly believed in the Bolshevik cause. Not in jest, he told the astonished Agnessa that he would not hesitate to execute her if he found her to be an enemy. He soothed her tears by adding, "After I shot you, I would shoot myself." Mirosha's biography put Ivan's to shame. Still, Ivan and Agnessa continued to live together in their modest quarters along with Mama and Lena, whose unhappy second marriage had ended.

Mirosha and Agnessa met secretly for an entire year before consummating their relationship, or so she claimed. After the sexual dam broke, Agnessa and Mirosha trysted regularly in his quarters, while Ivan pretended to know nothing. Their underground love went on for six years. During his visits to Rostov, Mirosha left his hotel room unlocked so that she could slip in unnoticed. Once, when Agnessa entered a dark room wearing Lena's overcoat, Mirosha whispered, "Why not Agnessa?" He breathed a sigh of relief (or pretended to) when he discerned Agnessa's face.

Stalin's January 1930 dekulakization campaign required ambitious and loyal Chekists to manage the flood of thousands of kulak families deported to such remote, inhospitable regions as the Urals, Siberia, and Kazakhstan. On August 17, 1931, Mirosha was promoted to second in command of Chekist forces in Kazakhstan, more than

1,200 miles away. No more weekend leaves for Mirosha. Agnessa had to make a decision: a humdrum life with Ivan or an adventure with the Cheka's rising star, Sergei Mironov?

Kazakhstan, Dnepropetrovsk, and Novosibirsk (1931–1937)

In early September 1931, Agnessa accompanied Mirosha to the train station as he departed for Moscow and then on to Kazakhstan. Mirosha was thirty-seven years old; Agnessa was nine years his junior. Waiting for departure in his compartment, Mirosha suddenly volunteered, "And what if I spirit you off to Moscow? You have never been there." Agnessa laughed, as he grew more insistent: "Just come with me for a while. Then you can come back." Agnessa's first thought was clothes. She wore only a light dress with a jacket and carried just a small handbag. "How can I go without anything?" she objected. "Don't worry," Mirosha assured her. "We'll buy what you need in Moscow."

As the train's warning whistle sounded, Mirosha held her hand in an iron grip: "I'll not let you go!" The train started. Agnessa planned to get off at the next stop, thinking, "Ivan, Mama, and Lena will be so worried." As station after station passed, Agnessa penned a telegram to Ivan. (Ivan telegraphed back to them in Moscow, pleading with Agnessa not to leave him.) Thoughts of home vanished in Moscow as Agnessa and Mirosha bought winter clothes for the cold of Kazakhstan. Ordinary Muscovites could not think of purchasing an entire wardrobe in a couple of days, but Mirosha frequented stores reserved for the elite.

Mirosha presented Agnessa with an ultimatum the day before his departure: "If you do not come with me to Alma-Ata, we should part now, and it will be on your conscience forever." Agnessa boarded the train with Mirosha the next day. Her life in Rostov-on-Don had ended. Her new life as the wife of the mighty Mironov had begun.

In his new job, Mirosha organized camps for the arrival of "hostile elements" in Kazakhstan. He observed feeble peasants dying along the tracks and in miserable rail stations. Mothers hid sick children under their coats until Chekist medics took them away. Many more children died after arrival at their final destinations. Kremlin superiors did not allot adequate provisions, a task that fell on Mirosha's shoulders.

Ensconced in their Alma-Ata villa in Kazakhstan, Agnessa had to contend with the advances of Mirosha's boss, Vasily Karutsky, the pot-bellied head of the Kazakhstan Chekists. Agnessa detested his profanity, drunkenness, and lewd behavior. His wife had committed suicide shortly before Agnessa and Mirosha arrived, leaving "Pot-Belly" free to harass the wives of subordinates. He hoped to add Agnessa to his conquests and invited Mirosha and Agnessa for private viewings of French pornography. Agnessa remembered one photo depicting an invading Turk raping a nun.

Pot-Belly's assistant and procurer, "Abrashka," would wait for Mirosha to leave and then enter bearing fruits, melons, and other assorted gifts. Mirosha raged when he saw these bounties: "Send them back. Kick Abrashka out when he comes." Later, spying an ashtray full of cigarette butts in their parlor, Mirosha burst out, "These are not mine. Who was here? Abrashka? Again?" The day after the ashtray incident, Mirosha returned with a surprising proposal. "Pot-Belly is sending me on a long inspection trip so he can have his way with you. They are giving me a whole Pullman car for my trip. You come with me." Thus Agnessa embarked with Mirosha in mid-winter on an extended 1931 inspection trip of camps for deported kulaks.

An elaborate Pullman and a sleeping car from czarist times decorated in green velvet and red plush fabric transported Mirosha and Agnessa to the far corners of Kazakhstan. Mirosha's team consisted of Chekist officers, a conductor, and a chef. The only other woman was a typist. Agnessa could scarcely stick her head out the window due to the extreme cold. At each stop, Mirosha and his team disembarked in heavy winter gear. Unlike other Chekist inspectors, Mirosha talked with local officials in a friendly manner and offered them hospitality. The Mironovs kept their chef busy, but they had brought more than enough food to go around.

The infamous Karlag (Karaganda Corrective Labor Camp) shocked Agnessa more than any other stop. Prisoners and "special settlers" poured into this godforsaken "city" after it was officially opened in December 1931 to mine the rich coal deposits. As Mirosha disembarked at Karlag Station, he rejected the bored Agnessa's request to tag along. Upon his return, Mirosha lay on the sofa in their sleeping car without saying a word.

The other inspectors told Agnessa of miserable families freezing in crude shelters. The female manager of the supply depot told them, "I've even forgotten what bread looks like." She pointed out her window: "Take a look at that hovel over there. The mother and father died, leaving behind three young children. The two-year-old died shortly after them. The older boy took out a knife and cut his brother into pieces, sharing them with his sister."

A cup of hot tea restored the company to good humor. They had probably seen worse. One man pranced around Agnessa and the female typist, declaring, "You can see that I am small, but no woman has complained." The men continued their bawdy boasts into the night. Agnessa retired to bed unimpressed.

Agnessa thought she would shock Mirosha with her story of death and cannibalism. His answer: "I know all this myself. When we went into the barracks there were bodies everywhere. What a trip!" Agnessa whispered, "But Mirosha, they can't all be guilty." His attempt at levity did not cheer her up: "Obviously you cannot believe, because you are my little White Guardist." Agnessa could not get out of her mind that they were sitting with a trainload of provisions in a non-existent city in which everyone was dying.

Agnessa lived in her Alma-Ata ivory tower until the end of September 1933 as famine ravaged Russia. In a letter to Rostov, she asked Lena what silk undergarments and cosmetics she wanted. Lena's immediate response: "Do not send clothes. Send us something to eat." There's a Russian saying: the well-fed don't understand the hungry. Agnessa, however, understood. She ordered a large package of food to be dispatched immediately.

Lena later told Agnessa that she had given all her rations to her son, Borya. One day as she walked by the corpses in the streets, she feared she would join them soon. Just then, a truck stopped in front of her house, and a military man emerged with a package: "This is for you. It seems it's from your sister." Agnessa continued a steady stream of food packages. When she was next in Rostov, her sister met her, crying, "Agnessa, you saved our lives."

Agnessa encountered hunger everywhere—even on their Georgian vacation. A police officer brought over their three-course meals, usually topped off with ice cream. One day, their housekeeper asked hopefully, "What should I do with the leftovers? I have three children." Agnessa's mother told her to take the food. The next day, the emboldened housekeeper asked, "Can I bring my children to play with your niece and nephew?" Their appearance horrified Agnessa: "You could see their rib cages." Eventually, the woman brought in fourteen relatives, some all the way from Kharkov in the Ukraine. Agnessa ordered meals for nineteen. The sanatorium administrators could not refuse an order from Mironov.

Each new assignment signified a move up the administrative ladder for Mirosha. In September 1933 the Master assigned him to head the regional Dnepropetrovsk office in Ukraine. Agnessa welcomed the move back to her South. They occupied a two-story villa that offered ample accommodations for Agnessa's extended family, which joined them from Rostov. Each wing had a full bath with the most modern fixtures. They had their own billiard room and movie theater. A chauffeur lived on the property. Mirosha's cavernous study occupied much of the ground floor.

Agulya, the daughter of Agnessa's brother, Pavel, joined their household as an adopted daughter. The family decided she was better off with Agnessa, not with her father who worked in Georgia and had been left with Agulya and her sister, Tanya, after his first wife left him. In her kindergarten, everyone recognized Agulya Mironova as the niece of the most powerful man in the city. Agnessa brought her own seamstress, who knew how to get the best fabrics and cosmetics. As Agnessa's mother observed, "You outshine them all."

Agnessa and Agulya, 1930s.

When they arrived in Dnepropetrovsk, Agnessa was still legally married to Ivan, and Mirosha to Gusta. At last, Ivan wrote asking for a divorce. He wanted to remarry. As the head of Dnepropetrovsk operations, Mirosha oversaw marriage registrations. Mirosha took Agnessa to the registration office and within half an hour the two divorced their respective spouses and registered as husband and wife.

On their next visit to Kiev, Mirosha's boss, Vsevolod Balitsky, demanded they have a real wedding ceremony in his own dacha on the banks of the Dnieper River. Agnessa called him "Siegfried" because of his stately blond good looks. (The vain "Siegfried" ordered his portrait hung in Chekist offices throughout Ukraine.) Siegfried's subordinates arranged everything. Agnessa politely rejected the white wedding dress they selected. She picked instead a bright green outfit with golden buttons.

As the guests chanted, "Kiss, kiss, kiss!" Mirosha objected, "We are already married twelve years." The guests retorted, "Your married

life begins today." As part of the ceremony, Agnessa carried around
a tray with shots of vodka. Each male guest had to drink, kiss her,
and then place money on the tray. Agnessa saved Siegfried for the
last. He downed the shot glass, kissed Agnessa, and placed a rare
silver ruble on her tray. As the festivities ended, the guests locked the
"newlyweds" in their bedroom. The exhausted Mirosha fell asleep.
Agnessa sneaked out to rejoin the revelers.

Agnessa's dreadful visit to the Karaganda camp and her encounters with the starvation of others revealed the dark side of the Master's socialism. Life was bad for others—but not for her, it seemed.
Her first comprehension that she could be in danger herself came in
1935 in Tbilisi. She had read that one of their friends in the Georgian
NKVD perished in an automobile accident in Tbilisi, so Agnessa
decided to offer condolences to his wife. Mirosha categorically
refused to go along. An elderly woman escorted Agnessa to a darkened bedroom. Upon recognizing Agnessa, the new widow broke
out in sobs. After she regained her composure, she whispered, "You
know, Agnessa, Beria (the head of the Georgian party) killed him.
He is a murderer. His people did it." The widow said her husband
and his chauffeur were found mangled beyond recognition. When
Agnessa told Mirosha, he warned her, "If you want to live, keep
quiet about this." Agnessa heeded his advice.

Mirosha got his big break in late 1936. Their first intimation of a
change came in September. Mirosha and Agnessa walked the Black
Sea beaches of Sochi, luxuriated in a well-appointed hotel suite, and
ate at restaurants reserved for the elite. They met the Frinovskys,
who were also in Sochi—the same Frinovsky who took Ivan's job
in Rostov a decade earlier. He held no grudge against Agnessa, now
the wife of his comrade-in-arms Mironov. Frinovsky's wife, Nina,
astonished Agnessa. Back in Rostov, Agnessa had looked down on
the vulgar Nina's amateurish choice of clothing and makeup. She
recalled sitting in a hot restaurant with Nina, repulsed by mascara-
blackened drops of perspiration dripping on the plate. The new
Nina dressed immaculately and applied just the right makeup. She
had just returned from Paris. The Frinovskys must be doing well.

Nina could scarcely conceal her excitement. The Master was about to appoint Nikolai Ezhov as head of the NKVD. She confided conspiratorially to Agnessa, "Ezhov is our good friend." On September 26, Agnessa learned of Ezhov's appointment as NKVD head and that he named Frinovsky as his deputy. As they accompanied the Frinovskys to the train station the next day, Nina, dressed in elegant black hat and shining gloves, gave her a meaningful glance: bigger things lay ahead for both of them. Nina did not disappoint. Soon, Ezhov ordered Mirosha to report to Novosibirsk in Western Siberia as the head of its NKVD.

On their way from Dnepropetrovsk to Novosibirsk, Agnessa and Mirosha stopped in Moscow to witness the Master's Report on the Draft Constitution. Stalin delivered the address in the Kremlin Palace on November 25, 1936. Agnessa sat in the balcony with other wives. Their husbands sat below in the main hall. Agnessa joined the others as they rose as the Master approached the rostrum to shouts of "Hurrah for Comrade Stalin!" "Long live Comrade Stalin!" "Long live the Great Stalin!" "Hurrah for the great genius, Comrade Stalin!" Agnessa strained to hear the Master's soft voice as he droned on in a thick Georgian accent. To escape the stale air, Agnessa left her seat to forage for oranges at the buffet. Back in her seat after security guards scrutinized her identification papers, the other ladies begged that she share with them. When the Master finally concluded, Agnessa, in a burst of diplomacy, praised the Master's wonderful speech to her neighbor. The other woman answered with unexpected sarcasm: "It is not for us chicken brains to understand such things." Someone overheard. Agnessa learned later that her balcony neighbor was arrested shortly thereafter.

Upon arrival in Novosibirsk at the end of December 1936, Agnessa set up court in the former estate of the czar's governor-general. Visitors entered through a spacious courtyard garden to a stage for local theater. The residence contained a movie theater and billiard room, where Mirosha and his friends gathered to play and smoke. Agnessa selected the films. And the food! Agnessa threw legendary dinner parties. After dinner, guests retreated to the theater. Waiters bustled

Mironovs family: Agnessa, Sergei
(Mirosha) holds Agulya, 1930s.

around serving flaming crepes, whose blue flares temporarily lit the
darkened screening room. Agnessa brought along her mother, sister
Lena, adopted daughter Agulya, nephew Borya, and her personal
"miracle-working" seamstress. The servants tried to anticipate her
every wish. Agnessa referred to them as "bootlickers."

In Novosibirsk, Mirosha stood second only to the tall and austere
Robert Eikhe. This Bolshevik legend had ruthlessly carried out collectivization without flinching. In Western Siberia, Eikhe personi-
fied the party itself, while Mirosha headed the "unsheathed sword"
that protected the party.

Agnessa knew how to move in Chekist circles. The wives and
girlfriends had flair; they tried to look their best. Eikhe's clan of
party true believers was another kettle of fish, Agnessa soon learned.
Mirosha and Agnessa arrived at the Eikhe mansion for their first
official visit in the extreme cold of Siberian winter. A bowing doorman admitted them to an antechamber. Servants descended to take
their coats. The grand staircase was adorned with live lilies. Silk covered the walls, and the table was laden with a first course fit for a

czar's palace. The tall and restrained Eikhe perfunctorily glanced at Agnessa, dressed in her finest. The other women wore modest dark outfits with scarcely any makeup, the worst kind of "blue-stockings" in Agnessa's book. Eikhe's wife had earned two university degrees. Agnessa had just made it through school in little Maikop. The elaborate printed menu confused Agnessa. Eikhe tried to help. She pretended to enjoy the veal fricassee he ordered for her.

The men left the women for the smoking room. Agnessa sat uncomfortably—"a bright canary amid gray sparrows." She felt the Eikhe women's "murderous glances" as they chattered about the latest political news and gossip. They bored Agnessa to tears. In Eikhe's mansion she sat as a "chicken brain" compared with the highly educated women of the Eikhe clan. She thought: maybe real "chicken brains" survive, as she recalled her experience in the balcony of the Kremlin palace before their trip to Novosibirsk.

As 1937 began, Agnessa reflected on her twelve years with Mirosha. She had placed her hopes on Ivan, but his career fizzled. In Mirosha, she had a handsome man to whom power came naturally. Sergei Mironov had risen, according to the estimation of some, to third position in the NKVD. Ahead of him was Nikolai Ezhov himself and Mirosha's mentor, Frinovsky. Agnessa wanted people to say: Mironov is an interesting man, but his wife is not below him. Mirosha once assured her, "Twelve years and I did not betray you once." Agnessa had a ready explanation: she made their life a "permanent romance" and helped his ascent to become one of the most powerful men in the Master's Soviet Union.

CHAPTER FOUR

Maria

Portrait of the New Soviet Family

Chita, Eastern Siberia (1922–1930)

Maria's life was intertwined with the progress of the Trans-Siberian Railway, which opened operations in the early part of the twentieth century. Before the railroad, Eastern Siberia consisted of "cities without people," as the history books taught. The czarist police needed remote sites to dump exiles and revolutionaries in places of no escape. The police dispatched the Decembrists, who rose up against czarist rule in December of 1825, to the provincial capital of Chita. Many of their descendants stayed on and gave the city a cultural life and architecture out of proportion to its modest size.

Maria entered the world in 1904 in the isolated village of Tolbaga, halfway between Ulan Ude and Chita. Her Cossack forefathers had moved there as free landholders to eke out a meager living from the earth. Her father worked odd jobs and farmed a small plot.

Tolbaga rested on the free-flowing Khilok River. Periodic floods threatened the town's low-lying wood cottages, painted in pastel greens. The Mongolian border lay less than 125 miles to the south, but there was no easy way to reach it. Only much later was a rail line built that connected the Trans-Siberian Railway to the Mongolian capital of Ulan Bator. As a child, Maria grew accustomed to seeing Mongolian, Chinese, and native Siberian faces among the largely Russian population. Eastern Siberia formed a melting pot of East and West. Villagers trekked to the *Barakholka* flea markets to haggle with Chinese, Georgian, and Russian merchants hawking their wares. Buryat farmers, members of one of Siberia's indigenous populations, brought their goods on crude horse-drawn carriages. Russian peasant women wheeled their baked bread to market on clumsy homemade carts.

Maria grew up in one of the most inhospitable climates in the world. In winter, temperatures fell to minus fifty degrees Fahrenheit, or even colder. Parents warned children to wear their winter coats, gloves, and woolen caps. They suffered from frostbite even from brief exposure. Parents also warned their children about wandering off into the woods, saying that packs of hungry wolves preyed on humans in the winter months. In the summer, Tolbaga residents contended with extreme heat, as high as 104 degrees Fahrenheit. The sun rose at 4:00 a.m. and set at 9:00 p.m. During heat spells, residents took refuge in the Khilok River. Few owned bathing suits, so men and women bathed naked, separately. In summer, huge mosquitoes made life miserable.

The young peasant girl's family name—Senotrusov—disclosed her peasant origins. The name means "haymaker." Senotrusov aunts, uncles, and cousins populated Tolbaga and nearby villages. (The remains of fallen Senotrusovs from World War II still rest in the local cemetery.) Some villagers departed in the morning to herd cattle, sheep, and even reindeer. Others tilled their small plots or mined local iron ore and coal deposits.

Maria would have settled for the life of a peasant's wife except for the rich coal deposits in the region. The Trans-Baikal administration ordered a spur line built to the coal mines, and a young engineer, Alexander Ignatkin, arrived to supervise. Maria joined the small workforce the railroad recruited from among the local villagers. Maria met her future husband in 1922 at the age of eighteen. The twenty-six-year-old Alexander was counted among the region's most promising engineers. Tall and thin with an angular face, Alexander wore the dashing uniform of a railroad officer. They married within a year.

Maria Ignatkina, 1920s.

Despite the growing persecution of religion, Maria and Alexander married in a traditional Russian Orthodox ceremony. They exchanged rings as pledges to share their physical and spiritual goods, their eternal love and devotion. The priest then led the couple into the middle of the church, chanting, "Blessed are those who fear the Lord and who walk in His ways." Alexander and Maria proclaimed that they came to be joined by God. After prayers, the priest placed golden crowns on their heads, declaring, "O Lord, our God, crown them in glory and in honor."

During their courtship, Maria learned that Alexander shared her humble origins. Alexander's father worked in the slaughterhouse in the Siberian city of Irkutsk. He earned enough to educate only one of his six children, and he chose Alexander as the most talented one. Alexander finished Irkutsk Technical Institute with an engineering specialty. He started work in 1920 as the civil war raged across Russia. As the war ground to its conclusion, Alexander and his fellow engineers restored track, working alongside inexperienced villagers. Fuel was so low that trains halted periodically as passengers gathered firewood for the boilers. Thanks to specialists like Alexander, the Trans-Baikal railroad was set back on its feet in record time.

Despite miserable rations—four pounds of black bread and a pound of salt-dried fish for a five day trip—they worked on. After all, they were better off than those who survived by selling their belongings. Only the relief efforts of the American Red Cross prevented mass starvation among Eastern Siberian residents. Refugees lived in abandoned rail cars. They slept on wooden pallets, nailed one above the other into the interior of rail cars.

Before meeting Alexander, Maria had scarcely been out of her village. As Alexander's wife, she followed him from one remote assignment to another. She became accustomed to shuttling back and forth long distances on the train. Everywhere she was greeted respectfully as the wife of Alexander Ignatkin.

They first lived on the Amur River bordering China. They then set up house at the site of a rich iron ore deposit. Daughter Nadya was born first. Then came Olga two years later and son Yury two years after that. At each location, Alexander was assigned a small wooden cottage, next to the railroad tracks. Maria turned each cottage into a "light and comfortable" home, as her son later wrote. She raised educated and obedient children, who would later, like their father, help to build socialism. Alexander's hard work rarely allowed him the luxury of taking time for any hobbies, even his favorite: fishing. There were times in their marriage when he returned home only after the safe passage at 2 a.m. of the Moscow-Vladivostok courier train.

The family's favorite activity was reading aloud. Although Maria acquired only an elementary education, she loved good books, a passion she imparted to her three children. They especially loved Russian poet Alexander Pushkin. At the centennial of his early death in a duel in 1837, the whole Ignatkin family went to see the film *The Poet and the Czar*. Their collection of books made a small but decent family library. The family reading circle contributed to the excellence at school displayed by Nadya, Olga, and Yury. All three children received the award of *otlichniki* (outstanding students).

Maria made sure not to spoil the children. They tended the family cow, chickens, and potato garden without grumbling. Maria headed the parents' school committee. She volunteered as an "activist" wife of railroad workers. Alexander and Maria made a point of not quarreling at home. Maria called him *Shura* (a nickname for Alexander) and he called her *Rodnushechka*, or "my dearest little one." Yury would later write in his memoir, "The welfare of our family was nurtured by the love and work of our parents. We had a happy family."

In 1930, the management of the Trans-Baikal Railway promoted Alexander to chief of engineering operations of the Chita sector. The Chita administration controlled almost 2,000 miles of track. It coordinated traffic to China and Japan with the Chinese Eastern Railroad, headquartered in Harbin, Manchuria. Alexander had reached the apex of his career.

The respect of his colleagues and subordinates, however, would be of little use when the Chita NKVD set its sights on both of them.

Chita (1930–January 1937)

Alexander Ignatkin worked out of Chita's stately, white, cupola-domed station as he organized track inspections and supervised the locomotive repair yards. "Soviet power" showed its appreciation. His rewards included advanced training courses in Leningrad, a generous salary, a gold watch, a hunting rifle, and a portable gramophone.

Chita's 120,000 residents endured the persistent clatter of trains on their journeys from points west to exotic eastern destinations. Chita's massive locomotive works serviced engines and rolling stock. Its Railway Transport Institute graduated engineers and specialists. As a crazy-quilt of East and West, Chita's patchwork of nationalities was reflected in its mix of Orthodox churches, mosques, and synagogues. Churches struggled to withstand official anti-religion campaigns, and most fell into a state of disrepair. Nevertheless, people still came to baptize their children and to exchange wedding vows. Chita's proximity to Mongolia due south and China to the southeast explained its large garrisons of military troops. The military maintained its own police and courts. Alexander, like other railroad employees, answered to military justice.

Maria Ignatkina kept their comfortable three-room wooden cottage on the grounds of the Chita railway administration spick-and-span. Nadya, Olga, and Yury slept together in the children's room. Maria understood her family was more fortunate than others. She pretended to reproach Alexander when she caught him giving his own money to subordinates. He shrugged: "Well, what should I do? They have many children and their pay is not enough for bread." In a rare show of anger, Alexander heatedly reproached Yury for tossing a piece of bread to a beggar who interrupted their Sunday dinner. Even the poorest of the poor deserve respect, he told him.

As the end of 1936 approached, the Ignatkins assembled at the local photographer's studio for a family portrait. They sat in front of an artificial backdrop while the photographer caught their image in natural light with his Leica camera. He retouched the large negative to remove unwanted shadows and created a family portrait for the ages. The photograph shows a proud father and mother with their three children in between. Alexander sits, dressed in his uniform. He is forty years old with a thin face, receding hairline, and a penetrating gaze—a self-made man, a person of authority. The portrait highlights the thirty-two-year-old Maria's pleasant, round face and short-cropped hair. She has put on her finest outfit with a shawl draped across her right shoulder as an attempted fashion touch.

Maria has paid more attention to her children's attire than her own. Nadya, age fourteen, and Olga, twelve, are dressed in neat dark smocks with white-silk embroidered collars. Olga's unruly brunette curls contrast with Nadya's tightly wound blond pigtails. They are both images of their mother. Ten-year-old Yury, in a dark sweater with a starched white collar, peers deliberately, almost defiantly, at the camera, as if imitating his father. The portrait captures a family of modest circumstances that made its way through hard work and discipline. This family portrait would be their last.

The purges that Maria read about in the local Chita daily, *The Trans Baikal Worker*, had nothing to do with her. When she read in

Ignatkins family: Alexander and Maria with their children Yury, Olga, and Nadya (sitting), September 1936.

July 1928 that eleven engineers from the Shakhty coal mines confessed to sabotage, she considered their death sentences justified. Alexander wondered how engineers, of all people, could deliberately destroy their own work. When Maria read, in October 1929, that five former generals confessed to spying, she believed, "No innocent person confesses to a crime he did not commit."

The NKVD administration occupied the largest building in town at 84 Lenin Street. Its Road and Transport Department (DTO), which protected the nation's railways from its enemies, occupied a separate building on Kalinin Street. Alexander considered the DTO an irritating nuisance. DTO officers saw enemies everywhere and insisted that Alexander follow their orders. The Chekists felt they could run roughshod over anyone in their way. Alexander clashed with the Chekists regularly. He thwarted their claim for railroad apartments they wanted for themselves. They would not forget his impertinence.

Alexander had already witnessed the dark side of Soviet power. The Chekists threatened him with jail if he failed to finish a repair facility on schedule. Alexander saw thousands of "special settlers" passing through Chita to the Amur province. These bedraggled, sick, starving families cooped up in wooden boxcars did not seem to be the dangerous enemies depicted by official propaganda.

The Chita Gulag administration assigned prisoners to Alexander's work crews, many of them women. As idealistic expatriate Russians returned from Harbin, Manchuria, in 1935 to their "Soviet motherland of equality and promise," the prisoners digging on the track beds shouted, "Just wait. Soon you will be working with us down here." Only the most fortunate of Harbin "traitors" survived to join this pitiful labor force. The Master ordered the others summarily shot.

The Ignatkins welcomed New Year's Day 1937 with their new family portrait on display in their modest apartment. The temperature had not risen above twenty-two degrees below zero all day, but they squeezed together next to the peasant stove. Alexander worked as usual. Trains had to be dispatched, the repair works inspected, and track conditions evaluated, New Year's Eve or not. Alexander had to be there to make sure nothing went wrong. As for Maria, the Chita women activists had chosen her to represent them at the upcoming Moscow Congress of Women Railway Activists.

Maria counted her blessings as a poor village girl from the most humble of origins. She and Alexander believed in the goal of building socialism and were willing to work hard to achieve it. They were the kind of New Soviet People that Soviet Russia desperately needed.

CHAPTER FIVE

Evgenia

Luxury with a Beast

Gomel, Odessa, Sochi, Moscow (1922–1932)

Surely better things lay in store for Evgenia Feigenberg than her provincial Belorussian birthplace. Gomel had no culture, no society. It lay on the border with the Ukraine, not far from Chernobyl, in the Pale of Settlement delineated for Jews. Gomel was known as a commercial center and a transportation hub, not for its society and culture. Evgenia belonged to almost half of Gomel residents who were Jewish. Small-town Evgenia dreamed of high fashion, elegant parties, and the finer things of life—if not in Paris, then at least Moscow.

The new Bolshevik leaders needed polished women who appreciated the arts and music and knew how to behave in diplomatic circles. In a rare turnaround, being Jewish gave her an advantage. Many of the Bolshevik leaders were Jews themselves or had Jewish wives. She had heard that Lenin himself had Jewish roots. But how to escape dull, dreary Gomel?

Evgenia's father, Rabbi Solomon Feigenberg, did not help. He bred a large family. Evgenia's brothers at least entered the gymnasium under the 15 percent Jewish quota. Evgenia had to satisfy herself with a lower level of education at Jewish schools for girls. Rabbi Solomon could not understand his daughter's literary and artistic aspirations. Daughters of rabbis marry into solid Jewish families and

37

bear children. Why spend time writing poetry and reading? Such things do not make a good wife or mother.

As Evgenia blossomed into a young woman, she made her plan: she would use her considerable appeal to the opposite sex to escape Gomel. Evgenia's individual features were not of great beauty. But she did maintain a slim figure and, while short, her upright bearing made her appear taller. Her thin face and beaked nose marked her as Jewish. Her dark luminous eyes and vivacious smile were her best features. She kept her brownish-red curly hair short with a curl fashionably positioned on her forehead. Men found her irresistible.

If she could enliven provincial Gomel, surely she could excite the fashionable salons of Paris, Berlin, or Vienna. Evgenia stood out in a world a generation or two removed from the peasant plot, the *shtetl*. As she looked around for a man on his way up, one who wanted more than looks and fashion, she was prepared to use her sex appeal to emancipate herself from her humble origins.

Evgenia scored her first major coup at age eighteen. She married the journalist Lazar Khayutin, also a Jew, in 1922. Through him, she escaped to the metropolis of Odessa, on the Black Sea.

The port of Odessa burst with intellectual life in the 1920s. Evgenia found work through her husband at a lively Odessa literary journal, albeit only as a typist. But at last she moved in the literary circles where she felt she belonged. She met the satirists Ilya Ilf and Evgeny Petrov. She got to know Isaak Babel, who later became Odessa's most famous writer. His *Red Cavalry* and *Odessa Tales* made him an international literary figure. Even the great Maxim Gorky admired him. His fame took him regularly abroad, including to Paris, where his wife lived.

Evgenia's marriage to Khayutin ended quickly. Evgenia traded him for the more promising Alexander Gladun, who directed the Moscow Publishing House and had good contacts in the foreign ministry. They met while he was on an extended business trip in Odessa. Gladun was ten years her senior.

Evgenia captivated Gladun, and they returned together to Moscow in 1924. However, she remained legally "Evgenia Khayutina." Evgenia and Gladun, it appears, did not register their marriage, a common situation in those liberated days.

Her dream of living abroad came true four years later. The Foreign Ministry posted Gladun to London as the Second Secretary in the Soviet Embassy. London was not Paris, and Evgenia did not speak English well. But she attended concerts, visited museums, and soaked up the culture—until the British expelled her husband on espionage charges. Gladun returned to Moscow, while Evgenia took up residence in Berlin, supporting herself again as a typist. In Berlin, Evgenia made her first physical conquest of Babel. After riding together aimlessly through Berlin in a taxi, Babel and Evgenia went to his hotel room, where Evgenia applied her talents. Babel was not her first conquest among the literary elite. She had already bedded a famous journalist and a prominent editor, both of whom would come in handy later.

Evgenia returned to Gladun in Moscow in 1928. Babel continued to shuttle between Russia and Western Europe.

Through Gladun, Evgenia enjoyed the privileges of the party's middle elite. Evgenia could afford to decorate their modest Moscow apartment tastefully. She obtained work as a typist at the *Peasant Gazette*, where a liaison with the editor brought promotion to the rank of "journalist." Evgenia used her connections to launch a literary salon in her apartment. The men who had been her amorous conquests created a stir when they attended. The great Babel read from his works-in-progress. But the wives of more important men also cultivated literary salons. They landed bigger and better guests than Evgenia, still a piker in Moscow's literary salon business.

The wives of the party elite qualified for government-paid "cures." Party officials and their wives surely needed their rest. They worked long hours under great pressure and strain. In September 1929, at age twenty-five and in the prime of her life and attractiveness, Evgenia began a cure in Sochi that opened up a new world for her.

It was in Sochi that she met a small man with the potential for a big future.

WHILE STROLLING ALONG THE BEACH enjoying the balmy weather, Evgenia saw a short man, almost a dwarf, approaching her. His clothing showed an appalling lack of taste. He had brown, tobacco-stained teeth and did not look at all healthy. If anyone needed a "cure," it was he. "Sleazy" summarized Evgenia's first impression. But Evgenia had seen him before and had made inquiries. She had learned that Nikolai Ezhov served as deputy to an undersecretary in the fabled Central Committee of the party. This small man had a chance of going somewhere! Evgenia always kept an eye open for such a prospect. She overlooked small matters like personal appearance and hygiene. In Ezhov, there was a lot to ignore.

Evgenia liked the fact that the short man did not hesitate to approach an attractive woman like her. He invited her to dinner, and she accepted. As she observed Ezhov closely that evening at dinner, she measured him at five feet or less in height with an oversized head relative to his body. His asymmetrical face broke out in a sudden childish smile when he was amused. A nimble man, he made exact motions with his small hands. Nikolai fell short in the conversational category, although a later biography described him as a "great orator who set workers on the correct path of Lenin and Stalin." This biography would disappear from the shelves along with him.

Fortunately, Evgenia did not tower over the diminutive Nikolai as they danced to the restaurant orchestra and later strolled along the promenade. Needless to say, they ended up in bed. Evgenia learned from Nikolai that he worked in the fabled Orgburo, the Organizational Bureau of the Central Committee. This very agency handed out the key positions in the party and state.

Evgenia also learned that Ezhov, like her, was already married. Ezhov had wed Antonina Titova in 1921 while on assignment in Kazan in the Tatar Autonomous Republic. Nikolai and Antonina, who worked for the agricultural ministry, lived with his mother and his sister's two children in a marriage that remained childless and loveless.

Evgenia sensed that Nikolai was meant for bigger things. He told his friends that he felt like "a cockroach in a frying pan" in remote provincial postings. However, he had worked his way into a position where his prospects were unlimited.

Their courtship lasted two years. The married Nikolai played the role of suitor to a married woman. He showered her with flowers and took to attending her evening salon, although he had no interest in things artistic. They then threw pretense aside. Nikolai spent long hours with Evgenia in the Gladun apartment.

In the meantime, Nikolai was named a Secretary of the Central Committee. His new office sat atop the Old Square overlooking the Kremlin. Visitors required special passes to even enter the top floor. Nikolai attended meetings of the Politburo, where he was privy to the most intimate secrets of the party and state. Evgenia needed no more convincing. In 1931, she demanded a divorce from the hapless Gladun. His career had hit a dead end, while Nikolai's knew no limits. Antonina accepted Nikolai's proposal of divorce without hesitation. She could not wait to get rid of an alcoholic, promiscuous, and abusive husband. Her decision to leave Nikolai proved fortunate. Antonina survived. Gladun remained on good terms with Evgenia. He even introduced his new German wife to Evgenia and her nephew, who was amused by her halting Russian. Neither Gladun nor his wife would survive.

Evgenia's marriage to Ezhov propelled her into a new life of luxury, privilege, and authority. Evgenia tried to teach the impossible Nikolai about the finer things in life. First they lived on the exclusive Ostozhenka Street on the Moscow River. Then they moved to a sprawling apartment on Neopalimovsky Street and then to Mamonovsky Alley. Evgenia covered bare wooden floors with expensive carpets and decorated walls with framed paintings. Her imported knickknacks revealed a woman's touch. She accumulated a vast wardrobe of more than one hundred gowns, dozens of fashionable hats, and five fur coats.

She and Nikolai were chauffeured around town in his gold-colored Chrysler Airflow sedan. The Chrysler also whisked them to their "dacha" in Meshcherino, twenty-one miles southwest of Moscow. Dachas are second homes, often modest, where Russians spend their free time, especially in the summer. The Meshcherino estate, however, was far more than that. It included a three-story mansion, gardens, and a tennis court. Evgenia took pride that artists had gathered at Meshcherino during czarist rule. She restored it to its former cultural glory. Evgenia spared no expense in decorating the massive estate as a haven of tranquility and luxury for her artistic friends.

With a rising star like Nikolai Ezhov at her side, Evgenia planned to realize her dreams. If he failed, she could always move on, she thought. Evgenia did not realize that, under Bolshevik rules, wives of traitors were traitors themselves. Marriage to one of the highest officials of the Soviet state carried with it untold privileges but also extreme peril.

Moscow (October 1931–January 1937)

Evgenia anticipated that life with Nikolai Ezhov would not be easy when they married in 1931, but she underestimated how bad it would be. Nikolai drank to excess. As one of her friends described it, "He drank to the point where he lost his sense of being a communist and a human being." Nikolai, a nasty, belligerent drunk, beat her. One neighbor, a man of the theater, heard her screams through the walls. In vain, Evgenia hid his liquor bottles. She herself did not drink. Nikolai bloodied the lip of the deputy minister of heavy industry, Yury Pyatakov, during a drunken orgy. They did not speak again until Nikolai personally turned Pyatakov into a "toothless skeleton" during his interrogation. Nikolai's coarseness grated on Evgenia, the self-declared sophisticate. He competed with his drinking partners as they pulled down their pants to see who could first blow cigarette ashes off of a five-kopek bill with their farts. Nikolai could not abide Evgenia's artistic crowd. When they arrived, he left without saying a word,

Nikolai was known for his child-like behavior. In a living room full of family, he handed his twelve-year-old nephew a rifle and proposed he fire at a phone book to see to which letter the bullet would penetrate. After shouts of alarm from Evgenia, he took the rifle back and ejected live ammunition.

Drunk or sober, Nikolai remained a notorious womanizer no matter how inappropriate. The wives of subordinates, household staff, and Evgenia's acquaintances could scarcely resist the advances of such a powerful man. Nikolai "cohabited" simultaneously with a female employee of the foreign trade ministry and with the wife of a diplomat stationed in Warsaw. After he arrested the diplomat's wife, Nikolai offered "protection" to her fifteen-year-old daughter. He later confessed that he "inclined her to cohabitation in an active form" which, in his language, meant sodomy. When he wasn't pursuing household staff and other men's wives, Nikolai consorted with prostitutes in his many safe houses.

Although Nikolai claimed that he had outgrown his homosexuality, Evgenia knew better. Nikolai's "sins of pederasty" dated back to "mutually active" sex with fellow factory apprentices. He took male lovers during his provincial postings. Nikolai invited his favorite couple, the Dementievs, for sex orgies and drinking. He urged Dementiev to remove his dental plate as he performed oral sex on Nikolai. He complimented Dementiev's wife on her sexual performance, even though "she was rather old."

Evgenia's sexual escapades could scarcely compete with Nikolai's, but her literary salon provided a string of prominent men who visited her private quarters behind closed doors. The finest writers, artists, scientists, and intellectuals attended her salon. She made sure her elegant table was laden with the finest delicacies. She chose a luxurious apartment on Mamonovsky Alley because of the illustrious actors, artists, and musicians of the neighborhood.

Their adoption of the five-month-old Natasha in 1933 brought some semblance of order to their bizarre lives. Nikolai may simply have emulated the Master, who adopted a son, but both Nikolai and Evgenia came to love Natasha deeply. They saw that Natasha had all the privileges: on her birthday, the photographer took pictures of her with the Master's daughter, Svetlana. She even tricked Svetlana

Far left: Natalia, Nikolai and Evgenia Ezhov. Center: Sergo Ordzhonikidze, 1936.

into tasting bitter mustard, saying it was honey. Natasha did not like Lead Butt's daughter. She had a special room full of life-sized dolls, and Natasha did not. Mama and Papa took her to other dachas—to Sergo's, to Lead Butt's. Once, they even visited the Master's dacha.

Natasha loved the Meshcherino estate outside of Moscow. Ezhov and one Iosif Arkadev, Moscow's only other Chrysler Airflow owner, honked at each other on their rare encounters. Arkadev was the husband of Russia's "Queen of the Russian Romance." At Meshcherino, Natasha loved the parrot, Petka, who once pecked her on the head. There Papa loved to sing, most of all the folk song, "And Why Do I Love You, This Quiet Night?" Papa had such a good voice that he was taken to a voice teacher when he was young. The verdict: he had promise, but his small stature would relegate him to the chorus. Papa noticed that Natasha too had a good singing voice. He arranged singing lessons for her.

At Meshcherino, Natasha played with her cousin, Josef, from Mama's side of the family. After Evgenia arranged for Josef to be treated in the special Kremlin hospital, Josef and his mother lived with them for months at Meshcherino as he recuperated. Josef's mother asked to be moved to the servants' quarters to spare her son the sights and sounds of Uncle Nikolai's drunken rages.

Natasha waited patiently for Papa. He came rarely because he always worked. But when he came, he picked her up and asked how many teeth she had, and if she had been sick. If she went too deep into the woods around Meshcherino, Mama warned, "The gypsies will catch you and steal you away." Mama and Papa played tennis against the cook. If the cook won, Natasha had to grab the plume of the pet peacock. The peacock's scream caused her to drop it in fright. Papa loved to play with Natasha. It was Mama who disciplined her and made her do her lessons.

Only Evgenia and Natasha knew Nikolai's darkest secret—so secret that even the Master did not know. Natasha discovered it while playing hide-and-seek in their apartment with her little cousin. She ran into Papa's study and hid behind the curtains. On the windowsill lay a thick album with cigarette paper positioned between pages to protect the photographs. Of course Natasha had to open it. The album contained photographs of dead children, dismembered and mutilated. Natasha remained frightened and upset for several days. No one knew why. Finally, she told Mama, who always locked the study after that. But Natasha feared walking past the study door. She imagined the children's bodies—not in the album but in Papa's study.

Evgenia basked in Nikolai's crowning achievement. On September 26, 1936, the Master named him head of the NKVD. Nikolai was now an integral part of the Master's inner circle. His thirty-eight visits to the Master's office in 1936 approached the fifty-eight of the indispensible Cobbler. Nikolai wrote names on the Master's notorious "shooting lists." If the Master didn't want them shot, he marked through their names with his red pencil.

Evgenia's cousins benefited from Cousin Nikolai's elevated position. They could freely use his permanent ticket to the party loge at the Bolshoi Theater. Nikolai had little taste for ballet. Nephew

Josef was a regular, although his mother did not allow him to tell his schoolmates.

Nikolai reigned supreme from Number 410 on the top floor of the Lubyanka headquarters. He personally interrogated prisoners brought up from the NKVD Internal Prison below. As prisoners approached his office, the escorting guards snapped their fingers. Occupants of each office closed their doors to avoid seeing the prisoners.

Nikolai's right-hand man, Mikhail Frinovsky, wrote Nikolai's correspondence and decrees. Without Frinovsky, the semiliterate Nikolai could not have coped with the vast bureaucracy of the NKVD. Nikolai wore the elegant uniform of an NKVD general major. The bold stars on its lapel and cap reminded Nikolai of an earlier day when sympathetic comrades had to buy him a winter coat. Nikolai and the fabled Marshal Mikhail Tukhachevsky were now of equal rank and wore the same uniforms. Nikolai would prove to be Tukhachevsky's master. Within a year, the Master had him shot based on evidence that Nikolai fabricated.

Evgenia knew in the back of her mind that high office carried risks. The wife, sisters, children, and elderly parents of Yagoda, Ezhov's predecessor, died either in the Gulag or by an executioner's bullet. A smart woman, Evgenia understood that she could share their fate. All depended on the Master.

Nikolai thought otherwise. Surely the Master loved him as he did the Master. He worked tirelessly and with devotion to exterminate the "enemies of the people." No worry that torture was illegal. The Master told him that such "measures of physical intervention" were necessary when the country was in danger.

New Year's Eve 1936 brought to Evgenia the realization that she had achieved her goals, albeit at a high cost. The small-town girl from Gomel stood in the Master's presence at his New Year's Eve party along with the wives of the Cobbler, Lead Butt, Sergo, Klim, and other Politburo members. She greeted the wives of Bolshevik legends as an equal. They greeted her with respect, tinged with fear.

They knew that her husband had become the Master's loyal executioner. They themselves could become his victims.

Evgenia awoke New Year's Day 1937 to Pravda's praise of the Master: "The Great Helmsman Leads Us: our great country is confidently and boldly entering the New Year 1937. We know that it will be a year of great labor and intense struggle, that it will be a year of remarkable victory. It will bring us closer to the promised goal— the creation of a communist society and the victory of socialism throughout the entire world."

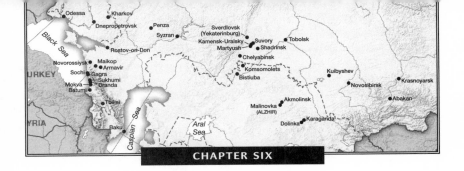

CHAPTER SIX

Adile

Princess Bride of Abkhazia

Sukhumi, Abkhazia, Soviet Georgia (1935–1936)

Adile Abbas-ogly, a fifteen-year-old schoolgirl, caught the eye of the dark, handsome, and brooding Emdy Dzhikh-ogly at a birthday party in the summer of 1935. Abkhazia's large families and intermarriage meant that most of the revelers were related to Adile, Emdy, or both. Adile blushed when Emdy—sixteen years her senior—approached and declared: "Such blue eyes! When she is older I will surely marry her." Who could resist such a beauty with a soft, round, angelic face, deep blue eyes, and an infectious smile that turned up at the corners of her mouth, dressed immaculately in a school pinafore? Adile already had admirers in school, but her strict Persian father kept a close watch on his only daughter.

In Abkhazia, girls married in their teens. Bridegrooms still kidnapped their brides, whether willing or reluctant. Adile sized Emdy up as a prize. Nestor Lakoba, his brother-in-law, ruled Abkhazia with a firm but paternal hand. Sariya, Emdy's sister, presided as the queen of Sukhumi society. Emdy headed the Sukhumi gas and electric works. Other eligible girls reacted with dismay when he set his sights on Adile.

The love-struck Emdy began to court Adile. He followed her home in his car and showered her with flowers and gifts. She answered his advances with, "I don't intend to marry. I am still a schoolgirl." His response: "Within a year or two, someone will steal

Nestor Lakoba and his wife, Sariya.

you. I don't intend to wait." Flustered but flattered, Adile feared her father's ire. Before the revolution, he owned a brick factory, among other assets, and had built the highway into Sukhumi. Her father hated the Bolsheviks, who had taken almost all his possessions. Adile worried he could spoil everything.

On October 20, 1935, Adile's father noticed a strange car circling the neighborhood. Adile feigned ignorance. Invited to a birthday party later that day, the large gathering and the buzz of excitement caught her by surprise. Adile scarcely drank, but her host insisted. A relative of Emdy dictated a letter to the slightly tipsy Adile. She dutifully scribbled that she wished to marry Emdy of her own free will. She now knew what was going on. Two of Emdy's relatives whisked her into Emdy's waiting car. He drove her to his plant, where the wedding guests awaited.

The exuberant bridal party escorted Adile into a separate room and covered her face with a silk veil. Each guest entered, raised the veil, kissed the bride, and handed over a present. The gift exchange completed, the men carried Adile back to the main hall and hoisted her on to the table to dance the *lezginka*, the national dance of Abkhazia. The wedding celebration ended at daybreak as a choir of local girls sang for the parting guests. Emdy retired with his fifteen-year-old bride to the Lakoba compound, a married couple.

Adile's father almost went mad when he learned she had married into the most prominent Bolshevik family of Abkhazia. Because of Bolsheviks like Lakoba, his family lived in only one room of their stately mansion. He also understood that Adile was in danger. The feud between Nestor Lakoba and Lavrenty Beria, the party boss of Georgia, could boil over at any time. No telling what would happen to Adile.

Such dark thoughts were far from the newlyweds' minds. Adile and Emdy moved into the Lakoba clan's two-story villa of white and red brick with a façade adorned by two balconies. Adile treasured her lavishly decorated bedroom, where the newlyweds spent their private time. Although they scarcely knew each other at first, she came to respect her doting and sometimes jealous husband.

Sariya, Nestor Lakoba's wife (and now Adile's sister-in-law), enthusiastically welcomed her brother's teenage wife into the family. She polished the naïve Adile and gave her *The Rules of Good Manners* to read. After Adile returned late from a visit to a girlfriend from school, Sariya reproached her: "You are no longer a girl but a married woman, whose husband occupies a high position. What you have done is simply not appropriate." A quick study, Adile did not have to be told such things twice. Adile and Sariya became close friends.

Adile was surrounded by in-laws much older than she: Sariya, Aunt Naziya (Sariya's younger sister), and Nestor's elderly but energetic mother. Closest in age to Adile was Nestor's and Sariya's teenage son. Rauf spoke fluent French, played tennis and soccer well, and stocked his own library with books that included a rare French edition of Jules Verne—a birthday gift from "Uncle" Lavrenty Beria.

Adile did not know that her father had written directly to Beria to complain of his daughter's forced marriage. As she got to know

Adile Abbas-ogly, 1936.

Emdy and enjoy the social whirl of the Lakoba household, she did
not understand that her presence would drive yet another wedge
into the deteriorating relations between the two party chiefs.

Sukhumi (May–December 1936)

Now sixteen, Adile lived with husband Emdy in the two-story wing
of the Lakoba villa, which covered a whole city block in Sukhumi's
best neighborhood. Three families of government officials occupied
the first floor. According to family legend, brother-in-law Nestor
Lakoba agreed to move in on the condition that the Armenian
owner keep the one-story home in the courtyard. Other rich families, such as Adile's, were crammed into one or two small rooms in
their own homes in the aftermath of the Bolshevik revolution. The
Armenian was counted among the luckier of the former magnates of
Sukhumi. Nestor, despite his almost complete deafness, was a gifted
orator. Although he received poor grades from the Tbilisi Seminary
(except in religion), he wrote clear, grammatical Russian.

Lakobas' house in Sukhumi.

Adile saw her new brother-in-law Nestor as a gentle, soft-spoken, and kind patriarch. She did not know his darker side. The Master would not tolerate a "soft" person in such a position. A crack shot, Nestor bagged more game than the Master's elite guards when they visited. During the revolution and civil war, Nestor used his rifle for human targets. Nestor did not shy away from self-enrichment, corruption, and patronage. Born humbly in an Abkhazian village, he robbed banks and committed mayhem as a revolutionary follower of Lenin.

After only a few months in the Lakoba household, Adile was in danger of being engulfed in the bitter feud between Nestor and Lavrenty Beria. As Beria launched investigations of his former mentor from his stronghold in Tbilisi, Nestor gathered compromising material on Beria. Nestor's spies reported on Beria's "secret games and intrigues." Only one winner could emerge from such a battle.

Nestor's special relationship with the Master served as his ace in the hole. After all, Stalin declared in public: "I am KOBA (the Master's preferred nickname for himself), and you are LaKOBA." A

Josef Stalin (sitting at the table), Nestor Lakoba, and Lavrenty Beria (in front), 1930s.

friend of the Master must be treated well, particularly a politically shrewd one, who confided to his private diary: "Praise of enemies curses them more than complaints." But Nestor's independent streak could irritate the Master. In defiance of Kremlin orders, Nestor spared Abkhazian vineyards and tobacco farms from collectivization, and he included former nobles in his government. His professed devotion to the Master concealed worries about "Stalinists" around him. As the Master consolidated power, Nestor praised Lenin and Stalin both as the true titans of history. The Master overlooked Nestor's occasional lapses, although he could not tolerate insubordination for long. But the Master loved his vacations in Sukhumi.

Nestor meticulously organized the visits by Stalin, Bolshevik dignitaries, and writers and poets. No one left without trophies from hunting and fishing or memories of Sariya's soirees. Nestor did allow one big mistake on September 23, 1933: on the Master's first holiday after his second wife, Nadezhda's, suicide, the Sukhumi police fired on Stalin's boat as it approached the shore. The Master's bodyguard

Sariya Lakoba (front row, second from the left), Sergo Ordzhonikidze (back row, in the center) holds Rauf Lakoba, Nestor Lakoba (front row, second from the right), 1920s.

threw himself on top of Stalin as the boatman steered back out to sea. The Sukhumi police claimed they fired warning shots from the cliffs to drive away unidentified foreigners, but Beria did not let this gaffe go by. Later he spun this incident into an assassination plot by the evil Lakobians.

Six months into her marriage, Adile found herself a pawn in the feud between the two giants of the Caucasus. It began with Adile's father. He burst into the Lakoba home upon learning of Adile's "kidnapping." He wrote letters to Beria, charging forced marriage of a minor. The "concerned" Beria saw an opening. He had no choice but to investigate.

Beria, his wife, Nina, and son Sergo threw the Lakoba household into a panic with an unannounced visit on a Sunday in May 1936. As Beria settled into his chair, he asked to talk with Adile. The worried Sariya rushed into Emdy's and Adile's living quarters. She instructed Adile to tell Beria she was seventeen and had married of her own free will.

As Adile entered, she spied Beria seated in the chair of honor, as if on a casual social call. Of middle height, almost bald, and sporting a reptilian smile, Beria exuded a coldness she had never before

(From left to right) Friends
Lavrenty Beria, his wife, Nina,
Sariya, and Nestor Lakoba.

experienced. Sariya instructed Adile to approach "Uncle Lavrenty" for a kiss on her forehead. The customary toasts followed, first to the Master, then to the beautiful women present and to the new bride. Noting her discomfort, Nestor whispered in Abkhazian that she should calm down or else Beria would suspect something was wrong.

After an interminable pause, Beria got down to business: what was her age, how did she come to the Lakoba family, and why was her father writing such defamatory letters? Adile stammered as Beria stared at her through his pince-nez with a penetrating and terrifying gaze. The artful Sariya headed off the developing fiasco by asserting her rights as hostess. She turned on the gramophone, noting pointedly that it was a gift from the Master himself. Sariya proposed that Adile perform the *lezginka* for the Beria family. As she danced, Adile tried to ignore Beria's metallic glare and his self-assured smirk. At the time, she did not know of his predilection for girls her age. The poker-faced Beria left with one more card to use against Nestor. Rumors began to spread that the Lakobas were rapists of young girls.

After this encounter, Nestor's and Beria's relations teetered on the edge of a total rupture.

Adile's unpleasant Sunday afternoon with Uncle Lavrenty evaporated in the heady swirl of Sariya's galas for dignitaries attracted by Sukhumi's balmy climate. Adile played her role as the new belle of the ball. After opulent dinners, the men repaired to the billiard room until the dancing began. The male guests stood in line to waltz or foxtrot with Adile, the most beautiful girl in the house. Years later, Adile remembered waltzing with the tall, thin Bolshevik legend, Yury Pyatakov. He returned her to Emdy with a deep and courtly bow. Admiring guests, especially the men, watched as Adile performed the swaying and graceful *lezginka*. The jealous Emdy often spirited Adile away early. He did not like all this masculine attention.

The Master himself visited regularly from his summer house in nearby Gagra. He did not pay a great deal of attention to Adile. Instead, he admired Sariya. He even ate the food she prepared for him, although, true to form, not without her tasting it first. Invited to a party at the Master's dacha, Adile mischievously sneaked into his private quarters and even lay on his bed before security guards shooed her away.

As the end of 1936 approached, Emdy began outfitting a four-room apartment on the top floor of the building that housed his employees. With new quarters located near her parents, Adile looked forward to regular visits with family. She dreamed of a bright future with children and other joys. But these dreams soon turned to dust.

ON DECEMBER 26, 1936, Nestor Lakoba received a summons from Beria to travel to Tbilisi. Beria claimed he wanted to work things out face-to-face. Sariya pleaded with Nestor not to go. She had a bad feeling. In a rare burst of temper, the mild-mannered Nestor announced to the family members assembled to see him off, "I am tired of hearing that my bodyguard-wife does not allow me to go anywhere." The car drew up. The front door shut behind Nestor, and a shot rang out. Sariya screamed in horror and burst through the door to find a grinning Nestor, waving a smoking revolver. He remarked, "I have just become convinced that if something happens to me that you, Sariya, will cry bitter tears." He got into the car and drove off. Sariya would indeed cry bitter tears, not only for Nestor but for herself and the rest of the family.

The news came early in the morning two days later when the special phone in Nestor's office rang. Half-awake, Aunt Naziya stumbled in to answer. The call also awoke Sariya, who rushed into the study. Naziya told her that the caller muttered that someone had died and hung up.

Pacing through the house in alarm, Sariya let out a bloodcurdling scream as she spied Nestor's closest friends in the doorway, their faces downcast. She knew immediately that Beria had killed Nestor. Roused by the hubbub, Adile summoned Emdy from the plant, where he had been working through the night. He joined the gathering clan of mourning friends and relatives. Through her tears, Sariya comforted her teenage son: "Don't be afraid. The Master will not let us down."

Early the next day, Sariya and her brothers set out by train on the 211-mile trip to Tbilisi. On the way, they met the special train carrying Nestor's body. Crowds of mourners stood silently as the train passed through their villages. The streets of Sukhumi filled as pallbearers carried Nestor's casket from the train station to the residence. As friends and family gathered around the casket, Nestor's mother sobbed to Adile in their native Abkhazian: "Our young bride, Adile, understood at first glance what kind of a person Beria was, and we received that disgusting snake as an honored guest." When a mourner asked for a translation, Adile complied. Beria later learned of this exchange.

Sariya asked to be alone with the body and closed the doors behind her. The next morning Sariya informed the family that she had called in a trusted physician, who diagnosed the cause of death as cyanide poisoning. Sariya had saddled Adile and other family members with a secret they could not escape. (Beria fired the unfortunate physician a week later. The Master personally signed his death sentence.)

On December 30, solemn mourners shuffled past Nestor's coffin on the stage of the Sukhumi Drama Theater. Among them stood the somber Beria and wife, Nina, bearing a black memorial banner "to our close friend and comrade." The next day, an honor guard laid Nestor's body to rest in the lush, tropical Sukhumi botanical garden. Orators delivered memorial speeches as Meri Avidzba, Abkhazia's own version of Amelia Earhart, circled her plane overhead in a solemn salute.

Nestor's family spent New Year's Eve 1936 going through the condolences flooding in from home and abroad. As each telegram or phone call came in, Sariya anxiously inquired whether it was from the Master. Stalin made sure a solemn announcement ran on the third page of *Pravda*, but he did not communicate with Sariya.

At sixteen, Adile had experienced her first personal encounter with death and tragedy. She did not know that New Year's Eve 1936 would mark the end of her life as the beloved princess bride of Abkhazia. She would see her world upturned in unimaginable ways.

CHAPTER SEVEN

Fekla

Child of the Kulaks

Suvory Village, Urals (1930–1931)

Fekla Andreeva led a carefree life until the men on horseback came for Father and Grandfather on February 10, 1930. The four-year-old Fekla did not understand that Papa, Grandfather, Mama, and even she and her little sister, Katya, were rich farmers, or "kulaks," as the Bolsheviks called them. They had a modest frame home, a barn, and farm animals. At harvest time, Papa hired peasants from the neighborhood to help. These characteristics put them into a class of landowners which the Soviet leaders had determined was hostile to the goals of collectivization and socialism. Fekla did not know her family had to be "liquidated as a class," as the Kremlin masters ordered.

Fekla's village of Suvory, in the Ural Mountains that divide Europe from Asia, scarcely showed up on any map. Sverdlovsk, former Yekaterinburg, where the czar's family had been massacred in 1918, lay sixty-two miles west, and sleepy Kamensk-Uralsky rested thirty-seven miles to the southwest. Only dirt roads connected Suvory with the outside world. Following Russian Orthodox custom, the Andreevs drew their names from the saints. Fekla's Russian Orthodox namesake, Saint Thekla, was miraculously saved from death by fire as a disciple of Saint Paul.

Before Soviet power came to Fekla's isolated Urals village, only the century-old Mir, a form of communal ownership, provided a semblance of village self-governance. Grandfather served as an elected

Fekla visits relatives (clockwise from back row, left): Fekla's aunt Agniya, her mother, Miropiya, aunt Evseviya, Fekla, cousin Maria, and cousin Avgusta, 1929.

elder, giving advice on the time to plant and arbitrating disputes. The Andreevs attended the village church, which was built with Grandfather's money. Fekla's eyes teared up as the bearded priest intoned the scriptures accompanied by the deep male voices of the choir. On Easter, the Andreevs joined the procession around the church, declaring, "Christ has risen. Yes, truly he is risen." The civil war lay a decade in the past, but it still divided villagers. Red Army veterans proudly displayed their red stars and other battle regalia. Those who fought for the anti-Bolshevik Whites, like Father, kept quiet, fearing the day of reckoning.

Soviet representatives from nearby Kamensk-Uralsky brought good tidings for the poor of Suvory: they should take everything from their kulak neighbors. They could revenge past grievances, such as Papa or Grandfather paying them too little, denying them seed loans, or simply living much better than they. The ragged men on horseback came to the Andreev farm, sporting red stars on their caps. They presented themselves as the Committee of Poor Peasants and declared without ceremony, "We have come for your things." A mob of villagers followed, equipped with sacks and carts to carry off the spoils. They hauled Father and Grandfather to the village, leaving Mama, Fekla, and Katya to watch the carnage.

The mob set about collecting pots, canned goods, cutlery, and the family icon, on which they trampled. They led away farm animals. They wrestled among themselves for linens. They left behind a house stripped of everything, except a few spoiled potatoes. The ragtag representatives of Soviet power wasted no time with Papa and Grandfather in the village. Respected farmers like Papa and Grandfather could turn naïve villagers against Soviet power. They ordered their possessions "socialized" and the whole family deported. The mob had already taken away their property. The family waited many months for the second phase of punishment.

Thrown out of their home with only a small provision of grain, the Andreevs slept in barns and used abandoned sheds as feeble protection from the bitter Urals winter. They begged for food from peasant families. Intimidated neighbors who helped them risked charges of collaborating with enemies. Soviet power had indeed come to Suvory.

The deportation order finally came in September 1931 from the overworked Kamensk-Uralsky Executive Committee. It should have sentenced Papa and Grandfather to prison, as "first category" kulaks, and deported the other family members. But Kamensk-Uralsky needed strong backs, even of children. The Andreevs should work for them in the adjacent Special Settlement of Martyush, rather than starving in Kazakhstan with other kulaks. The Andreev family had a stroke of luck. They were not to be separated.

With relief that their fate had finally been decided, the Andreevs boarded waiting wagons with their pitiful possessions along with several dozen other neighbors for the journey into the unknown in

September 1931. They did not know that their new home was a birch forest in the middle of nowhere.

Martyush Special Settlement (September 1931–January 1937)

Kamensk-Uralsky lay in the heart of the Urals metallurgical zone. Its planners placed dots on maps of ore and coal deposits. Each dot was to become a "special settlement" for "special settlers," or *spetsy*. One such dot was the Martyush Special Settlement. It would be Fekla Andreeva's home for the next fifteen years.

The Suvory Committee of Poor Peasants dispatched the "deku-lakized" Andreevs—Grandfather and Grandmother, Father, pregnant Mother, Fekla and sister Katya—in an open cart for the twenty-two-mile journey to Martyush. The Andreevs did not know that local authorities had no provisions awaiting them. Enemies of the people should take care of themselves anyway.

After what seemed an interminable journey, Fekla awoke as the driver shouted, "We have arrived." The date was September 18, 1931. Fekla remembered Mama's, Papa's, and Grandfather's alarm as they realized they had come to a halt in a birch forest. Among the trees, they saw only pits dug into the ground, cropping up like open tombs. There was no sign of human life, no barking dogs, nothing. No one in the open cart moved. A messenger sent by the commandant appeared. He petted the draft horse with his mittened hand as he ordered the wagon's occupants in a gravelly voice, "You have arrived. Get down, all of you."

Father took the tarpaulin from the open cart, and Grandfather laid it on the ground. They carried Grandmother, who could not walk on her own, and Mother, in her last month of pregnancy, to the cover. Next to them, they sat five-year-old Fekla and three-year-old Katya. Disheartened, Grandfather and Father surveyed their family sitting on the dirty tarpaulin in the middle of nowhere—the entire wealth of the kulak family. The adjutant of the commandant rode up on horseback. He nodded toward the open pits and ordered,

"Workers! Prepare the dugouts and make roofs for them." Out of nowhere, silent figures appeared with shovels and saws. They cut down birch trees and threw the limbs across the pits. They then covered the logs with branches and shoveled dirt on top. One of them muttered in a whisper, "Welcome to your new home."

The six Andreevs along with three other families descended into the pit. Mother and Grandmother leaned against the dirt wall and wept inconsolably. Fekla and Katya curiously explored the mud walls with their fingers. Father brought out a kettle, made a fire, and they drank hot tea. There was nothing else to eat. At least, they arrived before the winter cold. Spetsy who were deported in the winter had it much worse. Many did not survive the cold and disease. Grandmother did not last long, dying in 1932. The other Andreevs managed to survive.

Fekla's overland journey by cart proved a lark compared to the locked cattle cars that transported other special settlers to Martyush. The deportees from distant Voronezh and Lipetsk in central Russia were crammed twenty to thirty families in one rail car. Many had six or more children with them. The young and the elderly died along the way. Fekla's neighbors, the six Startsev children, had arrived before them in May. Their father died in prison, sentenced as a "bandit and exploiter." Their mother died upon arriving home from the prison. Despite the loss of both parents, the children were sent to Martyush as "dekulakized elements." The children, including the fourteen-year-old Kseniya, worked in the mines along with the adults.

At first, the Martyush spetsy lived like rabbits in burrows. They built thatched-roof earthen dugouts, about ten by twenty feet square, with their own hands. Seven families shared each burrow, sleeping stacked three-high on wooden pallets with no room "even for a mustard seed" between them. Mornings, they emerged from underground, filthy with mud and grass, to march off to work.

The Andreevs and the Startsev children cooked their meals and warmed themselves on open fires. The camp administrators considered the firewood they used to be "stolen" despite Martyush's location in a forest with plenty of kindling lying around.

MARTYUSH SPETSY SERVED as small cogs in the Master's industrial machine. They worked twelve-hour days, seven days a week. In the early years, their captors did not allow the spetsy time off for even the most sacred Bolshevik holidays, such as International Workers Day on May 1 and Lenin Memorial Day on January 22. They worked with crude picks and shovels to burrow down to depths of 130 feet. They fashioned their own crude wheelbarrows to transport ore to distribution points.

At first, Martyush spetsy worked in a nearby mine, but the Martyush dot on the map turned out to be at the wrong location. Their handlers therefore sent them to another mine, twelve miles away. Papa, Mama, and Grandfather set out at 3:00 a.m. on foot. (Later they used carts, for which they had to pay.) They returned exhausted in the evening, but sleep evaded them. The vicious taiga ticks left gaping wounds, some down to their bones. They also had to prepare for newcomers. Within weeks of their arrival, Papa and Grandfather marched ten miles to prepare dugouts for the next wave of incoming special settlers. The Andreevs also "volunteered" on nearby collective farms. After building a new stable, Papa and Grandfather concluded that the horses lived much better than they did.

All residents sixteen and older worked, including nursing mothers. Fekla's mother gave birth to her younger sisters, Nina and Klavdia, in Martyush, She received practically no time off for each birth. In one case, the guards locked a new mother in a hut for falling behind on her quota. Her children brought her infant to breastfeed through a hole in the wall. In another case, the guards ordered a woman caught secretly attending church to dig thereafter in her one good dress. At first, the guards kept the settlers under close watch. Armed guards herded them to the open-pit toilets—the filthy *nuzniki*. After the authorities realized the settlers had no place to run, "convoying" became more relaxed. The guards had other ways to spoil escapes.

The Andreevs focused on survival from hunger, typhus, cholera, and injuries at work. Like other spetsy, they bought food from their meager wages. Unlike their fathers, brothers, and sisters in the Gulag camps, they were paid, but the pay came to only sixty rubles a month, while a single bag of potatoes cost thirty-five. They paid six rubles for "living quarters," three for the carts that carried them to the mines, and another three for the school and kindergarten. They also paid special levies for the NKVD. The authorities punished spetsy who did not meet their quotas with a 25 percent reduction in pay. A woman they knew, who failed to pay her fees, worked three months without pay. Failure to meet quotas made camp administrators very nervous.

Soviet power did not provide the Martyush villagers with bricks, lumber, or mortar. But they improvised with what they had. After work in the mines, they built themselves crude barracks from dried layers of sod, split logs, patches of grass, soil, and clay. The camp authorities grudgingly gave them dilapidated stoves, one for every four families—a vast improvement over the open outdoor fires.

Drawn from the best farmers of Russia, the spetsy could have grown their own food. But Kamensk-Uralsky authorities located Martyush on forest land unsuited for agriculture. As a form of punishment for the slaughter of livestock during collectivization, camp regulations forbade spetsy to eat meat. But their neighbors had carted off their livestock before the Andreevs could eat them. Were it not for the food smuggled in by sympathetic villagers from nearby Brod, the Andreevs and their neighbors would not have survived, at least in the beginning. An arbitrary commandant could have confiscated the good Samaritans' internal passports, the essential documents which all citizens over age sixteen were required to carry, but the guards looked the other way.

No barbed wire surrounded Martyush. The graceful slopes and rock formations of the Iset River bank exuded an air of idyllic tranquility. In warm weather, the countryside invited. Escape looked easy and appealing. Scattered collective farms offered the only signs of civilization for scores of miles. But Papa and Grandfather could not think of escape. The girls could not survive the rigors of flight. If left behind, the children would have been made to pay dearly by the guards. Search teams caught most escapees anyway. Captured spetsy stood little chance of surviving the starvation, repeated beatings, and solitary confinement that awaited their return.

The guards had a second line of defense against escapes: collective responsibility as a deterrent. If someone in the barracks escaped, the guards hauled off one of the other men to barracks No. 25, no questions asked. The guards gave prisoners in "No. 25" no food. They toiled through the regular twelve-hour workday. After work, the guards beat them as they worked through the night. Family members tried to smuggle life-saving food into "No. 25," but its inmates had slim odds of survival.

Fekla saw the consequences of "No. 25" with her own eyes. After the guards released her playmate's father, her friend ran to Brod village to beg for milk. He returned to find his emaciated father dead. The guards dumped his body unceremoniously outside the settlement, where the wolves and scavengers took care of the rest.

The camp commandant represented Soviet power in the settlement. He dressed in a military uniform, wore a tunic-neck shirt, and sported a heavy black leather belt with a pistol in his holster. The commandant imperiously surveyed prisoners from horseback and carried a ready whip. He decided who could study outside after finishing school and who could marry, and he meted out punishment.

The Andreevs were lucky. Although they had cruel commandants, they escaped the habitually drunk "beasts" who ruled other special settlements, often carrying out a series of sexual assaults. They heard that a commandant from a neighboring settlement shot a seventy-two-year-old woman for "refusal to work." (She was too exhausted to get up.) A commandant from another settlement beat a spets to death in plain sight. He killed another by ordering him thrown into the freezing Iset River.

Martyush commandants came and went. Only disgraced NKVD officers received such a lowly assignment. They did their job grudgingly and perfunctorily. Only the sadists among them enjoyed their assignments. Even if they wanted to keep their prisoners alive, they received only meager supplies. In the end, the quotas counted more than people.

One commandant in particular treated spetsy as dirt unworthy of being spat upon. He haughtily ignored their respectful greetings as he rode by. His rudeness annoyed Fekla's ten-year-old playmate, Masha, who loudly declared as the commandant approached, "I'll not greet him as long as he does not greet me back." He heard her, and word got back to her concerned parents. They instructed her to be polite, no matter what the commandant did. Despite a reprimand, Masha continued her boycott. Settlers had to conceal their smiles when the proud and stubborn Masha refused the commandant's unexpected offer to ride on his horse on her way to school. He spoke to her, and she ignored him. Little Masha bested the camp commandant.

Martyush authorities followed health and sanitary regulations passed down from Kamensk-Uralsky. During one head-lice campaign, guards sheared off Mama's hair, and she returned home completely bald. As a joke, Mama dressed in Papa's trousers and shirt. Mama and the girls waited to surprise Papa. They burst out in giggles as their father stopped dead in his tracks at the sight. Their years in Martyush taught them to make light of moments that they earlier would have regarded as tragic.

THE ANDREEV FAMILY—Grandfather, Father, Mother, and the four sisters—had something to celebrate as the new year of 1937 began. The Andreevs had shown immense fortitude; they had toiled for four and a half years as slaves. They had all survived, except Grandmother. Few families had been so fortunate. Most had lost family members, mainly children, to cholera, typhus, and malnutrition. It looked as if the worst were over.

Fekla, now eleven years old, and her sisters knew only Martyush as their home. Fekla's memories of Suvory dimmed and then disappeared. Two years earlier, the Master had declared, "Life is becoming merrier." No one could characterize life in Martyush as merry, but it was getting better. In 1934, the families had moved from their mud dugouts into adobe barracks that had electricity, plus toilets only sixty-five feet or so from the barracks. They now had two bath houses, one for men and the other for women. True, they had to stand in a long line. But in the old dugouts, they had only one bath, and they could bathe only once a month. What comfort! Fekla and her sisters attended school and kindergarten. Children from nearby settlements had to walk. For Fekla, school—her refuge from harsh reality—was just around the corner.

Grandfather, Papa, and Mama would always be enemies of the people. For the eleven-year-old Fekla and her younger sisters, another life beckoned. Children of enemies could earn the right to leave the special settlement for a better life outside. The Master had already declared, "The son does not answer for the sins of the father." Fekla had her chance to become a model Soviet citizen. She would make her contribution to the building of socialism.

CHAPTER EIGHT

Stalin
The Storm Descends

The Kremlin, Moscow (December 18–31, 1936)

Iosif Vissarionovich Stalin began December 18, 1936, his fifty-eighth birthday, with a huge pile of papers awaiting his attention. As an exception, he had no official meetings scheduled for the day. Stalin liked to say he worked on behalf of the proletariat. He had few pleasures. Chronic indigestion prevented him from enjoying spicy Georgian food, and he drank moderately. Even the films he watched in his special screening room after midnight were there only so that he could protect his people from seeing the wrong things. He retired to a simple military bed in the early hours. His staff knew he would not wake before mid-morning.

Stalin's corner office on the second floor of the Kremlin's "Corpus No. 1" stood one floor above his own apartment. For Kremlin insiders, "being called to the Corner" meant a summons to Stalin. On this day, he worked alone with his personal secretary, Alexander Poskrebyshev, nicknamed the Silent One, who had already arrived at work at 5:00 a.m. as usual. The Silent One would leave at 10:00 p.m. at the earliest. With Poskrebyshev's photographic memory, little had to be committed to paper. All marveled when the ugly, bald Silent One wed a lithe and playful beauty. They were devoted to each other. Later, the Silent One continued to serve the Master after he had her shot.

Stalin's associates now referred to him as "the Master" behind his back. To his face, they addressed him formally, although old friends irritatingly continued to use the personal form of address (ty, in Russian). Their acknowledgment of him as "Master" confirmed his absolute hold on power.

Stalin's office measured 1,615 square feet, with five windows overlooking the courtyard. The walls were covered with oak paneling decorated with carvings from Karelian birch. Lenin and Karl Marx glared down from portraits encased in heavy wooden frames. In the corner stood an old-fashioned stove; central heat would not be added for a few years. It was from this office that the Master ruled the expansive territory of the Soviet Union and rained terror on his subjects. Over the next seven months, the Corner would be witness to planning that would cut huge swaths of terror through the state, party, cities, countryside, special settlements, and camps.

Three days later, on December 21, Stalin hosted a boisterous crowd of family and colleagues in the Kremlin. The Master decided what music to play. As at his other parties, the Master goaded his guests to eat and drink too much. At least, he did not order Lead Butt and the Cobbler to dance as at an earlier party. Sister-in-law Maria recorded in her diary that she danced until seven in the morning. Maria reminded the Master of his beloved Kato. Maria was as close as the Master had to "family." It was with regret that he would have her shot in 1942. The Master's exhausted guests departed in the early hours. They arrived sleep-deprived in their offices near noon.

As millions of Russian families gathered to greet the new year of 1937, they did not suspect that two years of terror stood before them. Stalin was about to set in motion a mass purge that would doom almost three quarters of a million victims, men and women, to execution pits and send a greater number into the vast Gulag system.

Stalin became the Master by patient and careful planning. He did not rush, especially when embarking on bold new measures. As 1937 began, he determined that it was time to eliminate all of his enemies once and for all time. For such an ambitious undertaking, he had to carefully prepare the stage. First he had to convince his minions that they were surrounded by enemies and that radical measures were needed.

In the early days, the enemies were "the others." Now, the Master concluded, the enemy had infiltrated the state, the party, and even state security. True Bolsheviks needed vigilance to root out enemies from their midst, even if they were friends and relatives. Those unwilling to do so revealed themselves as enemies.

Millions of his enemies were already under the ground or in camps and special settlements. He had swept the cities of anti-Soviet elements. But relatively few of his enemies had been executed. They remained a potential danger. He would not be safe until all his enemies were, as they said at the time, "no longer among the living."

Even more worrisome, the Master now suspected his enemies were banding into conspiratorial groups bent on overthrowing him. His worst enemies were even consorting with foreign powers. It was time to call his subordinates to heightened vigilance. They must seek out and liquidate the enemies in the highest ranks of the Soviet state and party. But high-level enemies have followers. They formed conspiratorial "nests" intent on harming Soviet socialism using sabotage or deliberate plan failure. Vigilant regional officials must be alert for any sign of disloyalty. Only vigilance would keep the Master and his regime secure. It was time to organize his followers to eliminate his enemies forever.

Moscow (February 1937)

Despite the success of collectivization and the execution of Trotsky's allies in August 1936, the Master still felt a sense of deep disquiet. Ezhov's expulsion of almost 10 percent of all party members was proof that enemies had infiltrated the party itself. His regional party bosses complained about returning kulaks and criminals. Almost every day, news came in of accidents, plant shutdowns, and fires. Surely much of this was deliberate sabotage by allies of Trotsky, Bukharin's right-wing factionalists—or "rightists," as he called them—or even enemy agents. Enemies still surrounded him.

The Master's rightist enemies twisted in the wind. Bukharin
and his young wife, Anna, remained confined in their apartment
just down the corridor from the Corner. Ezhov's couriers delivered sealed testimony against them almost daily. When he did not
like what he read, he told Ezhov. The upstart Bukharin challenged
Stalin's interpretation of Marx and opposed his policies. He would
get his come-uppance.

The Master did his best thinking in the Near Dacha. At Kuntsevo, he had the time and quiet to ponder the big issues and craft
his plans. His Kremlin office buzzed with too much activity, and his
apartment study shared a corner of the family dining room. Work
piled up on his office desk. The Cobbler and Lead Butt made him
decide too many things. At times, he barked at them in frustration,
"Decide something yourself!" But when they did, they usually got
it wrong. In the end, he had to do it himself. In the early weeks of
the new year of 1937, the Master turned his Kuntsevo thoughts to
liquidating his enemies "once and for all time." Ezhov promised the
Master he was up to the task.

At Kuntsevo, the Master lived and worked in his bedroom. He
had everything he needed there: a sofa for sleeping, a large table piled
with documents and newspapers, and an array of special phones.
When absorbed in work, the Master did not leave his private quarters. Attendants placed a tablecloth monogrammed with Stalin's
initials, "IVS," on the table and brought in his meals. The Master
didn't put much thought into food; he ate in haste. Stalin cared
little about creature comforts, but he had to think of his health.
The Master fitted the large bath off his study with imported sanitary equipment. He disliked foreign products, but he needed hot
water for his aching joints. His pains dated back to his exile, when
he froze while the soft Lenin and Bukharin luxuriated in cozy Swit-
zerland. His sacrifices earned him the basic amenities. An auxiliary
heater ensured that there was always hot water.

Valechka (Valentina Istomina) took care of Stalin at Kuntsevo.
She was in her early twenties, and Stalin admired her attractive peasant face, turned-up nose, and full figure. Valechka's constant good

humor and mirth livened up the place for little Svetlana. Valechka's officer husband went along, and he survived the purges and the war. Valechka supervised the Master's meals. He accepted medicine only from her hand. She tended to his frequent infections and diarrhea without telling others. A mighty Master could not be weak or ill. Valechka sometimes stayed in his bedroom until Stalin fell asleep, at 3:00 or 4:00 a.m. Years later, only Valechka clung hysterically to his body in the Near Dacha on March 5, 1953. The others feigned grief, while heaving sighs of relief.

By early February 1937, the Master was ready to act after much deliberation in the Near Dacha. He instructed the Silent One to send invitations for a plenum (a meeting of all members and candidate members of the Central Committee) to start on February 19 and last one week. The final list included 125 Central Committee members, fifty-seven members of control commissions, and fifty-one invited guests, including Sergei Mironov of Western Siberia. Ezhov, of course, would be a keynote speaker. An NKVD officer delivered Bukharin's invitation personally to his Kremlin apartment. Notably, his invitation limited his attendance to the first session only.

The Master had learned long ago that a true "Master" should remain almost invisible at plenums. Let Lead Butt, the Cobbler, Klim, and the Armenian—and now the faithful Ezhov—do the dirty work. A Master remains above the fray. They must all confess their lack of vigilance. They must name enemies within their own ranks. With the ban on high-level executions broken, accusations meant almost certain death.

The incoming delegates faced a delicate balancing act. To uncover too many enemies meant they lacked vigilance. Too few meant they sympathized with enemies or belonged to the enemy conspiracy. The Master constructed the plenum as a loyalty test. He would sit, listen, and decide.

The log of meetings in the Corner recorded the increasing pace of activity as the opening day of the plenum approached. On Monday, February 8, the Master met with eleven officials from 4:30 to 9:30 p.m. On Saturday, February 13, he met for five hours with various

officials. On Sunday, the Master invited nineteen officials—the largest group so far. The meeting included the keynote speakers from
his inner circle: "Lead Butt" Molotov, "Cobbler" Kaganovich, and
"Sergo" Ordzhonikidze, plus Ezhov.

The Master worried about Sergo, the keynote speaker on
"wrecking in industry" (the Master's term for deliberately under-
mining the economy). Sergo resisted throwing his own people over-
board. Sergo hated criticism. Why should he, of all people, admit
to a lack of vigilance? Sergo denied the requests of the NKVD
to arrest his subordinates. Instead of denouncing his deputies as
a true Bolshevik should, Sergo defended them. Unlike the Master's other cronies, who took the arrests of wives and relatives in
stride, Sergo vehemently objected to the arrest of his older brother.
Sergo's prison visit to his right-hand man—Yury Pyatakov—on
January 29 confirmed his unreliability. Pyatakov's mutilated face
disturbed Sergo, who even bent down to ask, "Is your testimony
voluntary, absolutely voluntary?" Vigilant Bolsheviks do not ask
such questions. Anyway, Pyatakov received the supreme penalty the
next day.

Sergo went from bad to worse. He telephoned the Master throughout the night after Ezhov ordered a search of his apartment on February 16. In the old days, the Master usually took Sergo's calls, but
not that night. Sergo met Bukharin's young wife in the Kremlin
courtyard, squeezed her hand, and instructed her to "be firm." On
February 18, Sergo did not get out of bed. His worried wife, Zinaida,
summoned his sister. In the early evening, they heard a shot. Sergo
had killed himself.

The Master came after a considerable delay from across the courtyard with his entourage. As they entered, Sergo's wife shouted at the
Master, "You did not protect Sergo for me or the party!" The Master
shot back, "Shut up, you idiot!" The Master tore Sergo's parting letter from his sister's hand. No embarrassing suicide notes allowed. As
relatives and party bigwigs came and went, Sergo's younger brother
overheard the Master say: "We will say to the press that he died of a
heart attack."

The inner circle then proceeded at 8:55 p.m. back across the court-yard to entrance No. 2 and up the stairs to the Corner to deliberate. The ledger shows Ezhov entering and leaving the meeting to carry out the Master's instructions. The emergency meeting ended twenty-five minutes after midnight. The official Politburo record lists two agenda items: "The speaker to point No. 3" and "About the Plenum of the Central Committee."

Stalin hated surprises. Sergo, his trusted friend, "spat upon him" like the others. His suicide betrayed the party and the Master, who decided on the spot to delay the plenum until February 23. He assigned Lead Butt to replace Sergo as the speaker to point No. 3.

SERGEI MIRONOV joined the other unsuspecting delegates pouring into Moscow for the February 19 Central Committee plenum. Many arrived on the very evening Comrade Sergo pointed his pistol to his heart. Before Stalin became the Master, delegates had joined their private rail cars together for a convivial trip, but no longer. The Master frowned on private meetings among delegates. However, luxuri-ous suites in the National, Metropole, and Moscow hotels awaited them. Attendants stood ready at their beck and call.

The delegates awoke February 19 to whispered rumors that Sergo had taken his own life, another suicide. Sergo had many friends. Instead of the evening plenum opening in the Kremlin, the delegates trudged to the Union House where Sergo lay in state. Not since Old Man Lenin's funeral had there been such an outpouring of grief. The Master himself pulled the leather strap over his shoulder as Sergo's lead pallbearer. Stalin himself joined the honor guard, standing at the four corners of the casket, as thousands of mourners trudged by. A solemn procession placed the fallen hero's ashes in the Kremlin Wall. Observers listened with sad but determined faces in the bitter cold as Lead Butt mourned the loss of "the most ardent and fearless fighter for the communist cause." In life, Lead Butt and Sergo could not stand each other.

Sergo's funeral ceremonies ended February 22. The plenum began the next evening. One "enemy" had revealed himself through his

suicide. Thousands of others lurked in the dark passages of Soviet
society. The first two days were devoted to the destruction of Nikolai
Bukharin and his ally, Aleksei Rykov (the former prime minister),
whose more moderate politics had no place in Stalin's vision for the
Soviet Union.

After the Bukharin matter, the plenum turned its attention to
rooting out and destroying the suspected thousands of traitors who
had infiltrated every level of society. Although delegates competed
to show their enthusiasm for purging these many traitors, few could
have imagined just how far the purge would go. In fact, many of
those calling loudest for the death sentence for Bukharin, Rykov,
and others were among the purge's first victims.

CHAPTER NINE

Agnessa

Crashing a Funeral

Moscow (February 1937)

Agnessa counted on going with Mirosha from Novosibirsk to Moscow for the February 19 plenum. She looked forward to a whole week of shopping, restaurants, and Moscow high life, while Mirosha attended those dreary meetings.

Agnessa did not conceal her disappointment when Mirosha rushed in on February 18 on his way to the airport: "You stay here. Our rail car is being repaired. I am going to fly to Moscow by myself." With that terse announcement, he drove off.

Mirosha could not deny her that easily. The offended Agnessa ordered a special train to be readied for the next day for the two-and-a-half-day trip to Moscow. The ladies of Agnessa's court clamored to be included. Going with Agnessa meant a free trip in luxury. Agnessa's household staff prepared provisions and packed her things.

As the train pulled out of Novosibirsk, Agnessa and her cronies began a game of poker that continued until the outskirts of Moscow. A male attendant played with them and lost all his money. Agnessa lost to him intentionally at the end, leaving him marveling at his poker skills.

Mirosha greeted her coldly on the platform: "Why did you come and why did you bring *these* people with you?" Agnessa refused to answer to that tone of voice. Her mood softened when she spied a bowl of fresh grapes and pears in their suite at the Hotel Moscow.

Mirosha had ordered it especially for her. "He missed me," she thought to herself.

As they entered the bedroom, Mirosha whispered, fearing they were bugged, "Sergo is dead. Only don't tell anyone. They say it was a suicide, but the official version is a heart attack." He continued, "And now you understand my cold reception when you arrived, especially with those ladies, playing cards the whole time. Why? I told you to stay home. What should I say when people ask why you are here?"

Agnessa assumed a somber expression and replied, "Tell them that I came to share your grief about the loss of our great leader." Mirosha burst out in laughter at her politically incorrect use of "great leader"—that title was reserved only for the Master! Agnessa's faux pas cheered up her Mirosha. To tell the truth, she couldn't care less who was who in the Kremlin hierarchy. Agnessa's ignorance of politics relieved Mirosha. Agnessa's political naïveté might save her. Mirosha's spirits lifted: "What could I do without you? You are like a small light in a dark kingdom."

Agnessa caught the tail end of Sergo's funeral. Crowds of mourners filled the streets with black banners. Eulogies and solemn dirges replaced regular radio programming. Newsreels explained that Comrade Sergo's indefatigable devotion to building socialism caused his heart to fail. Another fallen hero.

Sergo's funeral ended on February 22. Agnessa and her ladies-in-waiting had several days of shopping, cards, and restaurants ahead of them. Mirosha's speech was not scheduled until March 4. He spent time practicing with Frinovsky.

While Agnessa and her cronies had their fun, Mirosha's assigned chauffeur drove him through the Spassky Gate of the Kremlin wall separating Red Square from the Senate House. After passing the guards' inspection, he exited the car at the front entrance of Sverdlov Hall. Mirosha disposed of his winter coat at the wardrobe in the antechamber and queued up to sign the obligatory attendance sheets. It could not escape his notice that the printed lists included those "no longer among the living" or under arrest. Ezhov affixed his signature next to the name of a condemned childhood friend of the Master.

Those entering the magnificent Sverdlov Hall for the first time marveled at the beauty of the blue, white, and gold dome. Delegates craned their necks and whispered among themselves as Bukharin made his way hesitantly down the right aisle and sank to his knees before he reached the front. Weakened by a hunger strike, Bukharin defended himself as best he could before the jeering crowd. Of the thirteen "orators" heaping abuse on the hapless Bukharin, seven would "no longer be among the living" by the end of 1938.

The Master waited until March 1 to turn to the main agenda: Lessons from Sabotage. Ezhov spoke in a monotone with a slow cadence, but he had the audience's rapt attention as he accused the "feudal princes" of "defending their departmental uniform." Encouraged by shouts of "You are right" and "Arrest them," Ezhov berated his party colleagues: "Not once in my five months in the NKVD has some leader called me on his own initiative to say: 'Comrade Ezhov, there is something suspicious about this person, something is not quite right, can you investigate this person?'"

In paroxysms of panic and terror, speakers rose to engage in self-criticism and to point the finger of guilt. "Orators" vied to name the most enemies within their organizations and to show that they had eradicated these vermin. As they returned to their places, they shouted epithets at other speakers for their lack of vigilance and half-hearted self-criticism.

Mirosha's perfunctory March 4 speech followed the formula set out by Ezhov: "Comrades, the rotten chasm in which the NKVD finds itself has many reasons as highlighted by Comrade Ezhov. Despite the order to deliver a mortal blow against the Trotskyites and right deviationists, not one operational decree inspired our Chekists or mobilized us for battle against our enemies." Mirosha delivered the Master's message: We have not been vigilant. We must liquidate the evil enemies of Soviet power.

The Master played his usual role as the most moderate person in the auditorium. He warned that excessive expulsions from the party would play into their opponents' hands—or, in the Russian saying, "bring grist to the mill of our enemies." He condemned "zeal to expel thousands of excellent people prepared to sacrifice for the cause." The delegates, however, understood the message: investigate, arrest, and kill all those whom you suspect. Enemies could be anywhere, even within the NKVD. True guilt or innocence makes no difference.

Agnessa began to understand that politics were indeed important. Until Sergo's death, she thought that high politics were not "worth a sneeze." Mirosha's and Agnessa's fates were already intertwined with those of Frinovsky and Ezhov. If they fell, Mirosha and Agnessa could crash down with them.

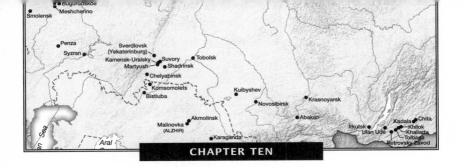

CHAPTER TEN

Stalin
Launching the Great Terror

Moscow (July 1937)

Its modest size and simplicity struck first-time visitors to Stalin's Kremlin apartment. Guests expected something grander. Thick walls and composite wood ceilings framed the impersonal interiors of small rooms connected by a narrow hallway. The bucket of pickles at the entrance provided a Georgian touch. The Master loved pickles. His adopted son, Artem, shared a small room with Vasily. Little Svetlana had her own. Svetlana complained that she rarely saw her father. Usually, he came home only to eat. Home, at least, gave him safety from poisoners. Artem complained about the bad food. For the children, guests for dinner meant better cuisine. The cook scolded the Master for not eating well and for staying up into the wee hours.

The dining room served double duty as the Master's study, where he crammed books into every nook and cranny. He had 25,000 volumes, including copies of many books which he had ordered to be removed from libraries. He could no longer keep up with the quota of reading 500 pages a day that he had set for himself in the mid-1920s.

It was against this backdrop that Stalin launched a "mass operation" against the enemies of Soviet power, big and small.

On the evening of July 2, 1937, the Master had important business to discuss with the diminutive Nikolai Ezhov. That momentous date gave the outward appearance of an ordinary workday. The Master's Kremlin office meetings started at 2:40 p.m. and ended at 7:05 p.m. In these four hours and twenty-five minutes, the Master had what appeared to be routine meetings with twelve officials. But something of great importance happened in the twenty-four hours of July 2. Twenty-nine days later, on July 31, the Politburo's records show that it approved the July 2 decree "About Hostile Elements." The Silent One placed the draft of this decree written in the Cobbler's scribble in the "special files" with the signatures of eight Politburo members affixed in the margins.

The Master and Ezhov met that evening to transform the top-secret Politburo decree into an "operational decree" for its executors. Stalin and Ezhov completed their work in one sitting. The Silent One distributed NKVD Directive No. 266 the next day by coded telegram to all heads of regional administrations of the NKVD. It instructed them, "Upon the receipt of this telegram, investigate all those kulaks and criminals in your area, returning after serving their sentences or fleeing from camps and settlements. Divide them into two categories: the first is the most hostile elements. They are to be arrested and shot; their cases are to be processed by troikas. A second category of less active hostile elements is to be deported according to NKVD directives. Send to me the numbers of first and second category elements by July 8. Instructions about the timing and procedures for this operation will follow.

"N. I. Ezhov, Peoples' Commissar, NKVD, July 3, 1937"

Over the next four weeks, Ezhov visited the Master's office seventeen times, for a total of forty hours. Only Lead Butt saw more of Stalin. The Master had decided to deal "once and for all time" with his enemies. He planned a mass operation dwarfing dekulakization in scope and brutality. Only his most trusted deputies could know for now.

Ezhov's July 3 telegram set off a frenzy in the sixty-five regions. Leaders of each rushed to prepare lists of enemies. They had but a few days to search personnel files, card catalogs, criminal archives, and any other records that might yield "enemies" for their lists. Telegrams began to flow into Moscow on July 7 and 8. The July 8 telegram from Eikhe and Mironov in Western Siberia expressed enthusiasm for the upcoming campaign: "The important and correct proposal of the Central Committee to purge collective and state farms and enterprises of fleeing kulaks and criminals suits our situation in Western Siberia. According to preliminary figures from 110 districts, the number of fleeing kulaks and criminals is 25,000. Of these, the most hostile and active are 6,500 kulaks and 4,200 criminals, whom it is necessary to shoot." Mirosha, unbeknownst to Agnessa, had pledged to shoot almost 11,000 residents of Western Siberia.

The regional officials chomped at the bit to get the bloodbath started. The Ukrainian party leadership, without consulting Moscow, recommended on July 10 that "the troikas begin their work." Frinovsky warned them: "Do not start the operation. I repeat: Do not start. A special instruction from the commissar will follow."

Ezhov ordered the regional NKVD heads to Moscow for a special meeting on July 16 to get the operation organized. As Sergei Mironov of Western Siberia traveled to Moscow, Ezhov scurried between the top floor of the Lubyanka and the Master's office to clarify questions coming from the regions: "Can we use incriminating evidence in place of confessions for the death sentence? Can the troika pass sentences in absentia? Should we exempt soldiers, war medal holders, and invalids?"

Ezhov's July 16 meeting with regional NKVD heads in Moscow took place behind closed doors under conditions of utmost secrecy. Upon his delayed return to Novosibirsk, Mirosha related to Agnessa only a few details: Ezhov gave general operational instructions to the assembled NKVD officers, while Frinovsky discussed with each region separately its "operational limits." Ezhov expanded the list of enemy categories to include "other assorted anti-Soviet elements," a catch-all term for anyone deemed hostile to the regime. Mirosha stayed on several days after the Moscow conference to consult with his mentor, Frinovsky. Ezhov received them both as frequent guests, and they joined his drinking bouts. Despite Mirosha's claims of faithfulness, he could scarcely have avoided Ezhov's and Frinovsky's orgies that involved sex with prostitutes.

Stalin assigned quotas of executions and imprisonments to each of the Soviet Union's sixty-five regions. As Sergei Mironov in Western Siberia and Lavrenty Beria in Georgia received their quotas, they had to be sure that they uncovered and punished as many or more enemies as other regions. As regional administrations competed for higher repression rates, ordinary families were increasingly drawn into Stalin's execution net.

The wives and daughters of prospective enemies of the people would have been hard-pressed to understand why their husbands and fathers represented a threat to Soviet power. Maria Ignatkina knew that her husband labored long and hard to build socialism. Fekla Andreeva saw Father depart for work every day and return exhausted. He had no time for hostile acts against the Master. The youthful Adile in Sukhumi understood better. She had witnessed first-hand what happened to those who tangled with Soviet authority.

Upon his return to Novosibirsk, Mirosha called his troops together on July 25 for a briefing: "As I acquaint you with our plan, the figures you hear should disappear from your memory. Anyone guilty of letting this information slip must answer to a military tribunal. I must acquaint you with the numbers so that you can appreciate the magnitude of the operation." After going through the numbers of executions and arrests, Mirosha ordered his subordinates to return to their districts on the first train out. He instructed them to submit their lists of enemies to the prosecutor's office only after completion of the operation to avoid interference from justice officials. He also stressed the importance of confessions. With a signed confession, they need submit only a brief protocol to the troika. Mirosha ended on a chilling "technical" note: "The head of the operational group should locate a place where the sentences will be carried out and a place to bury the bodies. If the place is in a forest, it will be necessary to dig trenches in advance with plenty of earth to cover the area so that the location cannot become a place of assembly for opponents and religious fanaticism."

Back in Moscow, the drafting of the full NKVD's Operational Decree 00447 proceeded at a furious pace. Frinovsky did the writing, while Ezhov consulted the Master. They feared word would get out and send panicked enemies into hiding. On July 29, Yezhov and Frinovsky met with the Master, Lead Butt, the Cobbler, and Klim from 3:25 to 7:00 p.m. Frinovsky remained behind an extra hour. As the author of the draft decree, he answered questions and entered corrections.

On July 30, 1937, the "Operational Decree of the NKVD Commissar N. I. Ezhov No. 00447" was dispatched by coded telegrams to the regions. It ordered the operation to start on August 5 and placed Frinovsky in charge. Anyone "hostile" to Soviet power was "subject to repression" of the "most merciless form." Anti-Soviet elements were to be divided "into a first category of the most dangerous and most hostile enemies to be immediately arrested and after examination by troikas—TO BE SHOT." The less active hostile elements were to be arrested and placed in camps for a minimum of eight years.

The first and second category "limits" for the sixty-five regions added up to 75,950 executions and 193,000 imprisonments. The sixty-five regions faced the monumental task of identifying, sentencing, and executing almost 80,000 people.

Ezhov buried a significant detail deep within the order: "In cases where circumstances demand a raising of limits," regional NKVD offices "must present to me petitions justifying the request." This seemingly innocuous note encouraged regional officials to compete among themselves for ever higher limits. As a result, at the end of the Great Terror, actual executions exceeded the limits in Decree 00447 by a factor of ten.

Throughout the Master's empire, there was a growing sense that something very bad was about to happen. Experts from NKVD investigative technology departments hunched over their desks wearing bulky headphones for *proslushka*, the secret monitoring of phone calls. They tracked down persons implicated in confessions and managed the network of *seksoty* (secret collaborators). Citizens were "taken" (the term arrest was not used) from their apartments or off the street in "black ravens" (vehicles used to transport prisoners).

Rumors of arrests in Kamensk-Uralsky spread through Martyush. For no apparent reason, Fekla's neighbor, Ponosov, disappeared. In Chita, the DTO headquarters on Kalinin Street buzzed with nervous energy. The prison cells began to fill with prisoners in anticipation of the big event. The clatter of typewriters preparing arrest orders filled the corridors. For Adile in Sukhumi, Beria's arrests of her friends and relatives accelerated. They were getting closer to husband Emdy and sister-in-law Sariya. In Novosibirsk, Agnessa noticed that Mirosha left early, and he slept poorly at night. For Evgenia Ezhova, Nikolai's regimen did not change. He still worked almost constantly. In his spare time, he drank and caroused. She did not want to know what he was doing. She had her life, and he had his.

NIKOLAI EZHOV, perched atop the Lubyanka, intended the "mass operation" to be his signal achievement. He would rid the country of its enemies once and for all time. The Master would love him and reward him for his loyalty. Decree 00447 made him the arbiter of who would live and who would die, no matter how mighty or small. His power was summarized by the boast of a Chita NKVD official: "I am the interrogator, the judge, and the executioner."

Nikolai's job was to carry out the Master's orders, not to question them. While playing billiards, Nikolai's teenage nephew Josef asked his Uncle Nikolai: "Is it not strange that so many of those who made the revolution and were with Lenin turned out to be enemies of the people?" Uncle Nikolai remained quiet and then responded: "There is your ball. Over there is the pocket."

Moscow (August 1937)

Mid-August 1937 found the Great Terror under way. NKVD officers busily organized arrests and interrogations and proposed punishments to the rubber-stamp troikas. To save time, death sentences required only a couple of lines of text. Troikas could approve hundreds of executions in one sitting. With rare exceptions, the troikas did not see the wretched persons they sentenced to death. It was all very antiseptic, but the execution itself was not. Each of the condemned received a bullet to the head at close range as his body was pushed into a ready pit.

The Master had one small detail to attend to. Operational Decree No. 00447 stated that family members were not, as a rule, to be repressed. But the Master worried that he had been too lenient to "family members of traitors of the motherland," known by the acronym ChSIR (chleny semei izmennikov rodiny).

On August 13 and 14, the Master met with his inner circle for five hours to correct this mistake. He invited Ezhov and Frinovsky to join his inner circle to draft an operational decree for the ChSIRs. The Politburo agenda approved, as item No. 646 on August 14, "Operational Order of the NKVD No. 00486: About the Repression of Wives of Traitors of the Motherland and the Placement of their Children."

It instructed the regional NKVDs as follows: "Women married to husbands at the time of their arrest are to be arrested with the exception of pregnant, breast-feeding and elderly women and wives who provide information that leads to their husband's arrest . . . All property with the exception of clothes and utensils the prisoner can carry with her is to be confiscated, and the apartment is to be reregistered. The wives of traitors are to be imprisoned, depending upon their social danger, no less than five to eight years. Children from ages three to fifteen are to be placed in orphanages of the ministry of health in other locations."

Unless the ChSIRs turned in their enemy husbands, they were to be arrested themselves and their children taken away.

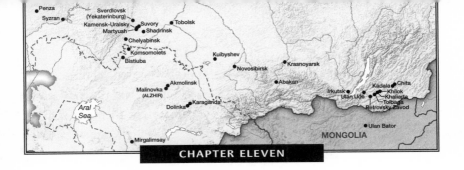

CHAPTER ELEVEN

Agnessa
The Purge Spreads Far and Wide

Novosibirsk (March–July 1937)

Upon her return from the February–March 1937 plenum, even the professedly naïve Agnessa noticed the increasing pace of arrests. As Mirosha's NKVD arrested the husbands of Agnessa's card partners, she sensed the fear around her, but she felt Mirosha was safe. After all, Frinovsky valued Mirosha, and Ezhov needed Frinovsky.

Agnessa heard from a Moscow friend how the worst had happened. She was sleeping with her sick husband, when, without warning, men in NKVD uniforms held her down. They yelled at her startled husband, "You are under arrest." They led him away after he collected some warm clothes. Agnessa's friend found Frinovsky relaxing in an easy chair in the living room. He kissed her hand in a perverted display of gallantry. Agnessa imagined that one day she could find herself in her friend's shoes with Frinovsky demanding more than a hand kiss.

Meanwhile, Mirosha held the power of life or death in Western Siberia. When Agnessa tried to plead for the arrested son of a Rostov friend, Mirosha's mood darkened instantly: "If he has been arrested in Rostov, the matter will be decided there. I will have nothing to do with this case. I would act the same if it were my own relative." Mirosha ended with a warning: "Never ask me again about such matters. We must agree on this once and for all. My work is none of your business."

91

But with arrests escalating, Mirosha drew Agnessa into his "business." In June, Frinovsky instructed him to host a commission headed by another Mironov, unrelated to Mirosha. Lev Mironov arrived with a retinue supposedly to conduct an audit of Western Siberian operations.

Mirosha arranged an elaborate dinner followed by dancing. Agnessa played the gracious hostess. Her guests had good manners and knew how to dance. The other Mironov sat playing with four-year-old Agulya, who was perched on his knee. Agnessa remarked to Mirosha, "Perhaps he is sad for some reason." Mirosha answered, "Why should he be sad? We received him with such honors."

A week later, Mirosha arrested the whole entourage. Frinovsky had sent them to him for a quiet arrest in the provinces. The other Mironov would be shot in August 1938. Henceforth, Agnessa thought of him whenever Mirosha went away on assignment.

Agnessa saw Mirosha growing increasingly edgy. On one of her regular visits to his office, Agnessa and Mirosha began a game of billiards in the side office. Agnessa was no slouch. They contested their games fiercely. In the midst of the game, Mirosha suddenly stopped short, the cue stick frozen in his hand. He turned pale. Agnessa followed his gaze. Through the large window, she saw three military men approaching in NKVD uniforms. Agnessa burst out, "What is the matter, Mirosha?" Then she understood. For an instant, he thought they were coming for him.

Agnessa could breeze in and out of NKVD headquarters whenever she wanted. On one such day in late July, she was surprised by the crowd of NKVD officers milling around the office in nervous anticipation. Among them were strangers she did not recognize.

With her nose in the air, Agnessa brushed through the crowd into Mirosha's office. He sat studying documents, frowning with creases in his forehead. Her surprise visit clearly displeased him: "Agnessa, can't you see I'm busy? Wait outside." The imperious Agnessa went into the next room. Mirosha ordered her: "No. Not there. Go to the reception." Agnessa shot back stubbornly: "No, I want to stay here."

The irritated Mirosha called his secretary. In a fit of pique, Agnessa rushed past the crowd to the main entrance, where the guards demanded her pass. Of course, she refused. Agnessa stayed away from home until nearly midnight to show her anger. Finally, chilled to the bone, she skulked home to find Mirosha in bed, not sleeping. As Agnessa lay down beside him, Mirosha volunteered, "That was something how you rushed by all the guards without a pass!" Mirosha confessed he could not sleep despite taking a sleeping pill. Heartened, Agnessa thought to herself, "This must mean he still loves me."

The next day, Agnessa learned that she had interrupted a top-secret meeting with all the district NKVD officers. Frinovsky had ordered Mirosha to inform his subordinates that the NKVD chief of the Tatar Autonomous Republic had been executed because he had made too few arrests. A sense of profound shock had filled the room. If you wanted to survive you had to produce arrests by any means necessary. The next evening Mirosha told one of his most trusted subordinates over the dinner table, "We cannot let that happen to us. We must keep up with the other administrations. Keep pace or face doom."

Unbeknownst to Agnessa, Mirosha piled up arrests, convictions, and executions. As a star of Ezhov's NKVD, he had already received the ultimate recognition: on June 28, the Master authorized Western Siberia to form a troika to expedite mass executions. He named Mirosha its head with Eikhe and the chief prosecutor as its other two members.

Weeks before Operational Decree 00447 became operational, Mirosha busily prepared to handle mass arrests. He reported to Ezhov on July 8 that he had prepared ten new prisons to hold 9,000 inmates. Mirosha's most notorious prison, called the "bird house," held 250 prisoners in each room. Conditions proved so horrendous that a prisoner committed suicide by immersing himself in a huge container of boiling soup.

As head of the Western Siberian troika, Mirosha signed death sentences right and left. In the July 10 meeting of his troika, Mironov sentenced 724, of whom 411 were executed. One night, Agnessa noticed that Mirosha, who usually snored loudly the minute his head touched the pillow, was lying awake, his eyes wide open. When she asked what was wrong, Mirosha told her that as he sentenced an engineer to death because of an explosion, "He looked me straight in the eye and said: 'I know what is waiting for me, and I only want to say that I am not guilty of anything. I wrote many times about the safety problems, but no one paid any attention.'"

Mirosha's appointment to head the Western Siberian troika made him the most important man in the region. As in other parts of the country, power shifted from the party to the NKVD. Eikhe himself suddenly became inordinately polite and deferential to Agnessa. He would sit next to Agnessa and discuss politics. He talked about China, about Chiang Kai-Shek. When Agnessa admitted that these Chinese names meant nothing to her, he gave her no sign of reproach. She understood that Eikhe knew that Mirosha was now superior to him.

Agnessa welcomed this elevation but understood the instability of her throne. Too many of her ladies-in-waiting had lost their husbands to arrest. She saw fear behind Mirosha's bluster. She knew too well what happened to wives of enemies of the people.

Ulan Bator and Moscow (July 1937–December 1938)

Japan's occupation of an area bordering the People's Republic of Mongolia alarmed the Master. He must ensure that Mongolia and its ruling communists not be undermined by enemies. And who better to cleanse Mongolia than Ezhov's right-hand man, Mikhail Frinovsky?

The vigilant Frinovsky began the Mongolian purge in Moscow. He arrested the "pro-Japanese" prime minister in July and Soviet Ambassador Vladimir Tairov on August 5. The Mongolian military chief of staff died of "accidental" food poisoning in Irkutsk. Frinovsky needed someone like Sergei Mironov, who did not shy away from blood, for the Mongolian operation.

As July 1937 came to an end, Agnessa feared the worst. Mirosha headed the troika that passed all sentences, usually the "highest measure." At night, he slept poorly. He complained that his own staff spied on him. Phone calls brought the distressing news that other regions were achieving "shining successes" while Western Siberia "slept." He knew of widespread arrests of his peers in other regions. Could he be next on the list?

In late August 1937, Mirosha's situation became clearer. Out of the blue, Stalin named Sergei Mironov ambassador to Mongolia.

Frinovsky gave Mirosha and Agnessa three days to pack their suitcases. Agnessa decided to take Agulya along. She dispatched Mama and Lena back to Rostov with the astronomical sum of 5,000 rubles in their pockets. Agnessa and Mirosha rode to the station with the Eikhes to greet Frinovsky's special train full of troops. Agnessa still feared an elaborate trap. As the train chugged to a stop, the radiant Frinovsky spied Mirosha, smiled smugly, and patted him protectively on the shoulder. The two scarcely glanced at Eikhe as they began an animated conversation. Eikhe bowed, fawned, and went unnoticed. He turned to Agnessa to tell her how much he regretted their departure and his wish that they "send him a little word if possible."

With this display, Agnessa's fears evaporated. What a success! They entrusted her Mirosha with such a responsible task in such a sensitive time. She observed the instantaneous return of Mirosha's self-confidence, imperial bearing, decisiveness, and relentless ambition. His eyes again glistened with the fire of success.

Mirosha, Agnessa, and their entourage boarded the train, leaving the waving Eikhes behind. Eikhe would be arrested six months later. He was tortured so badly that he was shot missing one eye.

In the train, listening to Mirosha's and Frinovsky's animated conversation about geopolitics, Agnessa breathed easy. She read diligently the "rules of conduct of Soviet envoys abroad" and learned to her disappointment that diplomats' wives must dress modestly—no ostentatious jewelry.

At a stop in the middle of nowhere along the way, Agnessa and Agulya were strolling along the track when they heard an inhuman shriek of suffering. Agnessa asked what it was, but no one answered. As the train resumed, Mirosha provided the answer, his face set in stone: "That was Tairov." Frinovsky had brought Mirosha's predecessor on the train to extract more evidence of perfidy and plots in Ulan Bator.

Agnessa and Agulya rode in a covered truck through almost 400 miles of desert, steppe, and rough terrain from the rail stop at Ulan Ude to Ulan Bator. The troops traveled in open trucks or on horseback in the freezing rain. After a day's travel, Mirosha informed Agnessa that he and Frinovsky had decided to fly ahead to Ulan Bator. Agnessa replied, "Let the others stay. I'll fly with you." Mirosha warned, "But the plane is made of plywood." Agnessa continued to insist after the pilot assured her, "The plane flies like an arrow." Mirosha backed down, to Agnessa's relief. She had never flown before. She was certain any plane she boarded would crash.

Finally, Ulan Bator. What a disappointment! Just open steppe, the Mongolian tent-homes called yurts, and dust storms. Viewing the ugly tent city, Agnessa vowed to teach the wives of local officials how to dress and behave properly.

As their first order of business, Frinovsky and Mironov presented Mongolia's acting head of state—Khorloogiin Choibalsan—with a list of Mongolian enemies and named him to head the Mongolian troika. His troika condemned the victims, while Frinovsky and Mironov stood in the shadows. Choibalsan expressed his gratitude with "warmth and affection" for the Master's generosity.

On their first day, Agnessa watched as Tairov's wife gave directions to the movers. Agnessa resisted the temptation to whisper to her, "Your husband has been arrested." Agnessa understood her private hell, but could give her no words of comfort. That evening, as talk turned to Tairov's wife, Frinovsky remarked matter-of-factly, "When she is in Moscow, we'll have a little chat with her." Agnessa understood the kind of "chat" he meant and imagined herself in Mrs. Tairov's shoes.

As Mirosha busied himself with uncovering and executing traitors, Agnessa attempted to improve the cultural milieu of Ulan Bator.

The rampant promiscuity of Mongolian girls particularly grated on the strait-laced Agnessa. With the exception of her extra-marital affair with Mirosha, Agnessa lived monogamously. (Not that she lacked opportunities.) Mongolia, Agnessa learned, suffered from low fertility due to a syphilis epidemic. Girls "circulated" with as many men as possible. The more men, the greater the chances of pregnancy. Agnessa was shocked when the parents of a "circulating" girl told Agnessa: "Let her play around a little more. Maybe she'll get pregnant. Then all the eligible young men will want to marry her."

When Agnessa appeared at a reception adorned with the latest beehive hairdo and clad in an evening dress, the wives of Mongolian officials looked her over from head to foot. At the next reception, Choibalsan's wife appeared with a hairdo and blue silk dress exactly like Agnessa's. No wonder the Mongolians took her fashion statement as an order. Her husband had the power of life or death over each of them. When Choibalsan's young wife suddenly disappeared, he explained that he had to get rid of her because she was "hostile" to the Soviet Union. Agnessa recognized nonsense when she heard it. He got tired of her and wanted a new young wife.

Mongolian food repelled the fastidious Agnessa. The host and guests stuck their hands in the common pot of greasy lamb to extract fat-laden hunks of meat, which they popped into their mouths with their greasy fingers. The fastidious Agnessa tried to pick meat from the corners where others had not touched. Mongolian hygiene revolted Agnessa even more. Mongolian women who felt the urge simply hiked up their robes and squatted on the ground, wherever they happened to be. Smiling, squatting women greeted Agnessa politely as she passed without interrupting their exertions.

Mirosha ended his duties in Mongolia and returned to Moscow in April 1938 after nine months in Ulan Bator. He left behind good statistics. Mirosha had repressed about 27,000 people, almost 3 percent of Mongolia's entire population of 900,000.

On April 4, Mironov summarized his achievements in a telegram to Ezhov: "We conducted additional arrests related to the united conspiratorial center. As of March 30, we dealt with 10,728, of these

7,814 monks, including their leaders, 1,555 Buryats, 1,555 feudalists, 322 responsible officials from the ministries, 108 officials of the Mongolian republic, and 408 Chinese. We concluded 7,171 cases of which 6,311 were death sentences."

Although Mironov was back in Moscow, Agnessa had to stay behind. Agulya had fallen ill with scarlet fever and could not travel. Agnessa sat at her bedside two days and nights. The Soviet military command flew in a specialist, who saved Agulya at the last moment. The military hospital even transported an X-ray machine to their house. The technician reminded Agnessa of someone in Maikop with the same name. When she asked, he responded, "That means you are either Agnessa or Lena?" Agnessa remembered he played the role of a guard dog, chasing away bandits in their games. In gratitude, Agnessa invited him to dinner, but she saw he could hardly speak from distress. His father, she remembered, owned a shop and his brother spent time in jail. Her guest spent the whole evening on pins and needles, fearing Agnessa would reveal his past to the authorities. Her good deed turned into an evening of torture for her guest.

With Agulya finally well enough to travel, Agnessa made the trip back from Ulan Bator in a car loaded with her purchases. In Ulan Ude, they boarded the train for Moscow. When they arrived at Yaroslavsky Station in Moscow, Agulya screamed "Papa, Papa" when she spied Mirosha on the platform. Agnessa could see he was happy not just because they arrived. He wore a business suit and not his NKVD uniform. He was still a diplomat, not a Chekist. Mirosha ordered his people to take care of their luggage, and they entered Moscow traffic. After Ulan Bator, Moscow struck Agnessa as a boiling kettle.

With an air of mystery, Mirosha refused to tell them their destination. Agnessa expected a suite in a hotel, but they passed the Metropole and National, and then Manezh Square with the Kremlin on their left. They crossed the Moscow River and turned into the newly constructed "Government House" built for the party elite.

Mirosha escorted them into a beautiful six-room apartment on the seventh floor, with fresh fruit and flowers to greet them.

Mirosha hugged Agnessa and whispered in her ear, "Are you surprised? I am now the deputy minister of foreign affairs for the Far East. Take a look." On his chest he wore the Order of Lenin, the nation's highest decoration. Agnessa knew well that look of success in his eyes. Agnessa called Mama to Moscow. Together they enjoyed the sight of the Kremlin domes from their windows.

The first of many invitations—to a reception in the Foreign Minister's ambassadorial residence—drove Agnessa into a frenzy of preparation. Moscow diplomatic circles understood fashion and could stand a new face. As Agnessa donned her brocade evening dress with the cinched waist, bare shoulders, train, slippers with gold weave, and high coiffure, Mama assured her, "You will be the most beautiful of all." Mirosha joined in the admiration: "You could imagine she was born a duchess." Mirosha cut a fine figure himself in his tuxedo, his grand wavy hair already graying.

The reception did not disappoint Agnessa. The young women wore low-cut dresses. Their necks, wrists, and fingers bore the finest jewels and gold. Even an "old" fifty-year-old woman caught Agnessa's eye in her bright red dress, with a red rose in her hair. Japanese diplomats stood with their helmets cradled in their bent arms. When one of them stepped on her train, Agnessa gave him a contemptuous glance. The embarrassed Japanese grinned what Agnessa considered a false smile.

Mirosha settled into the routine of diplomatic life. He received officials from China and Japan, and his old friend, Choibalsan, from Mongolia. Diplomacy called for fewer hours of work than the frenzy of his Chekist years. He spent more time with his extended family in their spacious quarters in the Government House. Agnessa played gracious hostess to his foreign visitors. At home, Mirosha enjoyed making up games for Agulya and her playmates.

But Mirosha's high spirits alternated with depression and despair. One evening, Agnessa quietly observed him putting on his medals for a diplomatic reception. His self-satisfied look evaporated as he turned to Agnessa with a sense of foreboding: "Whatever happens, you must keep my medals. You can always sell them. They can guarantee you a living."

Agnessa and Mirosha resumed their friendship with the Frinovskys. Nina Frinovsky's birthday gave them a first opportunity to see the Frinovskys' summer home. White columns adorned the front. An open terrace with chaise longues placed between blooming flowers graced the back. From the terrace, guests entered a glassed-in veranda for dinner. Spacious living quarters, a study, a movie theater, and a billiard room welcomed the dacha's inhabitants and guests. The Armenian's dacha stood nearby.

Nina bustled around with last-minute preparations, while Frinovsky greeted them as a feudal baron. He invited them to relax on the terrace, anxious to hear Mirosha's latest news from the foreign office. Agnessa, who had admired Nina's "new look" in late 1936, determined that her vulgarity was showing through again. She still had an air of Paris about her, but she painted her face like a prostitute.

After the other guests arrived and finished their meal on the terrace, they proceeded to the private film theater. In the next room, the older Frinovsky son was playing pool with Mikoyan's sons. Exclamations of jubilation from the billiard room interrupted their film: "Vasya has come!" Agnessa looked into the next room to see a pale, red-haired, pimpled youth dressed in a uniform. All the attention embarrassed him. His eyes darted to and fro, not knowing where to look. Frinovsky ran over to Vasya, introducing him as the younger son of the Master. He called for his secretary. At tomorrow's viewing of horses, he should take Vasya along and let him pick out one or two for himself. Vasya's face turned red with excitement.

Mirosha's island of safety began to look vulnerable. Frinovsky and Ezhov, Mirosha's protectors, appeared to have lost the Master's support. On August 22, Stalin named Beria Ezhov's "deputy." With Beria looking over his shoulder, Ezhov could only remind the Master of his unwavering loyalty and write that "despite all these large deficiencies . . . the NKVD did a healthy job in smashing our enemies."

On September 8, the press characterized Frinovsky's new assignment as minister of the navy as a promotion, but Mirosha knew better: "Why such a short announcement? Where is his portrait?" On November 25, the Master replaced Ezhov with Beria. Ezhov, exiled to the Ministry of Water Transport, appeared at work drunk, fashioning paper airplanes during meetings. He knew what lay in store for him.

Every day Mirosha appeared at work to find new people on the job. The next day, new people replaced yesterday's new people. Even the ambassadors were being purged. Not an evening passed without a "black raven" pulling up to Government House. It departed quietly with a new enemy of the people. Shortly thereafter, the wife or adult children disappeared, and a new tenant arrived.

One evening, Mirosha and a neighbor entered the lift. As the door was about to close, a stranger dressed in white *burki* felt boots entered. Both Mirosha and the neighbor froze. Mirosha's floor was the seventh, his neighbor's the eighth. They heaved a sigh of relief when the stranger exited on the sixth floor. Their eyes met without expression. It was not a time for pleasantries.

The tension overwhelmed Mirosha. In the middle of the night, he jumped out of bed, as if possessed, to rig a line from a ceramic pot in front of their door to the lift. If the elevator door opened in the middle of the night, the crash would awaken him. Agnessa understood. He needed a warning to have time to shoot himself. Mirosha sobbed hysterically, "They are taking the wives, too." Agnessa had never seen him cry before. She stroked him reassuringly: "An arrest does not mean the end. You will be freed. You are innocent. You still will have a life. If you shoot yourself that is really the end."

They agreed on a code. If he could write her from jail, "tender kiss" meant things were going well and "regards to all" meant the opposite.

Then everything seemed fine. Shortly before New Year's Eve, 1938, Agnessa heard Mirosha's hearty voice on the telephone, teasing her as in earlier times: "Do you have your wardrobe ready for the New Year?" Agnessa did not understand. She answered: "Yes, I have an evening gown for the ministry party." Mirosha could scarcely contain his excitement: "No, we are not going there. We are invited to the Kremlin for the New Year!" He hung up, after saying that only two people from the ministry had been invited. The other was the foreign minister himself.

Agnessa collapsed in her chair, almost crying. A weight fell from her shoulders. All these fears had been empty, almost comical. Her Mirosha was back on top. The Master valued him. They would both live.

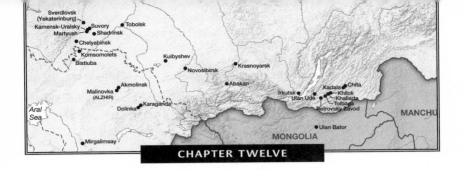

CHAPTER TWELVE

Maria

A Narrow Escape

Chita (June–August 1937)

Maria Ignatkina adhered to the highest standards for "communist activist wives" set by Comrade Sergo for "housewives to the nation." Maria shared the responsibility for her husband's production targets. His successes were hers. She groomed herself stylishly to mark her social status and to set a standard of "culturedness" for others. The curtains, tablecloths, and other decorations with which Maria occupied herself made for a comfortable and pleasant home. The meals she prepared followed state norms of nutrition. Maria played the benevolent mother figure for Alexander's employees. She established cultural circles for children and supervised meals at school. Maria volunteered in the worker canteens. She placed flowers and hung curtains in the miserable workers' dormitories. Her children consistently received among the highest marks at school.

The head of Chita's NKVD returned from the February-March plenum determined to show "good figures" of arrests and executions. His Road and Transport Department, known by all as DTO, occupied a three-story headquarters on Kalinin Street. DTO was his largest department, not unusual because it guarded Chita's major industry—the Trans-Baikal Railway. The Chita NKVD had to find enemies among the rail engineers and workers to show its value to Moscow.

DTO's Chekists chafed at being called "provincial tram inspectors" by the swaggering operational officers. They could brush off such slights by catching a big fish (and troublemaker) like Alexander Ignatkin. He had been a thorn in their side for too long. His fellows looked up to him. The DTO had much to gain if it made him an example.

The DTO Chekists got the evidence they needed in June. A defective freight car damaged track outside of Chita. Ignatkin dispatched a team to make repairs. A signal man mistakenly waved on a waiting train, which derailed with one fatality. This accident fell within Ignatkin's responsibility. Ignatkin's DTO adversaries wanted him tried under the notorious Article 58—an almost automatic death sentence. But DTO did not have time to conjure up witnesses to prove a conspiracy. Hastily fabricated evidence and uncoached witnesses threatened to make a mockery of the case in open court. They agreed instead for Ignatkin to be charged under Article 193 for dereliction of duty.

The Chita Military Tribunal set Ignatkin's trial for August 2. As an Article 193 defendant, Ignatkin continued to work. He slept in his own bed on August 1 before he and Maria departed for the court. The court ordered his arrest on August 3, and he spent the remainder of his trial in the DTO prison on Kalinin Street. He would never again be a free man.

Maria had no idea what to expect, but she prepared for a long trial. She sent Nadya, Olga, and Yury to a youth sanatorium at Petrovsky Zavod, a five-hour train ride from Chita. Alexander had headed Petrovsky Zavod station years earlier. She could count on the children being well cared-for. For the time being, she told the children nothing. Maria attended the trial every day, hoping that the court would take Alexander's more than twenty years of faithful service into consideration. Alexander, in his defense, explained that the wreck was the result of a series of unfortunate human mistakes. Throughout his career, he worked conscientiously to make his section of track safe. No matter how many precautions are taken,

accidents occur. The prosecutors argued that Ignatkin had been der-
elict in his duty. How could such an accident occur otherwise? They
hinted that Ignatkin had even more sinister motivations but did not
elaborate.

On August 17, 1937, the military tribunal sentenced Ignatkin to
seven years in a corrective labor camp. At least, the court did not
confiscate his property. The court ordered Alexander to serve his
sentence in a remote location, far from family and home. Maria
sat stunned in the courtroom. Consternation greeted Ignatkin's sentence throughout railway circles in Chita. His colleagues valued him
as a solid specialist and a fair boss, not groveling before anyone. The
DTO picked its example wisely. His subordinates muttered among
themselves, "If Ignatkin is in jail, who should be free?" The conviction of Alexander Ignatkin, chief engineer of Chita operations, demonstrated that a stellar professional career record did not help if the
secret police, the dreaded "organs," decided to go after you.

Then, apparently, a miracle: the authorities sentenced Alexander
to serve his seven-year term at Kadala station, only a fifteen-minute
rail ride from Chita. Kadala housed a labor camp, its forests and grass-
lands laid bare by strip mining. Over the years, Alexander had spent
much time in Kadala. He had fished in the nearby Ingoda River.
With Alexander close by, Maria looked forward to regular visits.

Still unaware of their father's trial, the children returned alone by
train ten days after their father's sentencing. In their absence, Maria
planned for seven years without her husband's salary. She found a
part-time job in the school cafeteria—not enough to pay the bills.
Maria surprised the children by boarding their train at Kadala. She
told them that their father was working in Kadala and that she would
take them to see him the next day. They bought the story. They knew
he often traveled to Kadala for inspections.

The next day Maria took the children to see their father. He told
them everything as they sat together in a field in front of the camp
gate within sight of the guards. Alexander explained that the Kadala
administrators understood what kind of a "criminal" he was. They

wanted him to supervise the building of a new rail spur within the camp. They would pay him a small salary. He could move around the camp without guards.

Alexander discussed matter-of-factly how they would get by until his situation was "clarified." Alexander instructed Maria, "My dearest one: sell everything that is not absolutely necessary including your wedding ring, but be sure to keep the fishing nets." Alexander intended to use his fishing skills to support the family. Maria knew the importance of the fishing nets to Alexander. Once, after someone stole his nets, he sent Maria all the way to Irkutsk to exchange his wedding band for a new net.

Alexander parted with Maria and the children with the words, "We'll make it through. Remember, they will review my sentence. Maybe they'll free me or reduce my sentence." Maria and the children left, prepared to accept their undeserved misfortune. Alexander and Maria were gratified that he had not been sent far away. This small bit of good fortune gave them the courage to confront the dark period that lay ahead.

Chita (September–October 1937)

In the 1936 portrait of the five Ignatkins, father Alexander appears clean-shaven and proud, dressed immaculately in his uniform. His prison photograph taken on September 7, 1937, shows a gaunt, unshaven, short-cropped man glaring at the camera with an expression of defiance and intense hatred. It is the portrait of a man subject to the most extreme miscarriage of justice—of someone determined not to be broken.

Maria and the children last saw Alexander in late August in the field in front of the Kadala camp. Maria learned that Alexander was no longer in Kadala on her next visit. The Kadala camp authorities refused to give any more information than that. A frantic search led her to the DTO headquarters on Kalinin Street. Maria, with daughter Olga in tow, queued up with other wives in front of the main entrance. Reaching the front of the line, Maria asked the officer at the desk whether an Alexander Ignatkin was inside. He told her: no. She rejoined the line until she heard the dreaded words on her third try: "He is here, inside."

Maria rushed home to prepare a parcel. When she and Olga reached the front of the line, the officer examined the package and asked, "And where is the tobacco?" Little Olga answered, "Our Papa does not smoke." The officer replied, cackling at his brilliant wit, "He doesn't smoke, but here he smokes." In other words, next time the guard expected tobacco. Maria continued her ritual for the next few weeks. She stood in line and handed over packages for Alexander whom she presumed was inside. Despite repeated entreaties, the guards gave her no information.

Maria and the crowd of wives and mothers congregating on Kalinin Street posed a threat to "Soviet power." As eventual ChSIRs, the Master needed them arrested, their property confiscated, and their children sent to orphanages. The Chita authorities could not act, however, until the traitors' sentences were passed. Only then was Maria officially a ChSIR. Until then, the women could assemble on Kalinin Street.

The Chita Transit Military Court sentenced Alexander Ignatkin on September 29 after a twenty-minute hearing. The full docket required the court to move on to the next case. With Alexander sentenced, the Chekists could move against Maria.

On October 7, 1937, eleven-year-old Yury Ignatkin arrived at school for the afternoon shift. His fourth grade teacher called him to the front: "They telephoned that they need you urgently at home. If you finish early, come back for the last class." His teacher did not know that she would not see him again. Yury dashed home, hoping Papa had returned. As he burst expectantly through the door, he saw his weeping mother standing in a corner, embracing Nadya and Olga. They were all crying. She rushed to him: "Thank God, we are all together." The officer in charge paced back and forth as he wrote down descriptions of their belongings. Curious neighbors peered in and hurried away. One of the men poked Maria's bosom for hidden articles. Olga innocently told her mother: "Look, the

'Uncle' put Papa's watch in his pocket." The DTO thief kept Papa's watch, awarded for outstanding service. He knew Papa did not need it anymore.

The officer in charge telephoned headquarters: "Send a car. I can't handle all this stuff by myself." The men loaded the confiscated possessions in the trunk of a black car. They hustled Maria and the children into the back seat. In the center of the city, they veered from Kalinin Street through the arch of DTO headquarters. The car halted. The officer opened the car door and ordered: "Ignatkina, get out of the car and sign the protocol." As Maria and the officer moved toward the front entrance, the driver revved the motor and the car began to pull away. The children screamed. Their mother lurched toward the car, and, before their horrified eyes, the men beat her to the ground. The driver took them to the NKVD orphanage at 26 Smolensk Street.

The Chekists hauled the distraught Maria into DTO headquarters. She did not react to anything. She sat motionless, as if in a trance. They searched her, taking her remaining money along with her wedding ring. At home Maria could not remove it from her swollen ring finger. But here they knew how to get rings off prisoners.

Within hours, a sergeant of state security began her interrogation. He had handled the "final stages" of Alexander's case and knew the Ignatkin case well. As the wife of a convicted traitor, he needed to confirm that she and Alexander were husband and wife and to determine the level of "social danger" she posed. Maria attested that she and Alexander had married in 1922 and that "I know nothing about any counter-revolutionary activity of my husband. He told me nothing about this." With that her interrogation ended.

On the next day, Maria was transferred with the wives of other "traitors" to the city jail at 1 Ingodinskaia Street. The prisoners slept in shifts on mattresses due to overcrowding. Maria scarcely noticed her surroundings. She wept the whole time. Following bureaucratic procedure, Maria had to confirm to a clerk the items confiscated from her. She reported, "Money and my gold ring." Consulting the record, the clerk confirmed the registration of 600 rubles, but he

The last photograph of Alexander Ignatkin taken in prison, September 1937.

failed to find a ring. Maria answered with indignation: "How can there be no ring? Tell me how I got this white stripe on my ring finger!" The clerk called in the admitting officer: "Where is the ring?" Stammering, he searched his pockets: "I forgot it at home in my other uniform pocket." He went home to fetch it.

On October 10, Maria learned Alexander's fate. The wife of one of Alexander's colleagues traveled from Khilok station to Chita that day with a package for her jailed husband. Upon arrival at the Chita station, she learned about the arrests of the other wives. As she prepared to flee on the next train, she glanced at the previous day's issue of the *Trans-Baikal Worker*. She read that the transit military court completed "the cases of participants in anti-Soviet terrorist and espionage diversionary organizations of Trotskyites and rightists on the railroad of Eastern Siberia." Attached were the names of 117 specialists of the Trans-Baikal Railway who had been shot. As she scrolled down the list, she saw her husband's name.

Publication of the list was delayed until all the wives were in custody. Only the Khilok station chief's wife had escaped the dragnet. The stricken widow hid the scrap of newspaper in her shoe shortly before the Chekists discovered her in the station. She brought the list with her into the prison cell. The other wives lined up to search for their husbands' names. Maria's face contorted with pain as she saw Alexander's name.

Maria and her cellmates could not avoid seeing the words crudely scratched high into the masonry of their cell by a previous inmate: "Better an end to horror than a horror without end." She did not know that Alexander had been in the same cell only a few days before. Now he was somewhere else.

CHAPTER THIRTEEN

Evgenia

Socialist Realist

Moscow (1935–December 1937)

At the end of 1935, Evgenia Ezhova found her calling as a "socialist realist." The Master invited her to edit the magazine that presented the new socialist paradise to intellectuals the world over. She had finally found her calling.

The Communist Paradise seemed too far removed from the reality of everyday life. Despite the Master's assurance that "life is becoming merrier," workers slaved in ramshackle factories under hazardous conditions. They cursed Soviet power and even told jokes about the Master. Stalin thought: if only workers and peasants could visualize the coming paradise, they could better accept their teeming communal apartments, shared dirty kitchens, and queues for filthy toilets. And who better to describe the Communist utopia than artists, writers, designers, and photographers? Even those who did not share the Bolshevik dream could create a new art form—socialist realism—to celebrate the achievements of Soviet power.

The Master needed Russia's greatest living writer, Maxim Gorky, for this bold venture. Stalin paid dearly for Gorky's return from Italy in 1933: he awarded Gorky the Order of Lenin and a mansion off of Tverskaya Avenue in central Moscow. He renamed his birthplace "Gorky." The Master avoided arresting artists whom Gorky protected, even the irritating Isaak Babel. The Master's investment in Gorky paid off when the famous author praised the redemptive rehabilitation of prisoners building the Baltic-White Sea canal. If Gorky wrote these things, wavering socialist and communist allies in Europe and America would believe them.

In June 1929, Gorky proposed a new illustrated magazine—*USSR Under Construction*—to depict a USSR as it should be, not as it was. The Master agreed and spared no expense. Like the oversized USSR itself, the new monthly appeared in enlarged format, on the best paper (with silk and gold etching), simultaneously in Russian, German, French, Spanish, and English. It sold for the unheard-of price of five dollars. Gorky sent out gratis copies to sympathetic socialists, among them George Bernard Shaw, H.G. Wells, and Romain Rolland, the French writer and essayist and winner of the 1915 Nobel Prize for Literature.

The *USSR Under Construction* depicted bronzed, muscular, heroic workers enthusiastically producing trucks, automobiles, combines, and textiles. Contented and joyous collective farmers steered shining tractors, harvested fields overflowing with grain, and recuperated in modern clinics. Diverse nationalities lived in harmony in a land of beautiful scenery, inspired athletes, and dedicated scientists and artists. The darker sides of Soviet life disappeared: the editors fed and dressed Gulag miners for the photo shoot. The benevolent Master loomed above all this happiness and joy with arms outstretched. As the March 1936 issue reassuringly announced a fictional Ukrainian saying, "What Stalin says will be done, will be done."

Unlike the radiant and joyful Soviet Union it depicted, the editorial board of the *USSR Under Construction* lurched on the edge of collapse. As its sixth anniversary approached, the infirm and unreliable "chief editor" Gorky chafed under house arrest until his death on June 18, 1936. The "responsible editor," Yury Pyatakov, was already a marked man. Of the remaining editorial board, only two had journalistic experience (as well as experience in Evgenia's bed).

The magazine needed a new editor. "Journalist" Evgenia Ezhova fit the intellectual profile. She wrote poetry and studied music and dance. She dressed in the latest fashion and cultivated an air of elegance. Noted intellectuals, writers, and diplomats frequented her salon. The vibrant Evgenia knew how to enliven boring Kremlin banquets, as she persuaded party leaders to dance or play cards. Evgenia herself wanted to be more than a social hostess. She should have a career like Isaak Babel's beautiful young engineer wife.

Evgenia was named deputy editor in late 1935. In June of 1937 she assumed the executed Pyatakov's title of "responsible editor." Evgenia—the self-educated provincial girl—found herself in charge of the avant-garde journal that presented the image of the Bolshevik state to the outside world.

As responsible editor, Evgenia confronted the logistical, artistic, and technological challenges that came with creating something entirely new each month. Each issue required teams of writers, illustrators, artists, and typographers. The cramped Spiridonovka Street offices burst with intellectual activity, coffee, smoke, and improvisation. Together, Evgenia and her team coordinated texts (in five languages) and printed and inserted foldouts of maps, paintings, illustrations, and other unique design features. (Today, copies are sought after by collectors, and its artwork and graphic designs are on display in museums of modern art.)

Evgenia's rock—Isaak Babel—had long since lost interest in Evgenia as a sexual partner. They formed instead a mutually beneficial business partnership. She lurked in her chauffeur-driven car in front of Babel's apartment to whisk him off to work. They edited text together in the editorial office on Saturdays. Evgenia used her massive budget to set salaries and bonuses. She sent her colleagues to exotic shoots at the best hotels and resorts. Babel particularly welcomed the opportunity to earn extra money to support his multiple families.

Evgenia's first issue in January 1936 featured sparkling rest homes and sanatoriums. Satisfied workers and peasants luxuriated in the sun, strolled in forests, frolicked on beaches, and enjoyed sumptuous cuisine. Another issue displayed smiling and contented collective farmers sitting in a sunlit field, all eyes on a charismatic young party propagandist. Doctors clad in spotless white treated farm children in immaculate clinics. Village girls in bright peasant costumes performed traditional dances for an admiring public. The April issue featured a tall, youthful, and bearded Master as he urged factory workers on to revolution in his native Georgia. Paintings showed Stalin as he should have been. Lavrenty Beria and Nestor Lakoba shared a small portion of the spotlight. Librarians later removed Lakoba's picture from copies printed in Russian, but they lived on in foreign-language versions.

Nikolai Ezhov refused to believe that Babel and Evgenia were not lovers. He did not mind Evgenia's other lovers, but raconteur Babel made fun of the Master. No telling what he said about Nikolai. Ezhov searched his apartment for Babel's love letters. He screamed and beat Evgenia. But as Nikolai flung himself headlong into the battle against enemies, he no longer cared that Babel and Evgenia consulted long hours behind closed doors. He faced more important tasks and challenges.

Throughout their married life, Evgenia and Nikolai kept their personal and professional lives separate. Evgenia's appointment to the editorial board of *USSR Under Construction* changed all that. With Nikolai's arrests striking closer to home, Evgenia fought to keep her tight-knit crew together. Babel's quip that "we are becoming accustomed to arrests as we do to the weather" got back to the Master. Beneath his bluster, Babel felt much less confident. He remarked after Gorky's death, "Now that he is gone, they will not let me live." The September issue failed to appear—clearly a sign of trouble. Neither did the October and November issues. Finally, the December issue, labeled "9–11, 1937," hit the newsstands.

As Evgenia's world crumbled, Nikolai's soared. The party and NKVD elite gathered in Moscow's Bolshoi Theater on December 20, 1937, to celebrate the twentieth anniversary of the founding of the secret police. Its staging honored Nikolai Ezhov—the indefatigable warrior against enemies of Soviet power.

Mikoyan, "the Armenian," served as the master of ceremonies. He nimbly sprang to the stage, a small man dressed in a service jacket and boots in the style of the Master. The Armenian burst into praise of "the talented student of the Master, the favorite of the

Soviet people who protects our security, and from whom all Chekists should learn." As the Armenian concluded, the members of the audience sprang to their feet in an ecstasy of applause and ovation, as if overcome by insanity.

Packed in the dense auditorium sat Sergei Mironov and wife, Agnessa. Like the others, they beat their hands together until they were raw. What else could they do? Such was the situation in Moscow. The guest of honor, NKVD Commissar Nikolai Ezhov, disappointed Agnessa to no end. On the stage sat a small, frail man with scars criss-crossing his face—an apparent nonentity. He looked anything but healthy. And he was Mirosha's boss. They said that his wife, Evgenia, was positive and cultured. She and Agnessa would get along well.

Life in the editorial office ceased to be a joy for Evgenia. She had wanted only the finer things in life. She enjoyed socializing and flirting with artists, scientists, and explorers. The creative energy of her designers enlivened her. But now she detested the atmosphere of fear in the editorial offices as she and her colleagues waited for the next arrests.

Worst of all, Evgenia understood that even Nikolai's powers were limited. Alone in their apartment, she appealed to Nikolai to spare a childhood friend who had been arrested. He immediately turned away and left the apartment. When she recounted to another friend what had happened, she put her finger to her lips and pointed to the ceiling. Even the head of the NKVD was being listened to.

CHAPTER FOURTEEN

Adile

The Master Will Not Abandon Us

Sukhumi (January–June 1937)

With Nestor Lakoba buried for more than a month, his portraits disappeared from public buildings. Horrible and disgusting rumors spread throughout Abkhazia. As the ultimate sacrilege, Beria moved Nestor's body from its place of honor in the botanical garden to the Mikhailovsky cemetery. Acquaintances avoided Adile, Sariya, and Emdy. People feared mentioning Nestor's name. As Adile later remarked, "They isolated us like lepers."

Anyone associated with the Lakoba clan risked arrest. The first of Sariya's brothers was arrested in mid-April as he visited Adile and Emdy. A stranger politely requested Sariya's brother to come with him "for just a couple of minutes to clear up a minor matter." They did not see him again. A month later, a second brother was arrested outside of Moscow.

Sariya departed for Moscow after the first arrest. Once Stalin knew of Beria's crimes, she was certain, he would come to their aid. Sariya took with her Nestor's collection of compromising material about Beria. Sariya also took with her what she thought to be the facts of Nestor's death.

This was the story that Nestor's bodyguard had reported to Sariya: Nestor's meeting with Beria deteriorated into a shouting match. The agitated Nestor returned to his hotel and warned his guard to stay by his side. The telephone rang—a call from Beria's mother: "Nestor,

---

please come to dinner. I have prepared trout just as you like it."
Nestor refused. Beria's wife, Nina, appeared at his door, tearfully beg-
ging Nestor to come to dinner. They should not allow anger to
spoil their long friendship. Nestor gave in. At Nina's insistence, the
wary Nestor ate one bite of trout and drank a little cognac. Within
minutes, Nestor's head spun. He told his bodyguard in Abkhazian,
"Take me away. They have killed me."

Back at the hotel, the phone rang. In a tone that defied refusal,
Beria told Nestor to come to the opera house for a premiere. After
the first act, Beria invited the ailing Nestor to join him and his company in his personal loge. As they drank a shot of cognac, the glass
fell from Nestor's hand as he collapsed, unconscious. Beria sent his
own doctor to the hospital, but Nestor's bodyguard barred the door.
Nestor died at midnight.

In Moscow, the Master curtly refused to see Sariya. Only after
persistent pleas did an indifferent Lead Butt receive her for a few
moments. He rejected Sariya's request to investigate. Sariya returned
home, a broken woman. But she kept repeating, "The Master will
not abandon us in our misfortune. He knows how devoted Nestor
was to him."

Adile desperately wanted to return to a normal life. She passed
the entrance exam for the State Pedagogical Institute with flying
colors, but she had to sit for an exam on the history of the party. The
examiner, a young party propagandist, launched into a tirade as she
entered: "You are one of those scoundrels, one of those Lakobites!
Who allowed you to take this exam?" He begrudgingly perused
Adile's exam results and declared her "admitted on probation" with
scarcely concealed disdain: "Well, let's see how well you can do."
Adile's academic career ended shortly after it began. The Institute
director expelled her before she "corrupted the youth." She ran home
to her parents, weeping inconsolably.

In early June, Nestor's replacement as head of the Abkhazian party
summoned Sariya. Adile accompanied her for moral support, waiting outside the office. Sariya burst out of his office, shaking, grabbed

Adile by the hand, and raced home. Sariya sat in a daze, not speaking a word. That evening, Sariya, Emdy, and Nestor's elderly mother disappeared. They did not return until the next evening. Adile learned what they had done when she overheard a conversation between Sariya and Emdy. The new party boss had told Sariya confidentially that Beria planned to quietly dispose of Nestor's body. She and Emdy dug up the coffin in the night and transported it to Nestor's village. Sariya did not allow Emdy to see where she reburied Nestor.

The whole city soon knew Nestor's body was missing. Beria and his minions rushed to Mikhailovsky cemetery to check for themselves. Beria arrested several Sukhumi NKVD officers for "insufficient vigilance" and ordered the cemetery guard shot.

Adile had her family to fall back on. Her mother spent more time in the Lakoba residence—one of the few willing to break the wall of isolation. Sariya withdrew into her shell. She sat silently, chain-smoking. They all hung in limbo. When would the police come for Emdy? So far, they arrested only the men. Did they intend to persecute Sariya as well? Would Adile's young age protect her? They would soon have answers.

Sukhumi (July–September 1937)

More than half a year had now passed since Nestor's death. Three of Sariya's five brothers sat in jail awaiting Beria's punishment. His NKVD claimed that "Lakoba's Nest" had plotted traitorous acts, including the assassination of the Master. Fortunately, Beria "vigilantly" uncovered their plots.

Beria played his cards brilliantly. The Master's July 3, 1937, telegram asking for lists of enemies gave him an ideal opportunity to move against the Lakobas. Beria dispatched his reply at 2:55 p.m. on July 8. His figures of 1,419 first-category and 1,562 second-category enemies, he stated, "do not include anti-Soviet parties engaged in active counterrevolutionary work . . . these add up to an additional 2,000 persons." Beria, in effect, asked for "limits" for 2,000 Lakobites.

As Beria responded to Stalin's order, Adile, Emdy, Sariya, Sariya's youngest brother, her teenage son Rauf, and her sister, Naziya, lived as virtual prisoners in the gilded Lakoba mansion. Sariya fell deeper into depression, chain-smoking in the parlor. Nestor's generous pension had been mysteriously withdrawn, and they had little money.

In late July, Emdy was fired. He left for the Black Sea port city of Batumi, where another brother lived, in hopes of finding a job. After a few weeks, Emdy wrote to Adile that she should join him in Batumi.

On her way to the harbor to buy a steamer ticket, Adile spied a friend from her school rushing toward her. He somehow knew Adile intended to travel to Batumi. He looked at Adile intently and said, "Go home; there is no need to go anywhere. I just returned from the port and saw police escorting Emdy and his brother. Emdy looked at me with a message for you in his eyes."

The devastated Adile rushed home to her own bedroom. She stealthily called in Aunt Naziya. As she told her about Emdy's arrest, Naziya's scream brought Sariya racing into the room. Of her four brothers, only the youngest was still free.

The women learned through a former housekeeper that Emdy was incarcerated in the NKVD prison in Sukhumi, across from the botanical garden where Nestor had first been buried. Sariya and Adile began their daily trek to the prison. Every day, a huge crowd of women gathered before the NKVD headquarters. Some sought the whereabouts of loved ones. Others, like Adile and Sariya, brought parcels. As the crowd waited forlornly, a gate opened and a rude voice announced that packages were being accepted. The prison authorities accepted only messages saying, "All is well at home. Everyone is fine." After the women spent hours waiting in line, the prison authorities handed out dirty clothing for them to wash.

On one occasion, as Adile prepared to wash Emdy's underwear, she discovered a tightly pressed wad of paper. She gingerly unwound it to discover a message from Emdy: "Who is still at home? How are you getting along? I do not know anything about you. I still do not understand how they can accuse us of such crimes. The investigation is brutal; our position is very dangerous. Some one has accused us, but why? Where is Sariya? I am afraid for all of you." Despite Emdy's understated tone, Adile now understood with horror that the red color on his underwear was his blood.

Emdy, at least, had a pencil to write with. Another prisoner wrote in blood, "Mama, this is my last letter. They are sending us away tomorrow." The massive crowd in front of the prison could only guess at conditions inside. Incoming prisoners had to be literally beaten into their cells. Prisoners stood to make room. Inmates died standing. Typhus infections swept the cells. The bodies were taken out to be burned. Beria himself informed the Master that over-crowding created "abnormal conditions in the holding of prisoners." Beria worried not about the health and safety of prisoners but that crowding enabled prisoners to exchange notes on interrogations.

So far, Beria arrested only the Lakoba men. But Sariya knew too much. A cautious man like Beria did not take chances. On August 17, 1937, a loud knock jolted the Lakoba household members sitting in the gallery. Startled, they looked at one another as Sariya's young-est brother went to the door to ask, "Who is there?" The visitors answered with another resounding knock. As the brother opened the door, three men burst in and proceeded to turn the house upside down. The intruders demanded documents. Sariya answered calmly that she had no idea what they were talking about. (Sariya and her youngest brother had hidden Nestor's papers in a special place under the floor.) One of the men approached her with a sneering smile: "Well, my beauty, soon you'll be dancing the *lezginka* for us, not for your high people."

Sariya signaled Adile to follow her into the living room. She hung her golden necklace embossed with black agate and rubies around Adile's neck, instructing her, "Wear this as a talisman." Adile recoiled as Sariya gave her a small woman's pistol: "If they find it on you, tell them I gave it to you. If they do not see it, give it to Mama." The men ordered Sariya to get some things together. They pulled the distraught Rauf from his mother's neck. Sariya put on her black scarf and turned back to them, trying to smile: "This is a mistake. I'll clear it up."

Three days later, three Chekists came to evict them. Adile recognized one as a former neighbor. As the other two started the search, he gave her a discreet signal to follow him into the corridor: "Do not give a sign that you know me. I'll try to help." He instructed Adile to place her most valuable possessions in a suitcase and pillow case and throw them out the window. Task completed, Adile collapsed in a chair pretending to be sick as the other Chekists entered her room. Adile's neighbor across the courtyard rushed out to hide her possessions.

The remaining Lakobas were resettled in a single room on Goriyskoi Street. Adile returned to her anxious parents. Nestor's antique ivory billiard balls were among the things Adile disposed of. As they sank in the Basla River, Adile felt her past slipping away with them.

Sariya's arrest did not alter Adile's daily routine, only now Sariya sat with Emdy in the Sukhumi prison. But in September, Emdy was transferred to Dranda.

Sukhumi (October 1937–January 1938)

October 1937 found the seventeen-year-old Adile standing in line with hundreds of other women outside Dranda prison, waiting to hand over parcels for her imprisoned husband. The evening before, Adile had traveled the nineteen miles from Sukhumi to Dranda, found a place to rest for the night, and then, at the crack of dawn, raced to be near the front of the line at the prison entrance.

Christians built the sixth-century Dranda Monastery to fend off marauding Turks. Dranda's turreted and domed cathedrals and administrative buildings rose above its three-story-high walls. The monastery was painted in pastel shades of blue, yellow, and green. Inside the walls, spacious grounds adorned with majestic trees and grass separated the cathedrals, living quarters, and other monastery buildings. Beria's people converted the monastery into a prison.

They took down the crosses, replaced the original wooden gate with steel, and installed iron bars in the windows. The thick brick walls divided the prison grounds into "traps of stone" that made escape almost impossible.

Adile's line moved slowly. The Abkhazian autumn heat stifled the waiting mothers and wives with small children. Once they reached the front of the line, they handed over their packages and hoped for some sign of life from their men. Adile noted that "the most terrible thing was the absolute silence." The women feared even to exchange whispers. "This evil silence was disrupted only by small children who pleaded with their mothers for something to eat, drink, or to sleep." Guards arbitrarily ordered women out of the line. After being driven away, they sat through the night to try again the next day.

Adile trekked to Dranda daily with her cousin, whose husband was also in the Dranda prison. Other than the smuggled note, Adile heard nothing from Emdy. One day, after she handed over her parcels, Adile left the line and gazed up at the prison windows. (Later, the prison officials covered them with screens.) Adile recognized Emdy's voice calling out her name. She searched the windows and saw Emdy, clinging to the prison bars and shouting: "Leave Abkhazia. Go as far away as possible. I fear for you. They are probably going to send us away. Do not believe that we have done anything wrong." As the guards tore Emdy from the prison bars, the people around Adile began to cry. A policeman grabbed Adile by the collar, dragged her to the gate and threw her outside to the ground. She returned home dejected.

Three days after this incident, an uncle spied Emdy among a convoy of prisoners being transported to Tbilisi. Emdy stealthily dropped a wadded paper on the ground. The guard pretended to tie his shoe, picked up the paper, and gave it to Adile's uncle, who rushed to bring her Emdy's message: "Dear Adile. They are taking us to Tbilisi. They are accusing us of fantastic crimes. They might imprison us for ten years. There has been some kind of mistake. I am still young and can survive, and I can prove my innocence. You must leave Abkhazia and disappear into the depths of Russia. Time

Gamid (Emdy) Dzhikh-ogly,
Adile's first husband.

will pass, everything will be clarified, and I will return. You are still young. You should consider yourself free, but I will wait for you. I will stay true to you. Read this and burn it. Do not say a word to anyone. My heart is hurting. I want to see you . . . Farewell, my Dearest. Your Emdy."

Sukhumi radio broadcast the "Trial of the Thirteen Lakobites," which was held October 30 to November 3, 1937. Beria himself attended at the Sukhumi State Theater. The defendants included Nestor's brothers and his closest associates. Sariya's youngest brother came over to Adile's house to listen. The whole city sat glued to the radio. The trial deteriorated into "bad theater," in Adile's words. Some defendants admitted their guilt but got confused on the "facts" of the case. A few asserted their innocence. One witness testified that Emdy had sabotaged the Sukhumi gas and electric works. Another witness became confused and testified that no crime had been committed.

On November 3, the court sentenced ten of the thirteen defendants to death. That evening, the wives of the condemned had a final meeting with their husbands. The guards had to pull them away, sobbing. The ten were executed the next night. Soon thereafter, the arrests of the wives and adult children began. People sat at home with their suitcases packed. They froze at every knock on the door. Beria arrested more than a thousand in the "Lakoba affair." Of these, he executed almost eight hundred.

Rauf sought in vain for two months to see his mother, Sariya, in jail. He appealed directly to "Uncle Lavrenty" during the Lakoba Thirteen trial. Beria received the young Rauf affectionately and promised him a meeting with his mother. The joyful Rauf ran home with the good news. Aunt Naziya accompanied Rauf to the NKVD headquarters. Police led Rauf off and told Aunt Naziya to wait in the reception area. An hour passed. Naziya paced back and forth, and finally knocked on the door. The guard told her she should not wait. Naziya returned overcome by grief.

On January 2, 1938, police arrested Adile's father. He had two strikes against him as a Lakoba relative and a "former person"— a rich bourgeois. His arrest followed the familiar pattern—a loud knock, the entry of several Chekists, and a search for documents and weapons. As a gold brooch that Adile was hiding fell to the floor, one of the intruders shouted, "Pick up your stuff before I think it over, you little thief." As they piled their loot on the table, they hissed, "You lived well. We should have taken care of you long ago." Two Chekists then began to fight over the spoils.

Other arrests followed: Aunt Naziya, Adile's Uncle Riza Abbas-ogly, "Aunt" Katya (a distant relation), Nestor's mother, and many of Adile's friends. As Aunt Katya (Adile's escort to the fateful birthday party where she met Emdy) was being tortured, she asked her interrogator, "My son, what would you think if I were your mother?" Unfazed, he screamed back, "Don't call me 'son,' you bitch. I would have shot a mother like you with my own hands." With that, he struck her, bloodied her nose, and knocked out two front teeth.

Adile saw her father one last time. One day as they were out shopping, he shouted to Adile and her mother in Abkhazian from the rear of a passing truck: "Tomorrow morning, go to the bread shop." Early the next morning, the waiting Adile and her mother saw him approaching, under guard, a large sack over his shoulder. Now an old man, he wore a shabby outfit with galoshes secured by a string.

His guard stood outside, smoking. They knew the clerk, a Greek. He rummaged around in the shop to cover their conversation.

Adile's father spoke hurriedly: "My little daughter, I am very afraid for you. You are a member of Nestor's family, and all of them have been arrested. Leave with Mama to some remote place in Russia. We are starving in prison. There is no tobacco. The most horrible thing is that we do not know what will happen to us." Adile, in a heroic sacrifice, shoved the family's last hundred-ruble note in his pocket as the guard entered the shop. Adile's father looked at his daughter and wife crying as the guard led him away. Shortly thereafter, they transferred him to Dranda prison and then to Kolyma in Russia's Far East, where he died.

The noose tightened. Both Emdy and her father had now warned Adile to disappear into Russia. A former admirer, now an NKVD guard, told Adile he saw her name on an arrest list. If Adile married him, he could protect her. As Adile rejected his proposal, her disgruntled suitor responded coldly, "Well, that was your mistake." At wit's end, Adile and her mother came to a fateful decision: Adile would travel with a neighbor to Moscow, where her neighbor's friend, an actress by the name of Anastasiya Zueva, would take Adile under her wing.

Moscow (July–December 1938)

Adile's mother had confided to her neighbor that Adile needed to disappear. Her neighbor planned a trip to Moscow and volunteered to take Adile along. She had rented her home to the famous Moscow Arts Theater actress, Anastasiya Zueva, in past summers. Zueva knew Adile from trips to the beach together, and had invited her to stay with her in Moscow whenever the occasion arose. But she could scarcely have anticipated the circumstances under which the teenage Adile would appear at her doorstep in July 1938 as arrests swept through Moscow.

Anastasiya Zueva began her career in 1926 at Konstantin Stanislavsky's Moscow Arts Theater. Half-joking, the legendary

Anastasiya Zueva (1896–1986), a famous Soviet actress, here in *The Winner* (1947), original title *Pervaya perchatka*.

director told the thirty-year-old, not particularly attractive Zueva that she should "play the eternal older woman." Zueva's favorite role was a mother vesting all her love in her children. Zueva was counted among the most-loved actresses of Stalin's Russia. As such, she held considerable influence in artistic circles.

Early in the morning on July 5, 1937, the seventeen-year-old Adile bid her mother goodbye and climbed aboard a bus for Sochi with her good-Samaritan neighbor. Adile's adventure almost ended before it began as four Chekists eyed them in the waiting room. However, the Chekists probably just enjoyed ogling such a pretty girl.

The train ride to Moscow took five days. Upon arrival, Adile's neighbor got no answer from Zueva's telephone. After all, she had not warned Zueva about her fugitive visitor. Adile's neighbor sought shelter with another Moscow acquaintance, a noted professor. They arrived bedraggled and unannounced to find he had died the day before. Despite the circumstances, the mourning family allowed them to stay. Each day they phoned until finally Zueva's son, Konstantin, answered to say that Zueva was touring for another week. The two exhausted travelers climbed aboard a train for the 250-mile trip to Smolensk, where the good Samaritan's sister and brother-in-law lived. After pleading their case, Adile and her companion were told by the fearful couple that they could spend three days, but that was all.

Upon their return to Moscow from Smolensk, they were instructed by Zueva to come right away to her apartment at 6 Kirov Street. She greeted them with a table laden with food. When she heard of Adile's plight, she volunteered that Adile could stay as long as necessary. Adile took heart in Zueva's lack of fear.

Zueva shared the apartment with another actor and his wife. They all used a common kitchen and entrance. The wife, older than her husband by seven years, looked at Adile with jealousy and distrust. Zueva warned Adile to stay out of sight. Any misstep and the wife might report Adile, an illegal alien in her own country.

Adile cleaned and shopped, while Zueva, an excellent cook, taught Adile the culinary arts. Zueva plied her influential network to find help for her teenage refugee. She started with top officials, but they asked too many questions. Zueva understood the danger of revealing too much and stopped making calls. Zueva did not conceal Adile from her artistic friends, who filled her apartment virtually every evening. Zueva's guests told stories and conversed about theater and art. Although the room filled with laughter and light conversation, they all bore the burden of the repression and terror penetrating the Moscow cultural scene.

Adile's artistic flair and elegant bearing so impressed Zueva that she invited a director to visit, who concluded that Adile spoke without accent and read with emotion. She should join the theater, he concluded. After the initial rush of excitement, Adile came to her senses, telling Zueva, "They will ask for my family name. I do not know how to lie. I'll have to fill out papers. They'll ask, 'What did you do before the theater?' and we'll have no answers." Talk of a theatrical career ceased.

At least Adile could witness the cultural life of Moscow. Zueva assigned her twenty-two-year-old son, Konstantin, to be Adile's escort. Konstantin dressed elegantly in his military uniform. They did not miss a production of the Moscow Arts Theater, watching Zueva perform in plays by Anton Chekhov and in other roles. With her hand tucked under Konstantin's arm, Adile felt safe. Konstantin called Adile his Caucasus savage. Adile felt he liked her—and she liked him. The moment came that Adile feared: Konstantin proposed marriage. She could change her name. They could use his mother's influence to keep her safe.

Adile rejected him gently: "If we marry, I cannot return home. All will say I betrayed a husband in jail. There is no way to hide, and you will end up suffering on my account." Konstantin never returned to this subject, but he continued his role as escort.

At last, Zueva went to a "big figure" whose name she did not disclose. She knew him well enough to entrust him with Adile's story. She returned crestfallen. The man had told her, "Do not go to anyone or say anything about this girl. This is very serious. I warn you." Beria's menacing reach extended into the inner sanctum of Moscow's elite.

Tragedy struck Adile's guardian. On December 15, Adile returned from shopping to hear Zueva sobbing in her room. She then was on the telephone for a long time, after which she disappeared into her closet and came out wearing a black dress. A car drove up in front. Zueva put on her black scarf, hugged Adile with trembling hands, and disappeared. Adile learned on the news that Valery Chkalov, the famous aviator (and one of Fekla's childhood heroes in Martyush), had perished in a plane crash. Later Adile learned that Chkalov was Zueva's great love. She mourned him long afterward, gazing at his portrait next to her bed.

Adile marveled at Zueva's compassion and fearlessness. While cleaning one day, Adile found a silver icon of the Virgin Mary hidden in the bedding. Zueva's belief in God explained her brave acts. When Adile told her about the icon, Zueva confessed that she prayed every morning and evening and before every performance. She ended her confession with a warning to Adile not to tell anyone: "You know nothing."

Even in Moscow, Adile could not hide from the notorious secret collaborators—the seksoty. One day in December 1938 she encountered in the subway a fellow classmate from Sukhumi. This acquaintance, Musya, gave Adile her phone number and invited her to visit. Foolishly, she did, and Musya's stepmother queried Adile about events in Tbilisi. Thinking herself in safe company, Adile answered truthfully, until she saw Musya gesturing to keep quiet. As she prepared to leave, Musya's stepmother insisted that they visit Adile—joking that she was such a fan of Zueva.

In the days following the visit, Musya and her stepmother unleashed a barrage of phone calls, insisting that they be allowed to visit. Zueva expressed her irritation. She wanted to be left alone. Adile's own suspicions heightened when Musya herself appeared unannounced at her doorstep. Oddly, Musya dragged a reluctant Adile to a photo studio, where they sat for a portrait. She again insisted that Adile visit. When the exasperated Adile refused, Musya responded with desperation: "I beg you to come. If not, my step-mother will kill me." Zueva saw no good solution to Adile's dilemma: "If you don't go, that witch might do something. It is best for you to go, but whatever you do, do not say anything."

After holding out as long as possible, Adile visited Musya to find a stranger awaiting her. The stepmother assured Adile that the stranger just wanted to help, describing him as a man of con-siderable influence. Adile repeated her story, leaving out the juicy bits, but she could not conceal the fact that most of her family had been arrested. Upon hearing Adile's censored narrative, the stranger remarked, "What a sad story, and the girl has done nothing. We need to help her somehow." And as an afterthought, he asked, "And how is Anastasiya Zueva involved in all this?" Adile replied quickly, "She would be very happy to be rid of me, but I have nowhere to go." The stranger soothed her: "Don't be upset. We'll try to work something out for you." A sheepish Musya accompanied Adile to the door. "I should be cursed. She is a witch, not a person. About the photograph—when it is ready, I'll send it to you." The photo-graph never arrived. It ended up in her NKVD dossier.

After this encounter, Zueva's phone began to ring off the wall. A "fan" appeared without invitation at their door—a young red-haired woman with an unpleasant face scarred by smallpox. Zueva understood that she and Adile had fallen into the sights of the secret informers. Zueva and Konstantin knew they were in danger, not only Adile. As these storm clouds gathered, Adile received through a messenger a letter from her mother, stating that the situation back home had improved, but it was still not time to return. Despite the dangers awaiting her, the homesick Adile decided to go home.

As a parting gesture, Zueva bought Adile a train ticket in "international class" where no one would bother her. Shortly before her departure, however, Adile's handbag was stolen as she queued up to buy a subway ticket. It contained her mothers' letters, her ticket, photographs, and internal passport. In a daze, Adile ran to the nearest police station. As the policeman began asking questions, Adile realized she stood just seconds from disaster. To her good fortune, the police brought in two teenage thieves, and Adile used the distraction as an opportunity to slip away. Back safe in the Zueva apartment, Adile realized the theft was not by chance. The NKVD and Beria knew all they needed to know, whether she resided in Moscow or Sukhumi. She might as well go home.

On December 27, 1938, a dispirited Adile boarded the train for a three-day trip back to Sukhumi. She was about to be thrown back into the cauldron of arrests, persecution, and torture. She would learn the fates of her husband, father, Sariya, and other family members. She did not know that Beria was fulfilling his promise to the Master to rid the world of the "nest of Lakoba vipers" who had plotted his assassination. He needed the young Adile to add to his narrative. The other Lakobas did not break easily. A teenage girl like Adile would be no trouble.

CHAPTER FIFTEEN

Fekla

Becoming a Bolshevik

Martyush, Urals (1934–1937)

The eight-year-old Fekla Andreeva watched as the special settlers of Martyush built a simple wooden building to serve as their school. Four to five students sat abreast on wooden benches. The library, cafeteria, gym, and special room for the Young Pioneers came later. The children attended in three shifts due to the crowding. For the next decade, school offered Fekla a refuge from all the pain and ugliness around her.

By the age of eleven, Fekla had become a true believer in the glorious Master and his Bolshevik cause. She learned that evil enemies surrounded their motherland. Fekla and her schoolmates "stumbling over their own words, in simple village language, pledged to defend their sacred borders," as she would later write. Fekla's parents toiled in the mines and fields, returned to the barracks exhausted, and kept their mouths shut. They hoped for a normal life for their four daughters. They knew it was not easy to create an educated person.

Teacher Belkina read the works of Alexander Pushkin and Mikhail Lermontov and told tales of Cossack legend Taras Bulba, daring aviator Valery Chkalov, and arctic explorer Otto Shmidt. As she did so, Fekla imagined skyscrapers, legends, adventures, and castles in the sky. She yearned to see the fascinating world beyond Martyush. Teacher Belkina encouraged her best students, among them Fekla, to enter poetry contests. They carefully packaged their poems and sent them to faraway Chelyabinsk. The Martyush children awaited the results with "rapidly beating hearts." Fekla treasured the postcard from Chelyabinsk announcing she had won a prize.

Teacher Belkina's sad, tired blue eyes gazed at the simple village children so compassionately and encouragingly that, as Fekla would later write, "against our own will we wished to accomplish pleasant and heroic things." Her teacher continued to radiate cheer and sincerity even after her husband was arrested. In Martyush, there was little distinction between the imprisoned and the "free."

With the appearance in 1936 of a real principal, the school acquired desks, geography maps, and a special club for the Young Pioneers. The principal was a tall, slender, charming Ukrainian with eagle-like eyebrows, a winged gait, and an open heart for all the children. (He died at the front during World War II.) He expanded the school to seven grades. The school soon boasted a string orchestra. Vanya and Kondrashin excelled on the violin and the bayan (similar to the accordion), while the other students played mandolins, guitars, and three-stringed balalaikas. Fekla remembered her principal as "the soul and creator of all interesting things in the school."

School was the only respite from work. Starting between the ages of ten and twelve, the children worked year-round with only two days off at the end and beginning of the school year. Zoya began to work in the fields at the age of ten. Anna had it better as a maid in the commandant's house. Dusya worked as a nanny from the age of five. The others worked alongside their parents, in the fields and mines. They planted grain, dug up potatoes, pulled weeds, and gathered sticks and branches for firewood. The children helped their parents meet their production norms but received no wages.

In the winter, the thinly dressed children pulled their sleds to the camp water pump. If it was broken, they walked a mile and a quarter to the Iset River for water. They returned frightfully frozen, red as a goose's webbed feet, trying to warm their fingers by rubbing them in their armpits. Children succumbed too often to work-related accidents. A runaway cart filled with ore crushed Kolya to death. He had come to the mine to share his parents' meager food rations. An errant rope strangled Misha, age 14, driving a horse-drawn wagon in mine No. 2. Thirteen-year-old Adyya drowned when she fainted while fetching water from the Iset.

In the summer, the children climbed trees, swam in the Iset, and gathered wildflowers. In the winter, they slid down snowy slopes on improvised sleds or skis. Their parents watched and worried. If children became ill, they died quickly. The adults tried, usually without success, to erect a veil of silence as the parents quietly mourned.

Despite work and meager rations, Fekla still found time to be a child. In the desolate swamp behind the village, the children staged battles, waving their wooden sabers and shouting "hurrah" as the "reds" drove the "whites" into the marsh grass. No one wanted to be a "white." Crying was simply not allowed, although the carnage often ended with bloody noses and other injuries. Despite the danger of quicksand, the children penetrated the depths of the swamp as clouds of mosquitoes hovered overhead. They imagined themselves aboard a ship exploring the unknown.

If injuries proved serious, parents carried their children to Dr. Emelyan Rogozhin. He was jolly and round like a snowball, but mobile like a rabbit. As Dr. Rogozhin examined patients with sprained ankles, maimed legs, or bloody faces, his light touch tempered the pain. He could do little, however, about the fevers and infections that claimed so many children's lives.

The children dreamed of spice cakes, candies, movie tickets, and books about valiant border guards. After school, they gathered in a circle to wager copper coins against buttons, pencils, dolls, knives, and ribbons. Drops of sweat fell from the foreheads of the obsessed gamblers. Fekla's mother crafted a miniature straw scarecrow, which she hung in a corner. When she caught Fekla gambling, she led her by the hand to the scarecrow and spanked it. That was her way of punishing her children. She did not use shouting, tears, or rebukes.

As the season changed from cold to uncomfortably hot, Fekla slept outside with the barefoot and hungry children from three neighboring barracks under blankets each household contributed. Fekla later ironically described this communal sleeping "as the communism that was being created in the Soviet Union."

Fekla's teachers taught her to love the Master and despise his enemies. She saw no reason to doubt. As an inductee into the Young Pioneers, Fekla shouted, "I am always ready," in response to the challenge: "Are you ready to fight for the cause of Lenin, Stalin, and the Great Communist Party?" "Activist" Fekla helped stage patriotic plays. She helped organize "political information" meetings that warned of omnipresent wreckers and those who pretended to be true Leninists. After the execution of Trotskyite traitors, Fekla and her fellow activists ripped the portraits of these "fake revolutionaries" out of their schoolbooks.

The Young Pioneers hosted "spectacles" on official Soviet holidays. Martyush's own nightingale, Anechka Guzhevnikova, brought sobs to the audience with her rendition of "Coachman: Do Not Drive Away." Some thought that informants used these spectacles to keep track of Martyush residents, but, if so, it was a small price to pay for this respite from the harsh reality of daily life.

Fekla's faith in the communist cause reached its zenith in May 1937 at the Kamensk-Uralsky May Day festivities. In the parade, one group of Martyush children carried a wooden plane they built in honor of the heroic aviator, Chkalov. Others marched as "Voroshilov's Riflemen" (in honor of Kliment Voroshilov, Stalin's henchman "Klim"). Fekla wore with pride the red stars she had crafted by hand. Teachers encouraged the children to emulate Pavlik Morozov, the legendary boy who denounced his traitorous parents and was murdered by angry relatives. This went too far, Fekla concluded: "Although we may have been deaf and dumb, nobody could demand of us, and God forgive us, if we denounce our own parents."

As summer 1937 approached, the special settlers of Martyush had a little more food, better living quarters, and some relaxation in their backbreaking work regime. Guards did not watch them closely. The vastness of the Soviet East, not barbed wire and guards, kept them in prison. Parents, exhausted from work and fearful for their children, came to consider their own miserable existence normal.

As for the children, Fekla would later reminisce: "We were young and innocent. We knew of our explorers reaching the North Pole, our valiant shock workers, and our Stakhanovites. We respected above all the ardent revolutionary companions in arms, Lenin and Stalin." (Shock workers were the over-achievers of the laboring class; Stakhanovites emulated Aleksey Stakhanov, who supposedly mined 102 tons of coal in one shift.)

Fekla's teachers failed to tell her the most salient fact: Papa and Grandfather were enemies of the people. Their November 10, 1930, sentence by the Suvory Executive Committee made this clear in black and white: "Andreev's farm was a Kulak household with 15 desiatins of cultivated land, two permanent employees and up to twenty seasonal workers, Andreev was a merciless exploiter of the poor. He deliberately reduced his sown acreage and destroyed his livestock at the time of collectivization. He agitated against Soviet measures. In 1918, Andreev voluntarily joined the White forces. Andreev is socially dangerous and is hereby deprived of his civil rights."

A "socially dangerous person" remained just that, no matter how much time passed. Dostoevsky's *Crime and Punishment* dropped out of the Soviet vocabulary. "Measures of social protection" replaced punishment and "socially dangerous persons" replaced criminals. Martyush families placed portraits of the "great quartet" of Marx, Engels, Lenin, and Stalin in their living quarters. As the arrests of friends, relatives, and parents began in late July 1937, the "quartet" remained and family pictures disappeared.

First, two policemen took the jolly Dr. Rogozhin away. He walked with his hands behind his back, a wry smile on his face. What was the village to do without its doctor? Next, they arrested the husband of Fekla's favorite teacher. She hid her grief in the classroom, but everyone knew. The arrests were coming closer and closer, but Fekla had faith in the Master and the Soviet state. There was no way they could consider her Father and Grandfather enemies of the people.

Martyush, Urals (Summer–Fall 1937)

Life in the Andreev family continued its routine. Father's skills as a carpenter and jack-of-all-trades landed him jobs in the "New Life" collective farm and on construction sites. He left every morning under guard with the work brigade. He never worked less than twelve hours. Mother continued to work long hours, despite a mine injury that rendered her a third-degree invalid. (First-degree and second-degree invalidity weren't allowed for kulaks, and third-degree invalids had to keep working.) In the summer of 1937, an operation confined her to bed. Grandfather, earlier a dynamo of energy and ingenuity, had become a frail old man at age seventy. He worked as a night watchman. At home, he muttered prayers in the direction of the "icon corner" where he hid the family icons. He defied the authorities by regularly attending church services. He no longer cared.

Fekla, now eleven and a half, excelled in school and looked after her three sisters. The youngest, Klavdia, had not yet reached school age. Martyush school now received its students in two shifts. Katya and Nina attended the morning session. Fekla raced to school for the afternoon session after tending Klavdia in the morning. She worked in the fields of the "New Life" after school. She faithfully attended Young Pioneer meetings and brought home excellent grades. She doted on her father, still a handsome man at thirty-eight.

At home, the Andreevs had to be careful. The dreaded seksoty reported "anti-Soviet" conversations. They listened to the radio's strident warnings that "nests of enemies of the people" lurked in every corner. The radio broadcasts did not mention kulak enemies in the special settlements. Not in their wildest dreams would they have understood they were the "enemy." But life relaxed a little. Father even got permission from the commandant to take his daughters to see the glories of the big city, Kamensk-Uralsky. For the first time, Fekla saw streetcars and tall buildings. Memories of her visit to Kamensk-Uralsky with Papa remained with Fekla the rest of her life.

The Master's July 3, 1937, order to liquidate "returning or flee-ing kulaks and criminals" confused the Kamensk-Uralsky authori-ties. Indeed, they had "kulaks," but they were confined to special settlements. They did not fall under the headings of "returning" or "fleeing." What should they do?

Kazakhstan raised the issue first. As its party secretary explained in a telegram to the Master: "Insofar as many kulaks located in spe-cial settlements have already served their time of exile but fall under the activities indicated in the telegram, we ask permission for our troika to also take up their cases." The fate of the Martyush special settlers hung in the balance. Would the Master include them for liq-uidation? In a telegram that would have chilled the Andreevs to the bone, he authorized "the expansion of the directive of the Central Committee to special settlements."

Chelyabinsk Oblast submitted on July 9 its list of 2,552 first-category enemies to be shot. The village of Martyush fell within its jurisdiction. In the spirit of "socialist competition," the vigilant NKVD authorities of Chelyabinsk then asked for and received per-mission to shoot 5,800. Surely, they needed some of the Martyush kulaks to fulfill their quota.

The arrests began in Kamensk-Uralsky in late July and spread to Martyush, gaining steam in August. The men marched off in the morning in what Fekla later described as "the warm layers of early snow." They did not know if they would return. The NKVD usually picked up the men at work and drove them away in trucks. Despite their heavy work load, women stole the time they could. They ven-tured out along the road to meet their husbands and sons returning from work. If they heard animated talk as the men approached, their gray faces lit up: "At least today they have all returned."

More often, the men returned in silence, averting their eyes, as if they had done something wrong. The thick snow could not mask the sobs of the soon-to-be widows and orphans. Panic broke out as wives, children, and parents of those arrested returned to their bar-racks, sobbing. Neighbors came running. They tried to comfort the grieving, but they could do nothing.

Not all were arrested at work. The NKVD came for some at night in a "black raven." Some sadistic NKVD officers made sport of their victims. They came for one in a horse-drawn cart. Instead of seating him in the back, they tied his hands to a rope attached to the cart and made him run two and a half miles—barefoot—to the prison door.

Father became even more quiet and morose. With the growing shortage of labor, he came home later and later from work. Despite his fatigue, he played longer with his daughters in the evenings. Only Fekla was old enough to understand the danger. On September 29, Father did not return. Most of the men did not return on that day. The Andreev home stood quiet as a tomb. Fekla observed long and short shadows flickering across her mother's dead eyes as she sat close to the peasant stove. Grandfather and the girls lost the power of speech. No one thought of sleep or of school the next day.

In the morning, a crowd of women and children departed for Kamensk-Uralsky. No one bothered to ask the commandant's permission. If he had denied them, they would have gone anyway. Each woman hopefully carried a parcel or a bag of food or clothing for her loved one. In Kamensk-Uralsky, they converged on the locked gates of the NKVD headquarters on Kommolodezhi Street. An indifferent official rebuffed them. "No visitors! No packages!" They stood together, a silent tear-stained mass of women and children.

Fekla, along with her playmates, discovered an arched half-window in the rear of the two-story building. Through this window, they could look into the prison basement where their fathers were held. The guards held back the wives and mothers but pretended they did not see the kulak children, who came to see their fathers for the last time.

The half-window provided enough space for one child at a time to peek through. The prisoners stood elbow to elbow in the cell. They could feel the heartbeats of their neighbors. Those at the one window stared intently at the outside world. As they recognized the

Trofim Andreev, Fekla's father, 1938.

face of the child peering through the window, they made room for the father to come forward.

When Fekla's turn came, she could make out her father's face and could hear his words: "Make sure your sisters are educated. You are now the head of the family. They cannot take your education away from you." Father wanted to say more, but emotion overcame him. The other prisoners carried him away to make room for the next. At eleven and a half, Fekla was made responsible by her father for her sisters.

The next evening word spread like wildfire: "They are taking the men away." The villagers rushed to Sinarsky Station in time to see a ragtag band of men in worn quilted coats, rumpled leather jackets, or half-length jackets shuffling through the streets. Guards herded the miserable pack toward the cattle cars waiting at the station. The prisoners stole glances at the crowd, hoping to make out familiar faces, as the guards prodded them along.

Women and children watching this spectacle wailed, wept, and howled. They waved their arms frantically as the guards shoved the prisoners into the wagons. The convoy of prisoners froze as still as an honor guard on parade before disappearing into the dark confines of the rail car. The guards slammed shut the doors of the cattle cars with a resounding clang. The train headed east toward Chelyabinsk. The distraught Martyush spetsy stumbled back to the west to their barracks, which had suddenly become less crowded. The parting whistle of the train haunted their memories.

No one slept in the Andreev family. Still, arrested husband or not, Mother had to work. Fekla's sisters lay on the bed. Without Father and Mother, it suddenly seemed too large. The freezing Fekla perched on the stove. Her temples pounded with the heartbreaking words of a young woman at the train station: "They are never coming back." Quiet reigned. Grandfather's muttering occasionally broke the silence. He knelt down, his head held back defiantly, blaming God for their misfortune. He repeated his query: "Why, Lord? Why?"

Fekla fell into a feverish sleep. She dreamed that they were strolling along a street. Father carried Katya and Nina. Fekla grasped Klavdia, her fingers tucked into Father's back pocket. "Where should we go?" he asks. As they think it over, he decides to go to the pub. They enter. There is no place to sit, but it is warm. Although children are not allowed in the pub, the men make Father and the girls welcome. Fekla and her sisters eat delicious spice cakes, making sure to catch all the crumbs. After an hour, Father calls out, "It is time to go home. Mother is finished with the cleaning."

Fekla awakes. Father is on a train bound east. Grandfather mournfully chants Bible verses. Her sisters lie on the bed. Mother is not to be seen.

Life returned to some degree of normality in a Martyush largely stripped of its male population. The women rose in the morning and left for work under guard. The children walked to the Martyush school. The fates of fathers and husbands hung in the air, a question no one dared to ask. The authorities themselves erected a wall of silence.

Fekla's childhood ended the day of her father's arrest. The oldest kulak children became breadwinners for their younger siblings. Work had to be done, and the fathers were no longer there to do it. When not in school or taking care of her sisters, Fekla worked in the "New Life" farm. Talk of vacations and days off vanished. The swamp, where she and her comrades fought imaginary battles and explored new frontiers, welcomed now only the youngest of the Martyush children.

Those who were still children played in the meadow near the barracks. They fought more often. The arrests of their fathers had unnerved them. They divided forever into those who bore the scarlet letter of a convict's child and those who didn't. Fekla's sisters complained that the other children ordered them to leave the meadow. Exhausted, she paid little attention.

But one evening as she returned home, she heard shouts from the meadow: "Get out of here. This is not your place to play. Your father is a convict. You have no father." Fekla saw her huddled sisters intimidated by the teasing. She raced toward the tormentors, swinging her hoe and shouting, "What do you mean, no father? You scum. You snot-noses!" She swung her hoe at the backs of the children as they scampered away. They continued their teasing from a distance: "What you say does not matter. Your father is still a convict."

Within the Andreev household, life assumed a new routine. Mother continued to work in the mines, often the night shift, despite her injuries. At home, she perched, small and thin, in the family bed. On wash days, Mother directed eight-year-old Katya and five-year old Nina as they washed clothes in an iron wash tub. Fekla watched as her two sisters divided the wash and poured in boiling water from the kettle. Katya's head was scarcely visible as she peered over the top of the tub. She then climbed in with the wash, her legs sticking up over the edge. As she tried to get out, the basin twirled as if trying to dance on its own.

Fekla and Katya shared one dress between them. As Katya returned to the barracks, she threw the dress to Fekla, who hastily donned it and raced to school. This arrangement broke down when Katya misbehaved and had to stay late at school. More than once, Katya's antics caused Fekla to arrive late. Some teachers refused to admit latecomer Fekla, to her great shame. Teacher Olga understood her situation and admitted her despite her tardiness. Fekla's school mates sympathized. She was not the only one to share clothing with a sibling.

After one such incident caused by Katya's antics, Fekla extracted revenge by hiding the one dress in the morning as the girls prepared for school. Katya searched everywhere, growing more frantic as school time approached. When Fekla, at the last moment, revealed the dress's location, the two girls fought until their exasperated Mother separated them.

The Martyush school did not allow its pupils to attend class bare-foot. Fekla wore either Father's galoshes or cloth footwear fashioned by Grandfather. The math teacher invited Fekla to her apartment on the pretense of preparing an application. When Fekla arrived in her galoshes, her teacher offered her lunch, which Fekla ate despite Mother's admonition not to eat in other people's homes. The teacher then rummaged through her things to find Fekla a pair of shoes. They agreed that Fekla would tend her garden to pay her back.

The four girls slept huddled together in the bed, covered by an ancient blanket that slowly disintegrated into threads as they tossed and turned. Little light entered their room as they tried to sleep. The frightened girls saw witches and evil spirits in the shadows. They pulled the old blanket over their heads and imagined the worst.

One night they awoke to see a monster standing in the corner. They screamed in unison, "Mama!" But she was at work. They awoke their next-door neighbor, "Babushka" Anna Kolotova, with their shrieks. She rushed in with a stick and showed them that their "monster" was a coat hanging on a hook on the wall. The girls' heads disappeared beneath the blanket, their hearts still beating fast.

Grief destroyed Grandfather. His pale cheeks sank even further. He forgot his work as he held a damaged boot in his hand and stared out the window, seeing nothing. Grandfather prayed constantly and attended church to pour out his grief. He no longer bothered to ask the commandant for permission.

At Easter, Grandfather took Fekla with him. In the church, the old people crossed themselves and bowed deeply as the priest chanted the sacred liturgy in a deep bass, "Lord, have mercy on us," as he swung his silver chalice to dispense incense. The church choir sang the ancient harmonies. The singing stirred Fekla's soul. Despite her mighty effort, she could not restrain the stream of tears that flooded her eyes.

Word of Fekla's "deviation" followed her to school. "Young Pioneers do not pray in church," rang her teacher's rebuke. Fekla turned red. Her cheeks turned gray. Tears overwhelmed her. She rose to her own defense: "No, I did not pray. I only listened to the music."

During the change of classes, the boys sang out "Amen" as she passed them. When she entered the classroom, giggles broke out. Fekla's teasing continued for several days. At wit's end, Fekla threw her school satchel at her torturers. The superintendent expelled Fekla, the model pioneer, for three days of tormented exile. Thereafter, a dream of standing in church making the sign of the cross and beseeching the Lord's blessing haunted Fekla. She dreamed that someone from her school spied her at church. After such a nightmare, she awoke in a cold sweat, hating herself, Grandfather, and the whole world.

CHAPTER SIXTEEN

Stalin

The Master Needs a Scapegoat

The Kremlin, Moscow (June–December 1938)

Official NKVD records show that 681,692 people were executed by the Master's NKVD in 1937 and 1938. A similar number—634,820—had been sentenced to the Gulag. The vast majority of these sentences were issued between August 1937 and November 1938. This fifteen-month frenzy of killing is appropriately termed the Great Terror.

The Master's initial order for Mass Operations called for only 75,950 executions, but as regional NKVD bosses, such as Sergei Mironov in Western Siberia or the head of Chita province, felt pressure to "achieve good results," requests for higher execution limits flooded in. Nikolai Ezhov, sitting atop the Lubyanka, was more than happy to approve them. The Master put the party's stamp of approval on these higher "limits," but he could scarcely keep up with Ezhov. Stalin, no stranger to arithmetic, understood that the Great Terror had its own limits. Executions simply could not continue at this pace. Even more alarming was the fact that the ranks of party officials were thinning. Most of the regional party sector leaders were no longer among the living.

As head of the party, the Master received frantic pleas from party secretaries to rein in Ezhov's NKVD. They did not shy away from relating the methods the NKVD used to extract confessions and fabricate evidence—no news to Stalin, but the word of excesses was spreading. NKVD officers boasted that they stood above the party. Even the loyal Ezhov placed himself above all except the Master himself.

The time had come to stop and to punish those responsible for these excesses. Of course, the Master bore no blame. It was his trusted satraps in the NKVD who disobeyed his orders. Perhaps they had fallen under the influence of foreign powers or Trotsky. The Master needed scapegoats. Nikolai Ezhov had served his purpose. It was time for him and his clique to go.

The Master's decision to end the Great Terror would not save those already in the repression pipeline. Their husbands and fathers had already been shot. They were left behind to suffer the aftermath, branded as traitors.

Nikolai Ezhov sensed that the Master's support was weakening. Too many news items praised the one he feared most—Lavrenty Beria, the party boss of Georgia. However, all was not lost, Ezhov thought. He would regain Stalin's confidence through bold action. The Master had praised "vigilance" in the February–March 1937 plenum. Nikolai would demonstrate his own vigilance by killing his own people.

Ezhov dispatched his right-hand man, Mikhail Frinovsky, to "inspect" regional NKVD operations around the country. Armed with a trainload of special NKVD forces to counter armed resistance, Frinovsky cut a swath of violence as he purged one NKVD administration after another. It never hurt to get rid of those who knew too much. (Mirosha told Agnessa that his good friend Frinovsky would have killed him had he not left the NKVD for the foreign ministry.)

Word of Frinovsky's purges spread. Agnessa's "pot-bellied" suitor in Kazakhstan shot himself in the night of June 13, at the very same time as the Azov-Black Sea NKVD head deserted to the Japanese. The defector had ordered his driver and guard to deposit him at the Manchurian border for a purported rendezvous with a secret agent. His Japanese contact failed to come, and his men found him asleep in a ravine the next morning. Using the same pretext, he returned the next night and successfully met up with Japanese intelligence. When an English correspondent asked him at his June 1938 Tokyo news conference, "What caused you to betray your country?" he answered, "We need to kill Stalin."

Ezhov and Frinovsky frantically debated how to tell the Master. There was no need—he already knew. After this intelligence disaster, Ezhov fell into a depression and wept before one of his subordinates: "It is over for me."

The next blow was the most telling: the Master named Beria deputy head of the NKVD on August 22, 1938. Ezhov drank himself into oblivion at his dacha. He remained away from the office for eight days. Upon his return, he sat in his office doing nothing. Beria took the reins of the NKVD as its de facto commissar. Now all significant orders went out under his name. The chief of the Ukrainian NKVD administration, visiting Lubyanka headquarters at the end of August, witnessed Ezhov in his office frantically ripping apart incriminating documents with his bare hands.

On October 31, the Master convened a Politburo meeting with Ezhov present. The noted novelist and favorite of the Master, Mikhail Sholokhov, complained of NKVD abuses in his native Don region. The stammering Ezhov denied personal responsibility. Local authorities had exceeded their authority, he claimed. At the November 7 military parade on Red Square, Beria stood near the Master dressed in a resplendent general's uniform. Stalin's orchestration presented Beria to the party and people as Ezhov's replacement.

Ezhov's loyalists understood that Beria would purge them just as they had killed their predecessors. Five days after the parade, the head of the NKVD Leningrad administration shot himself. On November 14, the head of the Ukrainian NKVD left a suicide note on the banks of the Dnieper and disappeared. (Beria's people caught up with him six months later.)

Beria replaced Nikolai's dwindling cohort with his own loyalists. One giant, Bogdan Kobulov, nicknamed "the samovar" for his girth, beat victims mercilessly with his huge fists. Ezhov's subordinates could picture themselves at his mercy. Under Beria, the screams of torture victims continued in Lefortovo and Sukhanovsky prisons. Beria took part with his rubber hose.

Stalin showed that he remained fully in charge, despite the apparent chaos. He ended the Great Terror as suddenly as it began. The Master issued a decree on November 17 that criticized "substantial deficiencies in the work of the NKVD and the prosecutor's office." Stalin's new decree forbade the NKVD from carrying out further mass operations and arrests. Most ominous for Ezhov was the statement that enemies had infiltrated the NKVD. Stalin had Ezhov in a corner.

The Master waited until November 23 to finish him off. He summoned Lead Butt and Klim to the Corner. Klim walked over from his large apartment in Corpus No. 9 of the Kremlin, arriving first at 8:30 p.m. Lead Butt joined them a few minutes later, driving down from the Old Square. Ezhov drove up at 9:25 from the Lubyanka in his Chrysler Airflow sedan.

The attendees navigated the security system with a nonchalance bred by familiarity. After passing the two officers of the "special sector" at entrance No. 2, they passed three more guards in the reception area at the top of the stairs. The presiding clerk registered their names and times of entry in violet, black, and sometimes red pencil. After registration, they entered a foyer with the Silent One's office on the right. Two guards posted at the entrance to the Master's office did not search the visitors as they entered. No one would dare to carry a revolver into the inner sanctum.

As the terrified Ezhov sat staring at the ashtrays, water pitchers, telephones, glasses for tea, and newspapers covering the huge meeting table, the Master, Lead Butt, and Klim reviewed Beria's report of "substantial deficiencies" in the NKVD's work. Stalin, in his usual indirect way of speaking, declared that it appeared appropriate for Nikolai Ezhov to resign his position. He was, after all, needed to head the Water Transport Ministry. Ezhov left the meeting at 1:00 a.m. after submitting his resignation and admitting to fundamental errors. The Master had his scapegoat.

The next day, the Politburo reviewed the "Declaration of N. I. Ezhov About His Mistakes" and named Beria as head of the NKVD. Ezhov justified his many mistakes by the fact that he "went out of his mind" after the desertion of the Azov-Black Sea NKVD head to Japanese intelligence. He said that he saw Beria's appointment as a vote of no confidence and that he considered Beria's criticisms as directed against him personally. It was not until December 8 that Pravda announced that Beria had replaced Ezhov. Ezhov sat drunk in the Water Transport Ministry lofting paper planes and doves into the air. He embarked on an orgy of drinking and homosexual and heterosexual sex, which continued until his arrest on April 10.

For thousands of Russians who were already in the pipeline, the Terror continued. Ezhov's replacement by Beria and the termination of the purge would not help innocent victims such as Fekla, Maria, and Adile. Agnessa's Mirosha was temporarily out of sight in the foreign ministry, but who would forget that he had been Frinovsky's right-hand man?

CHAPTER SEVENTEEN

Agnessa
New Year's Eve with the Master

Moscow (December 31, 1938–February 1940)

Agnessa considered Mirosha's embossed invitation to the Master's New Year's Eve dinner on December 31, 1938, as their talisman. Mirosha stood again at the top of the world. Only he and the minister himself had been invited from the Foreign Ministry. As a diplomat, he seemed immune from the firings and arrests in the NKVD. All her fears vanished. Agnessa had planned on wearing a flashy outfit to the Foreign Ministry ball, but "party wives" dressed in severe outfits. There could be no thought of bare shoulders among such blue-stockings.

On New Year's Eve, Mirosha's chauffeur delivered them to the entrance of Vladimir Hall, the unique center of the ensemble of Kremlin halls and palaces. As they entered the pink and white architectural masterpiece, Agnessa gazed at the glass cupola. Pink marble covered the walls and pillars. Ornate frescoes decorated the pastel walls. A huge, exotic carpet covered the ornate wood paneling. The three arched windows looked out on the Moscow River. The 21,500-square-foot grand hall offered space for 3,000 in concert seating. For this evening, guests sat at tables arranged around a huge fir tree in the exact center.

As a uniformed usher directed them to their table, Agnessa figured the closer to the Master the better. Her excitement rose as the usher brought them to the center, where their table stood in close proximity to Stalin's in the nearest corner. From her vantage point, she could see the Master in his resplendent white uniform. Such a seating announced they were in favor, or at least so Agnessa hoped.

The Master sat at one end of his large table with his inner circle. Opposite him sat Lead Butt's wife and other party wives. Each wore a slightly different shade of blue, as if they had orchestrated their choices. Polina Zhemchuzhina, Lead Butt's wife, Agnessa had heard, felt herself invulnerable. She greeted acquaintances cynically: "And have you not been arrested?" She too miscalculated when the Master ordered her arrest and forced her husband to agree.

Attentive waiters served caviar as a first course, fresh sturgeon as a second, shashlik as a third, and then brought out other delicacies for dessert. Each dish had the spicy flavors of the Caucasus, just as the Master liked it. A variety of wines stood on each table from which the guests could choose. The Master loved such nocturnal feasts. Although others said he ate and drank little, Agnessa saw that he ate heartily of fatted lamb. He ignored the warnings of his more coura- geous physicians who advised against such a diet at his age.

Agnessa saw Beria coming and touched Mirosha's shoulder to alert him. Agnessa's first encounter with the man who had replaced Ezhov a month and a half earlier lasted only a second. A short, bald man with a gray, unhealthy face, his golden pince-nez gleaming— Beria's eyes met Agnessa's without reaction. In replacing Ezhov's people, Beria surely examined the lists of all NKVD officers, even those in reserve like Mirosha. Agnessa repressed a growing anxiety. What if he remembered her friendship with the widow of his col- league, whom he had murdered in Tbilisi? She feared Beria's brief encounter with Mirosha could have bad consequences. However, Agnessa and Mirosha did not dwell on the unpleasant impression left by Beria. After all, the Master had invited Mirosha to celebrate the new year with him. That fact alone conquered all other fears.

The Mironovs spent the next six days—most of them official holidays—basking in their new-found sense of security. But on Jan- uary 6, 1939, Agnessa discovered a revolver hidden under Mirosha's pillow. So, Mirosha still toyed with the idea of suicide! Such thoughts should be behind him. She took his Mauser and hid it among her things. She and Mirosha then spent the day with Agulya and Borya. Mirosha played with them as if he were a child himself. An excellent skater, Mirosha fell on purpose to the delighted squeals of Agulya and Borya.

That night, the family dropped by to visit a colleague before an evening at the circus. In preparation, Mirosha donned his full-dress NKVD uniform. A phone call disrupted their animated conversation in the colleague's apartment. Their host handed the phone to Mirosha, puzzled. Agnessa saw growing concern on Mirosha's face: "But we had already agreed to that." Finally, he agreed with an air of reluctance: "Good, I'll come." He answered Agnessa's mouthed query: "They are calling me urgently to the Foreign Ministry." As he approached Agnessa, he whispered in her ear: "Maybe this is my arrest." Accustomed to his paranoia, Agnessa whispered in a jocular tone: "What are you talking about? Go quickly and we'll wait. Try not to be late to the circus."

Mirosha put on his coat. He borrowed his host's driver and car. Agnessa saw him off at the staircase: "Call me as soon as you get there." Despite the freezing weather, Mirosha did not even wear a muffler. Agnessa gave him her woolen scarf. He looked at the proffered scarf, and carefully wound it around his neck. Agnessa understood. This might be the only thing from her that he would have. He stood quietly a few seconds, gazed into her eyes, embraced her, and quickly descended the stairs, not looking back. She watched him descend until she heard the front door slam shut.

Agnessa rejoined the lively company. The phone rang. Mirosha must be calling to say everything was fine. But an unknown male voice demanded, "Call Mironov to the phone." Agnessa: "He is not here. He went to the Foreign Ministry." Voice: "How long ago?" Agnessa: "About twenty minutes." More than an hour passed before they heard a knock on the door. A polite man incongruously wearing white *burki* felt boots despite the cold entered. "Excuse me for the interruption, I am looking for Mironov." After being told Mironov had left two hours earlier, the stranger departed, excusing himself for the interruption. After he departed, Mirosha's colleague told Agnessa, "I know everyone who works at the ministry. He is from the NKVD."

The phone rang again. Agnessa's agitated housekeeper told her she should come home immediately, that her mother was sick. Agnessa responded: "I don't believe you. Tell the truth. Are there strangers in the apartment?" Agnessa heard the housekeeper's whisper: "May I tell her?" Agnessa's immediate answer: "Yes, I'll come."

Mirosha's chauffeur knew nothing. As they pulled up to Government House, he asked whether he should pick up Mirosha at nine as usual. Agnessa told him to wait for Mirosha's call. Agulya asked querulously, "Aren't we going to the circus? Where is Papa?" After an interminable ride in the elevator, Agnessa entered an apartment full of people. A man with a sunken chin, thin as the cigarette in his mouth, greeted her. Shortly thereafter, the man in the white *burki* felt boots joined them. Agnessa bent to take off her shoes. The disappointed Agulya asked, "But how about the circus?" Agnessa answered, "We have a circus here at home."

The men did not begin their search until she arrived. Agnessa followed them as they turned one room after another upside down. The man in white *burki* felt boots forgot his manners. He shouted at Agnessa, demanding to know Mironov's whereabouts. The agitation of her tormentors gave Agnessa a small measure of hope. Perhaps Mirosha had escaped? The telephone rang at two in the morning. She overheard the conversation. They had Mirosha—he had turned himself in. As the men left, a young officer handed her a telephone number. They will tell you everything you need to know, he said. After the search, the men sealed five rooms, leaving only one for Agnessa, Agulya, Mama, and the housekeeper.

Agnessa spent the next three weeks seeking out friends and acquaintances who might help. At midnight after she had returned from another frustrating day, the telephone rang. A polite young male voice instructed her to come to the NKVD reception at Kuznetsky Most 24. "They will know who you are. You need not come if you do not want to." They knew she would come. She must find out about Mirosha.

Agnessa donned her warmest clothes in anticipation of arrest. She gave her housekeeper and Mama instructions in case she did not return. She left their apartment at about 1 a.m. The doorman volunteered to accompany her, and the watchman said he'd stay up to open up for her upon her return. Agnessa and the doorman took the metro from Lenin Library to Kuznetsky Most. At the reception desk, she was given a pass, and an escort took her up the elevator. They walked along a dark corridor and entered a room. A polite young blond man bid Agnessa to sit and instructed her escort to "go about his business." (Agnessa worried his business might be preparing her arrest warrant.) The young man did not give his name, but the escort addressed him as Pavel Yakovlevich.

The blond man instructed her that he was handling the Mironov case. He handed her a letter written in Mirosha's hand: "Dear Wife and Friend: I only now understand the depth of my love for you. Everything is OK. Do not get upset. We'll figure everything out quickly, and I'll be home. I kiss you tenderly." Agnessa recognized their agreed-upon signal: "I kiss you tenderly." Everything was all right for the time being.

Pavel Yakovlevich tossed Agnessa's first draft of a response into the wastebasket. She could only write about herself and her family, telling him everything was fine. She ended her second draft with their signal: "I kiss you tenderly." The interview over, Agnessa's interrogator pushed a button and her escort reappeared. As they wandered through the dark corridor, Agnessa could not see signs of the elevator. She panicked, thinking he was taking her to a cell. Finally, she saw the elevator. The escort took her to the entrance and she exited onto an empty Dzerzhinsky Square. She sighed from grief and relief.

THE YEAR THAT FOLLOWED was one of alternating hope and anxiety.

Pavel Yakovlevich called in Agnessa periodically and gave her Mirosha's letters, all ending, "I kiss you tenderly." She answered with cheerful and brave letters. Maybe Mirosha could figure out a way to survive even an enemy like Beria. She wondered why they had not removed her immediately from Government House or arrested her. Maybe Mirosha could still pull some strings. Perhaps he leveraged his confession to help Agnessa.

Agnessa continued to live in the one room in Government House. The other five rooms remained sealed, but she could hear comings and goings followed by the moving of things. Once Agnessa encountered the men as they were about to enter the sealed rooms. One let her come in. Agnessa brought in a suitcase and packed her best clothes. As she picked up her fur coat, the NKVD officer told her she had enough. Next, Agnessa's housekeeper discovered that she could remove and replace the seals without anyone noticing. They could sneak in and no one would be the wiser. She and Agnessa removed the seals and began to collect Agnessa's possessions, substituting cheap for expensive items, as Agnessa remarked sardonically, "I am stealing my own things."

The eviction from Government House came eventually. Agnessa was assigned an apartment across the Moscow River on Kursovoi Street. She heard through the grapevine that her successor in her former apartment had been arrested. Government House was increasingly called the House of Tears, for good reason.

The more Agnessa thought about her things, the angrier she became. She submitted a list of confiscated items that belonged to her mother. Time passed, the phone rang, and a voice instructed her to come to the basement of Government House to collect her mother's possessions. The official at the entrance to Government House escorted Agnessa to the basement. Agnessa knew the guard. Her escort handed the guard the list of items she came to collect. Before he went to search for her things, the guard explained that thieves were breaking in all the time. Thieves even sawed off the bars and hauled stuff off through the window. The guard returned empty-handed and unapologetic: "Well, if you were all one family, you do not have the right to receive anything." Agnessa fully understood what had happened. The powers that be simply did not know her possessions had been stolen.

Agnessa continued to hope. Pavel Yakovlevich continued to hand over letters from Mirosha. He even gave her his own telephone number. Mirosha's letters hinted that everything would turn out fine. Months passed. Molotov and German Foreign Minister Joachim von Ribbentrop signed a non-aggression pact between their two nations in August 1939. The Finnish War (also known as the Winter War) began in late November 1939. In December, Pavel Yakovlevich summoned Agnessa and handed over a short letter from Mirosha: "Dear Wife and Friend: I advise you to leave Moscow. Regards to all." As Agnessa read these three dreaded code words, "Regards to all," she understood that Mirosha had lost his battle for survival. Pavel Yakovlevich did not understand why Agnessa broke out into sobs.

After a short while, Agnessa telephoned Pavel Yakovlevich. His tone changed from warm to cold: "I am no longer the investigator in the Mironov case." Agnessa: "How do I find out about him?" His cold answer: "Go to Lefortovo Prison and ask there." Agnessa began regular trips to Lefortovo Prison on the outskirts of Moscow. Each time she took a package and the magnificent sum of thirty-five rubles for the guards. If they accepted, that meant Mirosha was inside.

In January 1940, Agnessa arrived late, but she spied a young man exiting the guard booth. Agnessa apologetically approached, and he took pity on her. "What is the name?" "Mironov." He examined his list and told her there was no Mironov there. She could see from his look that he felt sorry for her. He instructed her, "You should go to Kuznetsky Most. They will know more."

Agnessa had had to find a job after her savings ran out. So she could go to Kuznetsky Most only after work. She arrived at 4 p.m. and joined a line of hundreds of women seeking news of husbands or sons. Several women were admitted at a time. She got to the front of the line at midnight. A middle-aged man in a prosecutor's uniform took her inquiry. She noticed exhaustion and beads of sweat on his forehead. After a short search, he found the name S.N. Mironov. He informed her that he had been sentenced to ten years under Article 58 without right of correspondence. He repeated the same to the women before and after Agnessa.

Ten years without right of correspondence. Agnessa did not know this meant he had been shot, but she later came to understand this terrible fact through gossip and whispers.

Agnessa usually slept deeply, especially in the early hours of the morning. But suddenly she felt as if someone had struck her a sharp blow. She looked at the clock. She felt a heavy weight on her heart. She wrote down the time and date: 6:00 a.m., February 22, 1940. She would later learn the significance of that date.

Kuibyshev to Kazakhstan (1940–1942)

Agnessa saw what happened to the wives of Mirosha's fallen associates. In the best case, they escaped notice and lived a quiet, modest life. In the worst, they and their children found themselves in the Gulag or before a firing squad. Her friend Nina, wife of Frinovsky, was shot on February 3, 1940.

Agnessa knew that no man could replace Mirosha, but she had her options. Her first husband, Ivan, wrote that he wanted her back. He'd gladly divorce his wife. Mirosha's first cousin, Mikhail Korol, offered a better option. A widower with two daughters, he had loved Agnessa since their first meeting. To the consternation of his younger daughter, he and Agnessa "married" without telling anyone. The daughter had no inkling until she caught "Aunt" Agnessa and her father engaged in noisy lovemaking. Family relations remained rocky, especially after Mikhail gave Agnessa the lion's share of his savings. Around Agnessa, he behaved like a love-struck child.

Mikhail himself had led a storied career that rivaled that of Mirosha. A civil war hero, he entered military intelligence, where he worked as an editor of the army's journal, *The Red Star*. In 1930, he became the deputy director of the state film agency, Goskino. While there, he wrote the screenplay for the prize-winning 1934 film *Chapaev*, about the legendary red commander Vasily Ivanovich Chapaev. From 1934 to 1938, he posed as a German-Jewish businessman in New York City. He was sent by military intelligence to establish business firms to funnel funds to the American Communist

Party. He returned to Moscow in 1938 during the height of the Great Terror. His party membership was suspended and he was dismissed from army intelligence, but was able to find work in the film industry. He lost his wife to cancer in 1939, and married Agnessa in 1940.

Agnessa, Mikhail, and their dysfunctional families remained in Moscow until the German bombing drove them hundreds of miles away to Kuibyshev, where they shared meager quarters with other refugees. Agnessa refused to leave her packed bags behind, knowing their contents could provide her with a livelihood. Hidden away in remote Kuibyshev, Agnessa figured the NKVD had more important things to worry about than the wife of Sergei Mironov.

In provincial Kuibyshev, Agnessa traded in the black market. Especially prized were her Mongolian silks. State and party officials, who had fled Moscow with suitcases full of cash, paid up to 200 rubles for Agnessa's treasures. Agnessa proved herself a survivor. While she bustled around night and day arranging her transactions, her do-nothing flat-mates expected her to share with them without making any effort themselves.

Agnessa's transgressions in the black market made her a prime candidate for arrest. At one point, state inspectors uncovered Agnessa's cache of goods and vodka, but they disappeared after accepting a bribe. If her neighbors had not been present, the inspectors would have taken everything. Agnessa saw the satisfaction in her neighbors' eyes as the inspectors carted off her things.

Agnessa avoided arrest until 1942. Shortly before her arrest, third husband Mikhail tried to obtain a pass for Agnessa and Agulya to return to Moscow. Perhaps that brought Agnessa to the attention of the authorities. After all, she was the wife of an important state criminal. Mikhail took Agnessa's arrest badly. He banged his head against the door. He wrote letters to everyone, including Beria himself: "If she is guilty, you should arrest me as well." The authorities obliged, and both Agnessa and Mikhail Korol disappeared into the Gulag.

After her arrest, Agnessa was brought back to Moscow in a Stolypin Wagon (the notorious railroad car used to transport prisoners in cattle car–like conditions). Agnessa slept in the crowded car in a stylish red cardigan, a cloth over her face to shield her eyes from the glare of the bright single light bulb. All of a sudden, a female guard rushed over to her. The guard, it seems, could only see the red color of the material through the peephole and assumed Agnessa had committed suicide on her watch. She kept Agnessa close in her sights the rest of the trip.

In Moscow, a puzzled Lubyanka interrogator could not figure out the reason for her arrest. Then he found in the file that Agnessa was the wife of the Chekist Mironov. Perhaps that explained it. That evening, a guard looking through the peephole called out for "Mironova." As she approached the door, she confirmed her name was "Mironova." Satisfied, he led her, not to the interrogator, but up the staircase to a higher floor.

They proceeded along a corridor covered with a plush rug, clean and beautiful. The escort led her into a large office dominated by a portrait of the Master. A well-dressed man with a pleasant face and polite voice greeted her: "Agnessa Mironova, if I am not mistaken." He examined her from head to foot and looked at the paper in front of him, as if checking something. "What is your full name?" He seemed puzzled.

As he read through her file, Agnessa spied in the neighboring room a table covered with a white tablecloth and loaded with appetizers and other exotic foods. Although earlier such a banquet would have been routine for her, after two months of prison food, the table seemed grand. The polite man inquired about her husband: "What was his full name? Whom did he replace?" She answered, and her interrogator picked up the phone and talked with someone at the other end. As he ended his conversation, he announced she was free to go.

The puzzled Agnessa returned to her cell. Later, she put two-and-two together. She remembered the other Mironov, whom Mirosha arrested in Novosibirsk in 1937. His wife had the reputation of having the combination of promiscuity and beauty attributed to the Roman empress Messalina. Men fought for her affections and favors.

Beria, the known fancier of beautiful women (and teenage girls), apparently heard that the wife of Mironov was in the Lubyanka. He sat at the table in the next room ready to enjoy a night with Messalina-Mironova. When he saw she was not the right Mironova, he sent her away.

In her glory days, Beria would not have rejected her. But Agnessa's days in prison and her hard work in the black market had dimmed her beauty. Beria's dismissal hurt her pride.

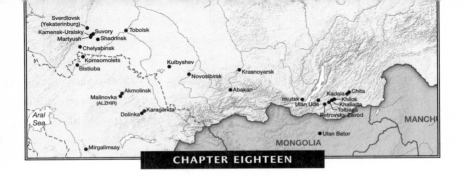

CHAPTER EIGHTEEN

Maria

Wife of a Traitor of the Motherland

Chita (October 1937–February 1938)

Maria Ignatkina learned of the execution of her husband, Alexander, in the Chita city prison on October 15, 1937. On October 17, the officer in charge indicted the grieving new widow: "In league with her husband, Maria Ignatkina, born 1904, aided the counter-revolutionary activity of her husband, who perpetrated crimes according to Article 58 of the Russian republic criminal code." On December 10, a shout roused the women inmates: "Transport is here. Get ready to go to court for your sentencing!" They went one by one. The first woman returned and burst out between sobs: "They sentenced me to eight years. Eight years!" The alarmed women thought she said "fifty-eight." Article 58 meant death. Panic broke out as the prisoners screamed. They quieted down when the woman repeated her sentence in a clearer voice.

When Maria's turn came, the court officer read her sentence: "Case No. 257 DTO, Maria Ignatkina, born 1904: As a member of the family of a traitor of the motherland to be imprisoned in a correctional labor camp for eight years, with a starting date of July 1937." The Master's August 15 order called for minimum sentences for wives of traitors of five to eight years. The Chita courts took no chances. They sentenced all of their "wives of traitors" to the maximum eight-year term.

On a freezing February morning in 1938, the prison guards marched the wives of the railway engineers in a column through Chita's streets toward the train station. Frightened passersby shied away from the miserable column shrouded in freezing fog. Suddenly the grown daughter of one of the women shouted out: "Mama!" Word spread. Chita knew the wives of the condemned railroad workers were being sent away. When the women arrived at the station, the guards ordered them to sit. "How are we to sit?" the confused women asked. There were no benches. The guards motioned to them to squat on their haunches. They squatted for several hours in the intense cold, choking back tears, burning with shame.

Crouching in the cold, Maria could not get out of her head the screams of her children as the car sped them off to the orphanage. She saw a commuter train approaching and in a mad moment of despair rushed into its path. A strong hand grabbed her hair and pulled her back from inevitable death with a stern reproach: "See here—that is the last time you try something like this. Don't ruin your children's lives. We will outlive our enemies. We will see our children again. Everything will be back in its own place. Believe me, the truth will win out."

The train arrived and they boarded. Maria's rail journey took her 250 miles to Karaganda in Western Kazakhstan. She toiled there in the notorious ALZHIR camp for family members of traitors, unloading rail cars. She would not see her children until 1946.

CHAPTER NINETEEN

Evgenia
Losing Everything

Moscow (1938)

The editorial office of *USSR Under Construction* buzzed at its usual hectic pace as illustrators, artists, photographers, writers, and graphic designers huddled together to get out the next issue. Evgenia Ezhova and her deputy, Isaak Babel, virtually lived in the office. The Master needed to show the world his socialist workers' paradise. Evgenia obliged, despite her shrinking staff. As autumn of 1938 approached, Evgenia realized that she was directing a sinking ship. The illustrated magazine's visages of smiling miners and joyous farmers masked the turmoil upending the socialist construction that Evgenia's magazine hallowed. Most of the managers praised in the July issue would be, within a year, "no longer among the living." The father of socialist construction, Comrade Sergo, had "spat" one last time on the Master with his February 1937 suicide.

Police arrested one editorial board member after another. The state bank chairman, one of Nikolai's closest friends, went in December 1937. Nikolai went to the torture room drunk, demanding that he confess more, mumbling to his officers: "We will beat, beat, and beat." Evgenia did her best to cover up the disappearance of her board members. If the arrest came right before the issue's publication, the designers covered the name with a black square. Finally, only Evgenia and two others remained on the editorial board.

Subsequent editions ceased printing the names of the editors altogether. When Evgenia herself disappeared, there would be no reason to mention this small fact.

The lively and exuberant Evgenia withdrew into her own shell. She sat alone in an apartment that had been full of laughter, chatter, music, and lovers. Daughter Natasha played alone with her nanny. Mama had lost interest in her. Nikolai gave her no comfort. She rarely saw him as he went about his business of killing people.

As his wife, Evgenia became more discreet in her own affairs. She could not afford rumors and gossip in this sensitive time. She knew too many people who sat in prison or resided under the ground. She had lived in England and Germany. She received letters and packets from abroad and used foreign currencies to buy luxuries from capitalist countries. Others were arrested for much smaller offenses.

In contrast to his wife's behavior, Nikolai's excesses worsened. Even his comrades in arms recognized that he was spinning out of control. One department head reported that not a day passed in which Ezhov remained sober. His absences from work were listed as illnesses, but everyone knew the real reason. He left to conduct interrogations at Lefortovo plastered with cognac. Frinovsky himself fell ill after each orgy. He complained that Ezhov drove him crazy. He could not continue in this way. Evgenia did her best to cover up Nikolai's excesses. She even arranged abortions for women he impregnated, even though she violated strict Soviet law in doing so.

Evgenia knew that fortune was turning against Nikolai. As the number of executions exceeded a half million in the spring of 1938, smarter heads realized that the terror must end. Those regional party leaders still alive began complaining directly to the Master. They wanted revenge on the NKVD and on Nikolai Ezhov. With a sense of dread and foreboding, Evgenia realized that she could go down with her husband.

On July 4, 1938, this abstract danger became real. During a meeting earlier in the day, Stalin questioned Nikolai about Evgenia's relationship with two Trotskyites, already executed. The Master casually ventured that Nikolai might want to think about a divorce. Nikolai returned home in a panic. A divorce from Nikolai meant the loss of her last protector, albeit a weakening one. Evgenia used all her powers of persuasion: everything will turn out just fine, she assured Nikolai. The Master's suspicions will pass. Nikolai must tell the Master he has full faith in her. Evgenia convinced Nikolai they should stay together, but she could not convince herself she was safe. She alternated between depression and manic activity. She had to keep busy. She had to keep herself occupied.

Nikolai failed to understand that the Master wanted him to sacrifice Evgenia to demonstrate his loyalty. He sealed his own fate by resisting. Nikolai went about getting rid of those who could incriminate him or his wife. Nikolai had already obtained permission to shoot Evgenia's second husband, Alexander Gladun, in June after holding him for two years. Nikolai also arrested another of Evgenia's lovers, the editor of the *Peasant Gazette*. He did not execute him in time, and the editor gave testimony against both Nikolai and Evgenia.

The desperate Evgenia saw her salvation in Mikhail Sholokhov, the author of *Quiet Flows the Don* and a favorite of the Master. He had Stalin's ear and did not fear using his influence. Unlike others, he did not tremble before the NKVD. He went directly to the Master to complain about the abuses of Nikolai's NKVD in his native Don region. Ezhov sought to smooth things over by inviting Sholokhov to their dacha, where he and Evgenia met for the first time. They hit it off immediately.

In August 1938, Sholokhov returned to Moscow, again to complain about NKVD purges. He visited Evgenia's editorial office under the guise of discussing a contribution to her journal. From there, they proceeded to his room at the National Hotel. Evgenia returned home very late. An enraged Nikolai confronted her. He became even more agitated when she confessed that she was "not indifferent" to Sholokhov. Evgenia did not know whether his rage was jealousy or because her new lover had a direct line to the Master.

The next day, Sholokhov and Evgenia again proceeded to the National. Unbeknownst to them, an NKVD bugging operator had recognized Sholokhov's voice the evening before and recorded their tryst in the hotel room the next day. The transcript provided explicit details: "They proceeded into the bath. They lay down together in the bed," etc. The chief of the secret department immediately dispatched the transcript to Ezhov.

Evgenia and her friend Zinaida spent the next day outside of Moscow at the dacha. As they readied themselves for bed, Ezhov stormed in. The women sat at the table while he drank himself into a stupor. After a while, he abruptly extracted a document from his jacket, and asked Evgenia point-blank: "Did you sleep with Sholokhov?" Evgenia stammered out a denial, whereupon Ezhov flung the document at her. As Evgenia read, her face turned pale, and she began to shake. Zinaida tried to leave the room, but Nikolai demanded that she read it, pointing to the key passages. Zinaida immediately understood: this was a transcript of Evgenia's lovemaking with Sholokhov. At this point, Nikolai sprang on the divan where Evgenia had collapsed and began to beat her. Zinaida intervened. Shortly thereafter, he destroyed the document in their presence.

Nikolai continued to waver, despite Evgenia's betrayal. As his career crumbled, Evgenia offered him an anchor. Unlike the Master's other henchmen, he could not find it in him to sacrifice his own wife, no matter what she had done.

Nikolai's resolve collapsed on September 18. The Master again raised Evgenia's Trotskyite past. He advised divorce without mincing words. That same evening, Nikolai informed Evgenia that he had decided to divorce her. Evgenia understood he had just sentenced her to death.

As Evgenia descended into a crippling depression, Nikolai dispatched her to a sanatorium in the Crimea, where the best specialists in nervous disorders awaited their illustrious patient. Her friend Zinaida accompanied her. Despite beautiful surroundings and attentive physicians, Evgenia did not eat. She scarcely slept. From her Crimean hospital bed, Evgenia launched her final effort to save herself with a forlorn letter to her husband: "My Dearest Little Nikolai:

In Moscow I was in such a bad state that I could not even talk with you even though I very much wanted to. I wanted to draw conclusions about our life together and about my own. I feel my life is over. I do not know if I have the strength to live. I cannot accept the idea that they suspect me of such crimes. These undeserved charges have left me a living corpse. All the time I think: why live? What offenses have I committed that require such inhuman suffering. I pray you to believe me, for my sake, for Natasha's."

Evgenia ended her letter with a plea that Nikolai speak with the Master: "If you could just speak with him five minutes, with this man who is so dear to me. I saw how he worries about you, how tenderly he speaks about women. He will understand me, I am sure. He understands. He cannot be mistaken in a person and allow that person to perish. How hard it is that I have no strength to write. How alone I am in undeserved unhappiness. And what will come? It is too horrible to consider. I wander the hospital room. I want to scream. But to whom? Who will believe me? You must believe all, I pray."

As Evgenia's depression deepened in the Crimea, evidence against her accumulated. The Master himself received accusations about Evgenia's trafficking with foreigners and misuse of state funds. Informants targeted Evgenia with denunciations. It was left to Frinovsky to acquaint Nikolai with the incriminating documents. He left Nikolai in an extreme fit of agitation. Nikolai knew that Evgenia could not be saved.

The day after Frinovsky's visit, Nikolai ordered Evgenia to return to Moscow. When Evgenia, accompanied by Zinaida, returned, Nikolai banished them to the dacha. He visited periodically. He scarcely talked to Evgenia. Instead, he spent his time whispering with Zinaida. On October 29, Nikolai placed Evgenia in the Vorovsky Nerve Clinic outside of Moscow. In the clinic, Evgenia's depression worsened. During one of his visits, she asked Nikolai for poison. He responded that he did not have poison, but he could give her enough sleeping pills to kill herself. They also agreed on a signal that all was lost. If he sent her a gnome figure, she should take a fatal overdose.

Shortly thereafter, Nikolai sent Evgenia a large box of chocolates in which he concealed a large quantity of sleeping pills. On November 8, Ezhov sent an associate to deliver a gnome figure to Evgenia. The messenger reported that she could not be consoled. She gave him a letter for Nikolai. He tore it to shreds after reading it. Back in Moscow, Nikolai waited for word that his wife was dead. Evgenia did not act immediately upon receiving the signal, but her last bit of hope evaporated when she learned of the November 15 arrest of her friend Zinaida. She knew that Nikolai could not be behind the arrest—Beria had arranged it himself.

In her final act of desperation, Evgenia penned a letter to the Master: "I beg you to read this letter. I could not decide whether to write, but I have no strength left. How can my doctors help if I am possessed by the idea that you suspect me. I beg you, in the name of my mother whom I love and Natasha who is the dearest to me, to believe that I did not exchange one word of politics with any enemy of the people. I, as an honest Soviet citizen, curse these criminal bands. I have made mistakes in my personal life about which I could tell you, but this is a personal matter. The physicians cannot cure nerves destroyed by years of insomnia, fever of the brain, and deep pain in my soul from which I cannot escape. I do not have the right to die. I live only with the knowledge that I am honest before you and the country. I feel myself a living corpse. What can I do? Excuse me for this letter, which I am writing in bed. I could no longer be silent. E. Ezhova."

The Master did not reply.

About 6 o'clock in the evening of November 19, an attending physician found Evgenia sleeping. He knew she did not sleep during the day. Attempts to revive her failed. Her pupils did not respond to light. Evgenia died at 7:55 p.m. November 21 of "pneumonia." It fell to Evgenia's brothers to arrange her funeral. The authorities did not allow them to use her married name, Ezhova, so she was buried under her first husband's name. Her remains were laid to rest in

Moscow's Donskoi Cemetery with the name "Evgenia Khayutina" on the gravestone.

AS THE VOROVSKY CLINIC doctors fought for Evgenia's life, Nikolai Ezhov fought for his own. He and Frinovsky sat in the Master's office surrounded by the Politburo. Beria sat menacingly opposite them. The grueling session began at 11:10 p.m. and ended at 3:20 a.m. The Politburo gathered to review the charges of "defective work" within the NKVD. Beria had reported with "regret" a complaint from the Ivanovsky NKVD, where arrested officers testified that "leading figures" in the NKVD were sabotaging the uncovering of enemies of the people. Nikolai Ezhov retreated into a world of drinking, carousing, sexual excess, melancholy, and depression. He had lost his wife and had nothing left to do but wait for his end.

CHAPTER TWENTY

Adile

Return and Arrest

Sukhumi (New Year's Eve 1938–February 1940)

Adile did not know Agnessa Mironova, Evgenia Ezhova, Fekla Andreeva, or Maria Ignatkina. They spent New Year's Eve 1938 in quite different ways. Agnessa sat just a few steps away from the Master in the Kremlin Palace, next to her husband, Sergei Mironov. Maria spent her New Year's Eve in the Chita city jail along with other wives of traitors, waiting to be sent to the Gulag. She already knew her husband had been shot. Fekla Andreeva spent her New Year's Eve in bed with her frightened sisters, grieving over the arrest of her father and hoping that he was alive. Evgenia's earthly remains rested in Moscow's Donskoi Cemetery, where her gravestone did not mark her as the wife of Nikolai Ezhov. Her former husband spent his New Year's Eve in a drunken stupor.

Adile Abbas-ogly, the sister-in-law of the late Abkhazia party boss, Nestor Lakoba, arrived in Sochi by train from Moscow on New Year's Eve. From Sochi, it was a short trip to her aunt's home in Gagra. The attention of two travel companions raised Adile's suspicions. Earlier, she would have interpreted their familiarity as flirting, but they had the smell of the "organs" about them. At the Sochi station, she refused their offer of a ride. When she looked out the rear window of her taxi, she saw her travel companions following. Her aunt greeted Adile with a warning that the "organs" intended to arrest her in Gagra. Adile proceeded immediately by bus to Sukhumi to her mother.

Agents met Adile as she arrived in Sukhumi and took her to NKVD headquarters. Awaiting her was none other than the notorious "Quasimodo," brought in by Beria to instill fear. Quasimodo's real name was Grigory Pachuliya, but he was nicknamed for the character in *The Hunchback of Notre Dame*. He shot his victims with his own hand; rumor had it he killed some by burying them alive. Admired by Beria as a soccer player, he did not disappoint with his brutality.

Quasimodo got down to business: "Why did you not report your passport missing in Moscow? With whom did you live?" Quasimodo confirmed that her stolen bag rested in her NKVD file: "Did not your mother write it was too early to return to Sukhumi?" He already knew the answers. Quasimodo listened to her stammered answers and then exploded, "What do you intend to do now, bitch?" Adile responded weakly, "I want a passport, I want to work." He terminated her interview abruptly: "We'll have to think over what to do with you." He dismissed her and sent her away. Adile returned home to her mother's arms after a half year's separation. Neither knew what to say. Her mother suffered alongside her in silence.

Adile began a routine of questioning by Quasimodo. He threatened to charge her with "political unreliability" under Article 39. He continued to probe: who sheltered her in Moscow, what did she do there, whom did she know? Then as suddenly as it began, they left her alone. The eerie silence convinced Adile that she had few days of freedom left. They could come for her at any time or place.

In mid-February, her friend Dina invited Adile to the theater. Adile did not want to go, but Dina pleaded, perhaps too much. In the theater foyer, Adile spied a group of men from the "organs" loitering in a corner. As she passed, one remarked loudly enough for her to hear: "Yes, 100 percent." Adile involuntarily looked up to see them laughing. The theater was cool, and Adile put on her shawl. Suddenly she felt someone tugging on it. Adile wanted to turn around, but Dina cautioned her to ignore them. Another tug and Adile turned to see one of the men from the foyer holding her shawl. "Don't be afraid," he said in Abkhazian, "We are only joking." Adile retorted, "I am not afraid," trying to appear calm. But she sat on pins and needles throughout the rest of the performance.

The play ended late. The men offered to escort them home. One wisecracked, "Someone may steal your purse as they did in Moscow." Adile rejected their offer, but they followed. Dina slipped away. Adile figured Dina set her up. When she hastily entered her house, the men loitered conspicuously outside. Adile understood the men came to harass her, not to arrest.

Adile's mother had to leave to take care of her ill father in the Abkhazian village of Mokva. She left reluctantly, crying. They both understood that it might be a very long time before they saw each other again. Adile remained home alone with her forebodings.

On February 22, 1939, at 11:30 p.m., Adile awoke to a loud hammering on the front door. A neighbor came to Adile's door to ask if she was expecting someone. Adile instructed her that if they were coming for her, they would have to break the door down. The banging continued, then silence. Adile slipped through the terrace to the neighboring house, where an aunt lived with four cousins. She asked one of her cousins to spend the night with her. As they returned, Adile took her ring from her finger and gave it to her cousin.

The men began to beat on the front door with renewed energy. Adile's neighbors saw it was hopeless to refuse, and opened. Quasimodo himself entered her apartment. Adile's neighbor, a schoolteacher, challenged the intruders: "Why do you need her? She is still a child." Quasimodo responded according to the NKVD operating procedures: "We need her to clear up some things. It will just take a second." Her neighbor answered: "Can't you clear things up during the day? I'll not let her go."

Quasimodo and his team proceeded to burrow through the apartment. They leafed through a photo album they unearthed and extracted a photo of Adile with Emdy. Adile's aunt came running from next door. Behind her came other relatives, protesting: "The girl's mother is not home. We'll not let you take her." However, Adile understood arrest was inevitable: "Just tell me what I should take with me." Quasimodo answered mockingly, "Why? Are you planning to stay with us a long time? You must feel guilty about something." Quasimodo assured her, "Everything is fine. You do not need to take anything with you."

Quasimodo whispered to one of his Chekists. After several minutes they heard a car idling in front. They bustled Adile into the car. Adile's aunt and the schoolteacher jumped in. At the headquarters, the men bustled Adile inside, leaving Adile's protectors helpless in the car. Her aunt remained outside until an officer threatened to arrest her.

The men took Adile to an interrogation room, where a former spurned suitor from her school days removed her hairpins. Criminals cannot have metal objects, he explained. Adile's hair fell down to her waist. He quipped, "A real-world Rapunzel," as Adile stood before him humiliated.

He escorted Adile to the office of the head of the Abkhazian NKVD, Varlam Kakuchaya. Adile's reception by Kakuchaya himself showed Beria's intense interest. Kakuchaya looked at Adile as if surprised to see her. He spoke politely in a reassuring voice: "You are not arrested. We just want to clear up a few things. You lived in the Lakoba household and may be able to explain certain circumstances. I advise you to tell us everything you know. And then you can go home." After this short exchange, the men took Adile to another wing of the building for the night. For the time being, they did not want Adile to hear the screams emanating from nearby rooms.

The guard locked Adile in the dressing room of the bathhouse. A dim light burned. Adile huddled into a ball in one cold, damp corner. The rats scampering around the room paid Adile no attention, but she screamed each time she saw one. The janitor heard Adile's shrieks. Adile's grandfather had helped out his family long ago. The janitor saw Adile being locked in the dressing room and hung around to see if he could help. He whispered through the locked door, "Why are you making such a noise?" As Adile sobbed about the rats, he comforted her: "Try to sleep. I will watch over you until the morning." He spent the night periodically knocking on the door to frighten off the rats. If his superiors caught him helping a political prisoner, he would pay dearly.

The next day, the guard took Adile back to Kakuchaya, who informed her that she was being sent to Tbilisi. Before her departure, they allowed an aunt and uncle to hand over a package of bedding to take with her.

After her photograph and fingerprints were taken at the Tbilisi NKVD headquarters, Adile was thrust into cell No. 38. The iron door clanged shut behind her. Adile's two new cellmates showered her with questions, and told her about themselves. The three could hardly turn around in the tiny cell. One identified herself as the wife of a prominent man executed as an "enemy of the people." She had undergone two years of physical and mental torture. The wounds on her arms and legs had not had time to heal. The other, the sister-in-law of Beria's wife, lay on her bunk, fresh from a beating. They had already shot her surgeon husband, who was Nina Beria's brother. Adile asked why Nina Beria did not help. The woman's whispered response: Beria had already disposed of all his relatives. She took a motherly interest in Adile. Her own daughter was only two years Adile's junior.

A bloodcurdling scream interrupted Adile's troubled sleep that first night. She shook all over and pleaded with her cellmates to tell her what was going on. They hugged Adile but only said, "You will know all these things yourself soon enough."

Adile began a routine of nightly interrogations. The guards led Adile through corridors of inhuman screams, groans, and curses. As they dragged prisoners from interrogation rooms, they ordered Adile, "Turn to the wall. Hands behind your back!" Her three case officers alternated questioning her. After all, they needed their own sleep. Of the three, Adile feared most "The Beast." A kind Ossetian guard would warn her on the way from her cell, "Get yourself ready, I am taking you to The Beast."

In their first meeting, The Beast showed Adile a document authorizing the use of torture: "I can skin you alive, if I wish." He grabbed her by her long hair and dragged her around the room. Adile remained silent despite the pain. He then commanded her to stand, sit, raise her arms, and get on her knees. She had to follow his commands no matter how exhausted she was. The interrogators beat everyone except Adile and another girl who was a little older than Adile. Even the NKVD observed some limits.

The Beast had means of torture more effective than beating. Adile watched as he beat half-naked prisoners in their private parts and forced them to run around on all fours. At times, Adile forgot where she was and ran to help them. A blow to her back brought her back to reality. Adile feared the narrow chamber nicknamed "the cage" most of all. She thrashed about like a caged animal in the intense heat and claustrophobia of this basement punishment cell. Her daily ration was a small piece of black bread, hard as a rock, and a cup of water. A nauseating bucket served as her toilet. Adile prided herself that she did not cry before her torturers. She never pleaded for mercy. In the cage, she cried for herself in her misery.

As a break in the routine, the guards delivered Adile to the opulent office of the NKVD commissar of Georgia, Avksenty Rapava. Portraits of Stalin and Beria stared down at Adile as Rapava examined Adile from head to foot. The Beast, her two other interrogators, and a handsome young blond man in a tailored gray suit sporting a walking cane joined the meeting. The young man smiled at Adile and then launched into a tirade: "Is it true that you consorted with that prostitute, Sariya Lakoba? If you remain silent, we'll turn you into a hag. You have no choice, you bitch. Confess how Lakoba planned to assassinate the Master in the spring of 1934. Confess that you arranged meetings between Lakoba and Turkish spies. If you confess honestly we'll let you go. If you remain silent, we'll finish off you and your mother." As Adile watched this handsome man turn into a monster, she felt her end looming before her.

In the days following the meeting in Rapava's office, Adile wrote as her interrogators dictated her confession. She "confessed" that she lured Emdy into marriage, that Sariya trained her as a conspirator, and that she obeyed Nestor Lakoba's criminal commands. She obediently signed her confession and, as she reached out to take it back to read, her interrogator grabbed her by the hand: "It is not allowed. Have you forgotten where you are?" But Adile could see that her tormentors were troubled. Although Adile's confession brimmed with lies and fabrications, they could not afford obviously inaccurate or ludicrous statements. One pointed out that Adile was only thirteen when Lakoba allegedly tried to assassinate the Master. She had no contact with the Lakoba family before the age of fifteen. The statement also misidentified Adile as Lakoba's daughter-in-law.

On their rare days without interrogations, the inmates of cell No. 38 exchanged stories. In an attempt to raise their spirits, Adile told a joke about Chekists. Shortly thereafter, she was summoned to The Beast and three other men: "We hear you are chatting in your cell about us. Tell us your joke." The flustered Adile pulled herself together and recounted the joke about a Jew, Abraham, who lived in the same house as a Chekist. The Chekist was puzzled that Abraham greeted him with "good evening" every morning. Finally, the puzzled Chekist asked why the Jew said "good evening" in the morning. Answer: "When I see you, all goes black in front of my eyes." The Beast and the others roared with laughter. They dismissed Adile without any punishment.

After Adile returned, her cellmates did not speak with her. They assumed that only an informer could get away with such sacrilege. They apologized after they learned that it was the wife of a prison official, posing as a prisoner, who tattled to the prison authorities—not Adile.

Adile's interrogators continued to edit her confession. At long last, they handed her the indictment. Adile objected that she had no idea what the articles of the criminal code under which they charged her meant. They explained that this article meant espionage, the other treason, the other disclosure of secrets, and so on. Adile wrote as they dictated: "I plead guilty according to all the articles." The interrogator took the signed confession and declared with satisfaction: "We have enough to stand you up against the wall." Adile felt nothing but fatigue and apathy. Adile's final indictment contained far less serious charges. Who could make sense of what went on inside the Georgian NKVD prison?

As they concluded the session, Adile's investigator asked her out of the blue, "Adile: if you live through this and encounter me on the street, how will you behave?" Her answer: "If I see you, I'll immediately go to the other side and pretend that I did not see you." Her answer irritated him. He brusquely ordered her taken back to her cell. Adile never understood why he asked this question.

A TELEGRAPH-LIKE TAPPING SYSTEM kept Adile and her fellow inmates in cell No. 38 informed about the goings-on in the prison. Through the prison telegraph, Adile learned that Sariya, her sister-in-law and mentor, occupied cell No. 16. Sariya's son, Rauf, resided one cell down from Adile in cell No. 40. Three members of the Lakoba family occupied the same floor of the same NKVD prison, but they never came face-to-face. The resourceful Sariya could hear when Rauf's cell was opened. She counted the guards' steps and cried out in anguish when they passed her cell with Rauf: "My miserable son is passing by his mother, and I cannot do anything." Rauf's presence nearby soon made Sariya physically ill. Rauf took off his shoes and went barefoot past her cell. His ruse worked. She concluded that Rauf had been transferred into a regular prison.

Interrogators beat Sariya with whips and stomped on her prostrate body. Knowing her fear of snakes, they put her in a dark chamber full of snakes. As they brought in her oldest brother and Sariya rushed to embrace him, her interrogators demanded that they both confess to conspiring with Nestor to kill the Master. Her brother looked pleadingly: "Sariya, forgive me. We must do it." She screamed, "You have lost your conscience. I'll never sign such lies. Take this traitor away."

As a final resort, Beria ordered a face-to-face meeting between Sariya and Rauf. When Sariya remained unbent, Beria screamed, "Beat that little bastard. Stomp on him. Let that woman hear the groans of her son!" As he was beaten mercilessly, Rauf begged, "Save me, Mama. Tell them all they want to hear." But Sariya answered, "Bear it all, my son. Your father was an honest man. They will not let us go, anyway."

In May 1939, Adile was transferred from the central NKVD prison to the dank, rat-infested cell No. 1 of Tbilisi's Ortachalskaya Prison. While she was there, word of the transfer of the deathly ill Sariya spread through the prison telegraph like wildfire. In her delirium, Sariya asked for Rauf. Her fellow inmates lied that he was healthy and in good shape. She cried constantly and sometimes laughed like a mad person. As Sariya's condition worsened, she was taken to the prison hospital, where a sympathetic physician smuggled in pain medication. In her delirium, she cried out to the Master: "If only you knew what a snake you kept in your presence. No, Nestor never betrayed you. He did not eat without first drinking to your health."

On the morning of May 16, the state prosecutor came to the semi-conscious Sariya, demanding that she sign her "confession," saying, "Sign or we'll finish off your son." Sariya rose from bed and hurled the paper at him: "In ten or fifteen years, you will have to answer for your crimes." At three in the afternoon, Sariya Lakoba died at the age of thirty-five. News of Sariya's death spread through the prison, evoking a wave of sympathy even from hardened criminals. On the same day as Sariya's death, Adile learned she had become a widow at age eighteen. The prison telegraph spread the word that Sariya's four brothers, including Adile's husband, Emdy, had been shot. Only the youngest brother survived.

Adile periodically received letters from her mother. She enclosed fifty-ruble notes for the guards and received back from Adile short messages that all was well. Adile knew her mother could not even imagine the circumstances in which she lived. After Adile suffered a bout with typhus that landed her in the prison hospital, the guards mocked her swollen face and thin body: "You arrived as a beautiful mermaid. Now you are a witch."

ADILE ENTERED THE NKVD SYSTEM in February 1939. In December 1939 she was sentenced to three years in remote Kazakhstan as a member of the "Nestor Lakoba gang." In January 1940 guards loaded the nineteen-year-old Adile, cane in hand, into a railway car to begin her odyssey to confinement in Kazakhstan. Along with Adile in the locked Stolypin Wagon traveled common criminals and political prisoners.

Along the way, she stopped in a series of transit prisons. One transit cell had water dripping down the walls, and the usual rats scurried on the floor. Inmates outnumbered the beds. On Adile's third day, a guard instructed her to gather her things and come with him. At first, Adile did not understand why her cellmates looked at her with such pity. Adile sensed something was very wrong. The guard led Adile through a long hallway and down some stairs, and shoved her into a basement lit by a blindingly bright light bulb. The cell had only a pile of hay in the corner. Water dripped on walls covered with mold. After three days, Adile had lost hope. But then the door opened and a guard escorted her back to the transit cell. Her comrades met her with joy and relief. The assumed she had been shot and had declared a hunger strike on her behalf.

At another stop, the guards drove the slow-moving crowd of women like animals, their tears turning to ice in the cold wind. The local people averted their gazes. Inside the dark building, the usual command came: "On your knees!" The roll call determined who had died along the way. The guards then drove them into the bath. The women waited for the guards to withdraw, but the guards made it clear that the women were to undress in their presence. Adile could hardly stand, but two women poured hot water into a tub and lifted her inside. All the while the guards gawked and pointed, laughing at the naked women.

Adile arrived in February 1940 in the desolate village of Bistiuba in northern Kazakhstan, her home for the next seven years. Much suffering, a marriage, childbirth, and a hazardous return to Anastasiya Zueva in Moscow and her mother in Sukhumi remained ahead.

CHAPTER TWENTY-ONE

Fekla
Face of the Future

Martyush (1938–1941)

Time passed slowly in Martyush. In May 1938 Mother was transferred from the mines to work as a janitor. During the day, Grandfather repaired shoes, often with the help of his granddaughters.
Mother awoke early along with Fekla's sisters. Mother poured milk
in a large bowl, meant for washing dishes. Each girl had her own
"sector" in which to dip the bread. If one sister dawdled, the others
got more milk. After breakfast, Mother left them with the same
admonitions: "Do not fight among yourselves. Behave at school. Do
not be late. Do not be afraid." After Mother left for work, the girls
ran to Grandfather, if he was at home. Each received her cobbling
assignment: to clasp the wooden heel while Grandfather hammered
in wooden nails, hold the needle steady while Grandfather inserted
the thread, or polish leather with a bit of soap.

The girls performed all of Grandfather's duties faithfully except
hair-cutting. Once the duty fell to mischievous Katya, who could
barely grasp the huge scissors. Grandfather's hair emerged from the
ordeal looking like a ladder of steps and empty spaces. Fekla tried to
even things out, but the end result was a Grandfather who looked
like a Tibetan monk. Grandfather's reaction upon seeing himself in
the mirror: "What a mangy-looking guy!" When Mother returned,
she asked why he was wearing his cap at home. He shrugged his
shoulders as the girls broke out in laughter.

Fekla, nearing graduation, felt herself superior to the "children" in lower grades. Yes, at the age of fifteen she was classified as an adult. Fekla and her fellow classmates decided that the singing class was beneath their dignity. They decided to show their indifference to Teacher Evgenia by mouthing words but making no sound as she directed them. She thought she had become deaf but caught on and rebuked them: "You are now adults. What would your fathers say?" It was not customary to remember their fathers, but the children remembered and waited. In unguarded moments, relatives praised the missing men. Fekla and the other children gradually forgot the faces of their fathers. There were few if any photographs left. But Fekla continued to hope.

As graduation day approached, the teachers called in the students to discuss their futures. No matter what their grades, their teachers advised them to stay in their village. The impending graduates were not fooled. They knew from the sad experience of recent graduates that universities and institutes did not take children of kulaks.

On June 20, 1941, graduation day, fifteen-year-old Fekla strolled with her schoolmates through the birch forest, past the ravine, to the banks of the Iset River. They remembered how they had clambered as small children on the "stone gate" of the sloping embankment, searching for wild garlic. They recalled how a passerby stole their clothing as they bathed in the cool river, forcing them to cover themselves with leaves and branches before they returned home, freezing and cursing the thieves.

On the river bank, the Martyush graduates sang from their hearts. Ahead lay their whole lives. Maybe their fathers would return. Perhaps, they thought, we can become arctic explorers, brave soldiers, or captains of mighty ships. The graduates shouted out from the rocks and waited for the echoes. Fekla felt a rare burst of happiness. She felt like flying and even imagined wings on her back.

Two days later, the new graduates of Martyush heard the frightful word "war." Their laughter and smiles disappeared. Their mothers sighed: "What will happen to us?" Fekla immediately thought of Father. Where is he? Perhaps he must go to war? Fekla believed in victory. She believed in the Master. She had no idea. Fekla had to wait almost five years to learn about the death of her father, and then the authorities told her a lie.

CHAPTER TWENTY-TWO

Aftermath

With the exception of Evgenia Ezhova, our Women of the Gulag survived to tell their tales. Evgenia died of an overdose on November 21, 1938. She left behind a husband, who would shortly join her in death, and an adopted daughter. The stories of the women who survived tell of life in the Gulag and of return to "civilian" life—to an unwelcoming society that viewed them with suspicion and even fear.

AGNESSA

Agnessa Mironova's life in the years immediately following her husband's death were a roller-coaster ride of hardships, horrors, and near-death experiences. Through it all—and despite her marriage to a third husband who worshiped her—she preserved her loyalty to her beloved Mirosha. During the 1950s, when recognition of Stalin's excesses led to the posthumous "rehabilitation" of many victims of the purges, she even tried to gain rehabilitation for Mironov. But that would have taken a miracle—one which didn't happen.

That Agnessa survived long enough to even think about rehabilitating Mirosha was a miracle of sorts. In September 1942, she was arrested in the provincial city of Kuibyshev after her roommates—jealous of her successes on the black market—accused her of anti-Soviet statements. Specifically, they denounced her for "anti-Soviet remarks about electricity blackouts and frozen water pipes." Little Agulya, eleven years old, was left alone in the communal apartment until Agnessa's husband, Mikhail Korol, fetched her and took her to her Aunt Lena in Rostov. Agnessa endured the indignity of transport with other prisoners in a locked Stolypin Wagon to the Lubyanka in Moscow, where her interrogators established that she was indeed the wife of the notorious Sergei Mironov. Korol's irate protest of Agnessa's arrest brought him to the attention of Beria himself. Korol would not return from the Gulag until 1956, almost a decade after Agnessa's own release.

In Moscow, Agnessa was sentenced to five years of corrective labor in Kazakhstan. Even in the Dolinka camp, the headquarters of Kazakhstan's sprawling Karlag, Agnessa demonstrated her survival skills. Since she had briefly studied nursing in Dnepropetrovsk, she was assigned to work in the camp hospital. Throughout her five-year term, Agnessa managed to work either in camp hospitals or in farming. She knew that, in both cases, her chances of getting enough food to survive were better. Soon, Agnessa could scarcely remember her earlier visit in a luxury Pullman car stocked with delicacies as Mirosha inspected the starving tent cities of Karlag.

The fastidious Agnessa learned to tolerate the miserable conditions in the Dolinka camp hospital. Prisoners died in droves in the winter cold. They could not be buried in the frozen ground, so prison officials stacked their frozen corpses in a corner of the hospital room. Their grim visages became a part of Agnessa's daily routine and a constant reminder of the closeness of death. In 1943, Agnessa was transferred to the Aratau Camp, also in Kazakhstan, for a life of hard agricultural labor. The Gulag emptied of able-bodied men, who were needed to fight the Germans, and the flow of meager supplies to Karlag from the outside ceased. In a state of near-starvation, Agnessa fell deathly ill but somehow pulled through in the camp infirmary. She spent the rest of her sentence working as a nurse in the Aratau camp hospital.

On September 8, 1947, Agnessa completed her prison term. However, like other released prisoners, she was forbidden to live in

Agnessa with Mikhail Korol, her third husband, no earlier than 1956.

the one hundred "regime cities," the country's major urban centers, which included Rostov. When Agnessa discovered that Lena and Agulya were living in the port city of Klaipeda, Lithuania, she traveled from Kazakhstan to join them. Eventually, Lena's second husband and their son, Borya, also joined them.

Mikhail Korol, confined in the SIBLAG forced labor camp in southwestern Siberia, learned of Agnessa's release but couldn't join her. Two years later, after serving his term, he was "released" to a small village in northern Kazakhstan. But in 1950, as he was awaiting a visit from Agnessa, Korol was arrested again, sentenced to ten years, and returned to Karlag in a Stolypin Wagon.

Meanwhile, Agnessa used her mastery of networking and relationship-building to wheedle a "clean passport" which omitted reference to her years in prison. With a clean slate, Agnessa moved with Agulya in 1950 to a suburb of Moscow. Agnessa worked in a kindergarten, while Agulya studied in Moscow and lived in a dormitory. Korol finally returned from the Gulag in 1956. His applications for rehabilitation, restoration of party membership, and a pension were approved, and he and Agnessa lived in one room of a communal apartment on Tverskaya-Yamskaya Street in Moscow. Agnessa worked as a nurse in a hospital. Korol died December 1, 1959, at the age of sixty-nine.

Despite Agnessa's first-hand knowledge of Mironov's crimes, she began a quixotic quest to rehabilitate her beloved Mirosha. The response from the military tribunal was, of course, negative. There would be no rehabilitation of Sergei Mironov.

In the course of gathering material for his rehabilitation, Agnessa needed a copy of Mirosha's death certificate. The prosecutor's office directed her to the civil registration office. A young female clerk asked in a cheerful tone whether she had come to report a birth. "No," Agnessa replied, "I need a death certificate." The young woman gave her a form. As Agnessa filled it out, she remarked to no one in particular, "I don't know when and how he died." The curious young woman asked, "How could you not know that?" An older clerk overheard the conversation. She pulled out a file and gave it to Agnessa. She read: Date of death February 22, 1940—the day Agnessa felt the blow to her head in her sleep. The cause of death had been marked through with a thick ink pen. The young clerk informed Agnessa the charge would be fifty kopeks. The older woman wrote: "Free of charge."

As she left the counter, Agnessa remarked for all to hear: "Well, you gave me fifty kopeks for my murdered husband. He did not die. They shot him." The young clerk lowered her eyes and was quiet.

The story of Agnessa's remarkable life would have been lost except for her sociability and extroverted nature. Agnessa began meeting regularly with Mira Yakovenko, an activist who spent hours in the mid-1950s sitting in the prosecutor's office and in the courts listening to Gulag survivors spilling out their stories, many for the first time. She believed that the real history of the Stalin period lay in the memories of those who experienced its excesses.

Among all those with whom Yakovenko became acquainted, Agnessa showed a remarkable ability to recount accurately and dis-

Agnessa, 1950s.

passionately her two lives—one as the privileged wife of one of Stalin's killers, the other as a survivor of the worst of his Gulags. She did not conceal her great love for Sergei Mironov and her ability to see him in his best light. But in no way did Agnessa gild the lily. She related what she saw and what she felt, while demonstrating a remarkable memory for dates, places, and events. After each conversation, Yakovenko wrote drafts which captured not only the story but Agnessa's exact words. After twenty years, Yakovenko published the story of Agnessa's life, titled simply, *Agnessa*. Into her sixties and seventies, Agnessa continued to attract male admirers. She died February 13, 1981, at the age of 78. Upon Mirosha's arrest, most of Agnessa's photos were confiscated, so the story of her fascinating life must be told with words and not with pictures.

Agnessa had no children of her own, but is survived by her niece and adopted daughter, Agulya, who lives today in Saint Petersburg.

MARIA

On December 10, 1937, the Chita military tribunal sentenced Maria Ignatkina to eight years in the Kazakhstan Gulag. Once her interrogator established that she was the legal wife of Alexander Ignatkin, her sentence—as a family member of a traitor of the motherland—followed automatically. At the time of her sentencing, her children were held in the Chita NKVD orphanage.

Ironically, Maria's marriage to Alexander doomed her and her children to years of privation and separation. Yet, when her marriage should finally have worked to her advantage, she was turned down for a widow's pension because Soviet law considered their marriage invalid.

Maria, like Agnessa and her husband, Mikhail Korol, served her eight-year sentence in Karlag, which occupied a territory of 23,000 square miles in Kazakhstan's Karaganda province. Karlag was an agglomeration of corrective labor camps and colonies, farms, and manufacturing and processing centers. Its administrative center was located in Dolinka (where Agnessa worked in its hospital). Its most notorious camp was the ALZHIR Camp for Wives of Traitors of the Motherland. Upon her arrival in Karlag in February 1938, Maria worked in ALZHIR, where, as the wife of a prominent railroad engineer, she unloaded freight cars.

Maria lived in total isolation in ALZHIR—no radio or printed material, and no news of the approaching war. Maria's greatest concern was the whereabouts and well-being of her children. She longed for just one line from them saying they were alive and doing well. The hope for eventual reunification sustained her. In 1939, Maria was permitted to send her first letter. Even then, she was not allowed to tell her children where she was—only that she was alive and doing well, whether that was true or not.

In 1940, Maria was transferred as a reward for exemplary work to a prison farm within Karlag, after completing a course in animal husbandry taught by eminent agronomists who were also fellow prisoners. The outbreak of war in June 1941 brought little change to the already miserable conditions of Karlag. Inmates continued to receive their miserly daily ration of bread.

The major change was the arrival in ALZHIR of male prisoners, held in a new barbed-wire zone outside the women's sector. Although the male prisoners lived separately from the women, they shared a common canteen. The camp hospital soon expanded to include an obstetrics ward for the children being born inside the prison. Maria noted that theft was rare among the prisoners. There was nothing to steal except food. Those caught stealing food were beaten within an inch of their lives, according to the thief's code: "Do not steal from your own."

Women feared delivering food to barracks 101, where the elite male thieves lived according to their own laws. They did not have to worry about getting enough to eat. They received bulky packages of food from outside. There were no limits to their violence and cruelty. In one instance, a thief-leader paid off a gambling debt by castrating one of his men and nailing his scrotum to the wall. Barracks 101 gamblers also paid off debts by forcing women to deliver sexual favors to their creditors.

Maria and her fellow inmates counted the days until their eight years were up. On October 7, 1945, the last day of Maria's term, the prison officials handed her document No. 256491, which stated: "Not to be used as a residence permit. Not to be reissued if lost." The document stated that Maria had served her term and designated Karaganda province as her chosen place of residence. "Freedom" meant being moved to barracks beyond the barbed-wire zone. She was expected to perform the same work as before, but now as a "free laborer." In 1946, Olga Ignatkina received permission to visit her mother in Karlag for the first time. They had not seen each other for almost a decade. Olga prepared the way for her mother's return to Chita in the same year. Finally freed from Karaganda, Maria moved in with her older daughter, Nadya.

Back in Chita, Maria applied for a review of Alexander's case. According to rehabilitation procedures, she had a right to the record of his interrogation and trial. At the end of 1956, Maria requested a copy of Alexander's death certificate. She would later learn from internal KGB documents that her request set off a flurry of activity.

In a memo dated January 14, 1957, the Chita KGB archivist reported to his superior that Ignatkin had been condemned to death on October 9, 1937, and was executed shortly thereafter. His widow now wanted a copy of his death certificate. The archivist proposed that a fake death certificate be issued stating that Alexander had died of natural causes. Internal records show that a KGB colonel approved the archivist's proposal. The Ignatkins, like thousands of other families, received a false death certificate to conceal the fact that their husband and father had been shot.

Maria's request for Alexander's rehabilitation brought forth the truth three months later. Maria received a letter dated April 13, 1957, signed by the main military prosecutor, stating that Alexander had been condemned to death without justification, after being subjected to torture with falsification of evidence. The letter also said that Ignatkin's case officers had been sentenced in 1940, but did not specify their punishment. On October 17, 1957, the supreme court of the USSR declared Alexander Ignatkin's case closed because of the "absence of a crime" and stated that he was posthumously rehabilitated. Eight days later, the Trans-Baikal military tribunal informed Maria that her case was also closed and that she was rehabilitated.

Even with official recognition that she and Alexander had been arrested, tried, and sentenced without justification, Maria's troubles weren't over. In 1959, Maria reached retirement age and became eligible to receive a widow's pension of thirty-eight rubles a month, along with an old-age pension. However, the authorities denied her claim for a widow's pension on the grounds that she had married Alexander in a church, and thus the marriage was not legal. The records of the Church of the Holy Trinity showed that Alexander Ignatkin and Maria Senotrusova were married on January 27, 1922. However, the pension authorities stated that only civil marriages would be recognized, not church weddings. During her interrogation in 1937, Maria's simple admission that she was the wife of Alexander Ignatkin condemned her to eight years in the Gulag. Twelve years

Maria Ignatkina with her granddaughter Natalia, 1959.

later, in 1959, Soviet power decided that she was not eligible for a widow's pension because she was married in a church ceremony. Fortunately, Maria pursued the issue and eventually persuaded a court to declare that her marriage to Alexander was valid.

Despite the trauma of their father's death and their mother's exile, the three Ignatkin children turned out well. Nadya, Olga, and Yury managed to stay together during their forced removal to an orphanage and then, luckily, were taken in by an aunt in Irkutsk.

Nadya first lived in the orphanage and then, along with Yury and Olga, with their aunt. She returned to Chita to study in its mining academy. Upon graduation, she worked for the Trans-Baikal Gold Works. Before taking in her mother when she was released from exile, Nadya married and had two children. Nadya died in 1969, and Maria then lived with her granddaughter Tanya, who lives in Chita today. Nadya's son lives in Moscow.

From the orphanage, Olga moved in briefly with a family which employed her to tutor a daughter who was doing poorly in school. She then moved in with her aunt and eventually returned to Chita, where she also studied at the mining academy and eventually worked

Nadya and Olga Ignatkina, 1950.

for various companies. Olga married and had two children and a number of grandchildren. She lived in Saint Petersburg with her daughter, Natalia, until her death on November 30, 2012, shortly after we filmed an interview with her.

Yury, who was only eleven when his mother was arrested, lived first in the orphanage and then with his aunt, eventually returning to Chita, where he studied mining engineering. Yury worked in gold mining his entire career in the Trans-Siberian Gold Mining Trust, earning awards as a distinguished inventor and receiving a gold medal as a veteran of the gold and platinum industry. For twenty years he was chairman of the board of the Chita orphanage where he once lived. Yury authored technical books about gold mining and published his *Tale of 1937*, the story of his father and mother, with his own resources in 1992. He died in 2008.

In the course of writing his tragic family history, Yury learned for the first time about the final days of his father. Documents showed that on September 7, 1937, the Chita Road and Transport Division of the NKVD issued a warrant to transfer Alexander Ignatkin from the Kadala camp to its headquarters at 56 Kalinin Street. A five-person

Yury Ignatkin and his sister Olga.

team interrogated him in shifts around the clock. They used sleep deprivation and promises of leniency. They beat him in the face, body, and genital area. They showed him a fake arrest warrant for Maria. In short, he was subjected to the full force of NKVD torment that had wrung false confessions from so many others. Torture was so ferocious at 56 Kalinin Street that suicide attempts among prisoners had become routine. In response, the interrogators strung barbed wire along the staircases to prevent prisoners from jumping to their deaths.

Alexander held out longer than most. On the fifth day, he signed a handwritten "declaration," which he knew was his death sentence. He confessed that he belonged to a diversionary group that planned rail accidents. The terse protocol of his twenty-minute court proceeding of September 29, 1937, describes his death sentence:

"The session began at 3:00 p.m. to consider the Article 58 case of Ignatkin. The prosecutors had no witnesses." (Alexander's accusers had already been executed.) "The defendant retracted his confession that he belonged to a counter-revolutionary organization, but he failed to explain why he confessed under interrogation." Apparently, the court refused to put his claim of torture in the record. "In his final statement, the defendant admitted he was guilty of bad work and admitted his mistakes but he never engaged in diversionary or espionage activity."

Upon return from a brief recess, the presiding judge read the verdict: "The guilt of Ignatkin has been established according to Article 58. The court sentences Alexander Ignatkin to the highest measure of punishment—shooting with confiscation of all property. The sentence cannot be appealed and should be carried out quickly." Alexander Ignatkin was shot late at night, creating confusion as to the exact date of death. One record gave the date as September 29 but another document said September 30.

Maria herself died in November 1992, age eighty-eight.

ADILE

Adile was nineteen when she was sentenced to be deported to Kazakhstan for three years as a member of the anti-Soviet Lakoba bandit nest. Her life since she married Emdy had already been a succession of almost unbelievable twists and turns of fate. More of the same awaited her.

A dozen years later, when she described her life to an official in Moscow's dreaded Lubyanka headquarters of the NKVD, he brought in another official to listen: "Why read a novel? Before us stands a real live novel, a victim of fate." Even after that, in yet another twist, she attended the trial of one of the men who interrogated her when she was imprisoned by the NKVD.

But first Adile had to survive the Gulag. Her journey from Tbilisi to Kazakhstan took more than a month, as the train stopped at holding prisons along the way. Finally, Adile and seventy-two other prisoners were loaded like cattle into a truck at a remote rail stop in northern Kazakhstan. The guards covered them with a tarpaulin as flimsy shelter from the February cold. Their heads spinning from hunger, the prisoners felt the truck stop in the middle of a desolate steppe. No civilization was in sight. Panic broke out among the prisoners. All they could see was the deserted plain stretching as far as the eye could see. Either they were to be left there to die or they were to be shot, they thought. But an old man appeared out of nowhere and directed them to barely visible earthen dugouts. These mud holes in the ground were to be their new homes for the next few years. Their village, Bistiuba, scarcely appeared on any map.

The prisoners began a routine of work from morning until night, cutting the hard brush and tending cattle and other livestock. An ill-tempered Chekist officer supervised their little settlement of local residents and prisoners. Adile, the youngest of the bunch, had a dreadful fear of cattle, especially the lumbering oxen. She suffered attacks of hysteria as she approached the dreaded beasts. Seven of Adile's fellow prisoners fell victim to the cold and hunger before spring came.

Help arrived from an unexpected source. The NKVD overseer broke out in a rage at the sight of Adile's mother arriving in a truck, her suitcases loaded with provisions. Anastasiya Zueva had used her influence to locate Adile and obtain permission for her mother to travel to Bistiuba. Adile rushed to embrace her mother and refused to let go. She shared the food that Mama brought with her. They parted, both sobbing, ten days later. Few trucks came through, so Mama had no choice but to take the next one.

The local residents of Bistiuba were native Kazakhs or dekulakized farmers from Ukraine. The Kazakhs took a liking to the Persian Adile, although their NKVD overlords discouraged fraternization with prisoners. Adile survived by trading her few possessions for food. During periods of famine, there was no food to trade for. Only the young and healthy survived.

Adile could not decide whether the winter cold or summer heat was worse. During the summer, the prisoners worked in the fields from morning to night, wilting under the torturous sun. Water was scarce; they returned at night dehydrated. As the youngest prisoner and a woman, Adile usually worked in fields that did not require heavy lifting. One day, Adile ran away, spooked by a coiled snake. As punishment, she was ordered to toil alongside the sturdiest men, doing backbreaking work.

In a rare stroke of luck, the local authorities assigned Adile, one of the few educated prisoners, to the accounting office. She welcomed the relief from field work. The administration office was located a few hundred yards from her earthen dugout. One day, on her way to work, Adile was caught in a blinding snowstorm. After wandering in circles, she was ready to lie down in the snow when a local Kazakh spied her and brought her to safety. Adile kept her life but lost her office job. She could not write thereafter because of frostbitten fingers. Adile was again close to starvation when another food package from Mama arrived.

Food shortages and weather were only two among many sources of mortality. Epidemics felled not only the local residents and prisoners but also the cattle. The NKVD seemed more worried about the loss of the cattle. After a rash of livestock deaths, a commission arrived to investigate whether the prisoners had poisoned the cattle. Until its decision was reached, prisoners were denied their bread rations. Remarkably, the commission absolved the prisoners, who again received their meager ration of black bread.

During the winter, Adile worked in the veterinary department, which inspected livestock on farms within the district. Adile traveled with the veterinarians from farm to farm in an open sled, no matter how bad the weather. On one such trip in minus forty-degree weather, Adile, sitting in the back, fell off the sled, unbeknownst to her companions. They turned around after noticing that she was missing and found her unconscious in the snow. They thought she had died, and were about to leave her body for burial in warmer weather, when she came to.

In the spring of 1941, fifty new families of Poles, Chechens, Koreans, Germans, and Chinese joined the Bistiuba prison community. Adile, with her knowledge of many languages, found ways to communicate with most of the newcomers. Friendships developed, and the diverse group of prisoners formed a "club" in which they

performed theater and classical music. Adile even danced the Abkhazian *lezginka* to the violin of one of the Poles.

June 25, 1941, was a hot day. The prisoners returned from the
fields too exhausted to sing or dance at their club. As they prepared
to spend the evening at the cool river bank, an officer from the district NKVD office arrived. He informed the prisoners that war had
begun "because of people like you." He then pronounced matter-
of-factly that, because of the war, their sentences had been made
indefinite. Adile had sustained herself with the knowledge that her
term would end within a year and a half. Her shoulders sagged like
those of her fellow inmates as they realized that there was no end in
sight. The war also meant that food had to go to the front and to the
cities. The Bistiuba "enemies of the people" were the last claimants
on the dwindling supply of food. Bistiuba had to feed itself or perish.

Among the prisoners was an elderly Greek, who sang the praises
of his engineer son, Ivan Vasiliadi, who had earned an engineering
degree despite being the son of an enemy of the people. Ivan, first
assigned to southern Kazakhstan, finagled a transfer to Bistiuba to be
near his father. Upon his arrival in Bistiuba, the NKVD gave Ivan his
own earthen dugout. The NKVD officials wanted to keep him happy,
as he was the only trained engineer for hundreds of miles. Adile and
Ivan became friends, and more. One day he came to Adile out of the
blue and said that he had permission from the NKVD authorities to
marry her. Ivan did not press Adile for an immediate answer, but he
told her that he also had her safety in mind. They married in October
1941 and had their first child, a son, Edik, in 1942.

In the summer of 1942, two Bistiuba women, accused of stealing
small amounts of food, stood before a circuit judge and a prosecutor.
As they pronounced sentences of five years for each woman, Adile
shouted out a protest. The startled judge declared that he would
send Adile to the camps as an enemy of the people. As luck would
have it, the judge's truck broke down. Ivan bargained for her freedom in return for repairing the vehicle.

By 1944, a baby daughter named Leila joined Adile's and Ivan's
growing household of son Edik, a cow, chickens, and a pig. Adile

was increasingly worried about the lack of medical facilities in Bistiuba. When she approached the NKVD for permission to take the ill Leila to a real medical facility, an official rudely told her, "One child dies, another is born. Not a great misfortune."

The war ended, and Ivan was transferred along with his family to a village in western Kazakhstan near the border with Siberia. In his new job, he taught engineering at a technical school. Their tiny apartment was without heat, and the children often were sick. When Leila fell and broke her wrist, the local doctor told her that without special treatment Leila would be deformed for life. The frustrated Adile decided to somehow return to Sukhumi with her sick children. She had been taken off the registry at Bistiuba and not put on the new registry. In a state of limbo, she decided to risk the journey to Sukhumi through Moscow without any papers. She could be condemned for fleeing from her place of banishment without permission—a criminal offense. But her daughter's health was at stake.

Adile was twenty-seven when she departed with a suitcase full of food, carrying two young children. Ivan accompanied them, walking across a frozen river, to a small station where they waited for a train. Each train arrived terribly overcrowded, but finally Ivan bribed a conductor to find a place for his family on board. A sixteen-year-old neighbor, Stella (also a Greek), had heard about their flight and joined them on the train. At Chelyabinsk, the inspection of documents began. Adile, having none, sat on her bulky baggage. She told the inspector, "My husband died in the war. I am going to my mother." She claimed her papers were somewhere in the bottom. As she moved to open her bags, the impatient inspector let her pass.

It took Adile a month to make it to Moscow. The trip was a nightmare, with Edik and Leila sick most of the way. At one stop, Stella went to get hot water for the children and accidentally spilled it in the eyes of the conductor. He wanted to throw them all off, but Adile convinced him that Stella was a mentally ill orphan whom she was taking to Moscow for treatment. Just as the train pulled into Moscow, Adile faced another check of documents. As the inspector approached, Adile sat on her luggage and sobbed, "Do what you must. I do not have the strength even to move." He mistook her for an evacuee, returning from the eastern part of the USSR after World War II, and left her alone.

At the Moscow station, Adile found a sympathetic nurse at the makeshift medical center, left Stella and the children, and rushed to Anastasiya Zueva. When Anastasiya saw the haggard Adile, she exclaimed, "Dear God, what in the world has happened to you?" Zueva gave Adile food and agreed to help Stella get to her home city. Adile spent the next three days trying to buy a ticket to Sukhumi. On the fourth day, she got a ticket on the steamer *Molotov*.

From Novorossiysk, Adile sent Mama a telegram, and every day Mama came to the port to await Adile's arrival. When she arrived, Mama and the relatives looked at Adile and her sick children with shock and sympathy. Through family connections, they arranged for Leila and Edik to receive the best medical attention that Sukhumi had to offer. Finally, the children lay safe in Sukhumi hospitals. But Ivan was stuck in Kazakhstan and Adile was harassed by the omnipresent security forces.

Adile's joy at returning to Mama and family proved short-lived. The Sukhumi Chekists sought to arrest her under Article 39 as a "politically unreliable person" who had unlawfully fled from her place of banishment. Adile cowered in closets and hid with relatives in nearby towns. Every knock on the door filled her with fright. Ivan finally succeeded in making it to Sukhumi from Kazakhstan, but as a Greek he had no right to stay. He found work in a nearby city where he repaired cars, including those of the local Chekists who tolerated his presence because of his mechanical skills.

Edik and Leila entered school, but with difficulty. They had no papers, and they could not say who or where their mother was. Adile trained them never to answer questions honestly. They could get by only by lying about themselves and their families.

Adile had an acquaintance who had once lived in her home and who had risen to an influential position in Moscow. He learned of Adile's plight and called her to Moscow. In December 1951, the thirty-one-year old Adile arrived in Moscow with her daughter, Leila.

Her acquaintance instructed her to write a petition to the Supreme Soviet of the USSR, advising her to keep it short, as otherwise no one would read it.

Her petition submitted, Adile sat for a straight week in the waiting room of the Supreme Soviet. When she was finally called, the stern president of the Supreme Soviet himself met her. After hearing her story, he ordered his assistant to place her in an official black car, which took her to the Lubyanka. An official, apprised of her case, led her through endless corridors. Adile entered a room occupied by a middle-aged man surrounded by a bank of telephones. He asked her to tell her story and listened in fascination. He called in another man to listen: "Why read a novel? Before us stands a real live novel, a victim of fate."

The assistant asked Adile to write down her story in detail. The next day, Adile returned to the Lubyanka, where the official from the day before smiled and said, "We gathered the necessary evidence about you. We have decided you can live in Sukhumi." He gave her a telephone number which Adile had to memorize. "If you have any trouble in Sukhumi, telephone us," he instructed.

Upon Adile's return to Sukhumi, she was called to the local Chekist office. Her interrogator asked, "Who is your lover in Moscow? Who helped you?" As advised in Moscow, Adile kept silent and refused to answer their questions. Finally, the interrogator said, "Well, they called from Moscow and told us to give you a residence permit. Go to the head of the police." Thus began a normal life for Adile. She entered the university in the Sukhumi Pedagogical Institute and eventually worked there from 1957 to 1965, first on the faculty and then as an archivist in the department of the history of the Communist Party.

In 1955, Adile attended the trial of Beria's associate, Grigory Pachuliya, the notorious "Quasimodo" who had personally interrogated Adile upon her return from refuge with Anastasiya Zueva. Lavrenty Beria had been executed in December 1953, nine months after Stalin's death. Beria's associates feared he would become the next Stalin. Their purge of Beria loyalists extended to Sukhumi.

Although Quasimodo was a professional soccer player with little education, Beria had appointed him to bring fear to the residents of Sukhumi.

Before the court, Quasimodo admitted to his crimes and tried to justify himself: "I just followed orders. I did not have the right to question them." His judges asked, "But did you not show restraint at least one time?" Quasimodo's answer: "Yes, I showed mercy to one victim. We did not shoot him. He got twenty-five years instead." Adile thought to herself, "And it was to such a person that I had to answer when I returned to Sukhumi." Quasimodo was sentenced to death, but his term was changed to twenty-five years.

On December 30, 1956, Adile was rehabilitated by the Supreme Soviet of the Abkhazian Republic. Her case was closed because of the absence of evidence of criminal activity. In the same year, Ivan was also rehabilitated. However, he could not get a job without a residence permit. Adile stormed into the office of her case officer and threatened that, if her husband did not get a residence permit, she would throw herself under the officer's car. His surprising answer: "Bravo." Ivan got the permit.

However, Ivan had constant trouble at work. He taught engineering at the technical college, but his boss required that lessons be taught in Georgian, which Ivan did not speak. Ivan, who never did find a stable job, died of a stroke on May 20, 1975.

Adile's otherwise normal life was shattered by the growing mental illness of her son. Edik had trouble in class and, although he was an excellent student, he moved from school to school. Edik was teased that he was a Greek and that his father was in exile. In 1959, Edik finished school and was admitted to the university. On the state examinations he did so well that he was admitted to graduate school in Tbilisi.

Edik had an uncanny ability to predict the future, often telling his family in advance of events that later occurred. In August 1992, shortly after the break-up of the Soviet Union, a thirteen-month-long war broke out between Georgian forces backed by local Georgians on one side and Abkhazian ethnic forces backed by Russia on

Adile Abbas-ogly, 2011.

the other. In the misery of this bloody conflict, Edik's health went from bad to worse. In December, he predicted that he would die on February 27. Edik died in Adile's arms on February 27, 1993, at the age of fifty-one.

Adile retired in October 1988. A few months earlier, on June 26, 1988, she was named a distinguished cultural worker of Abkhazia. In the first decade of the new millennium, she met with victims of Stalin's repression in the Lakoba Museum, housed in the former Lakoba residence where she had lived as Lakoba's sister-in-law. Adile appeared often in radio interviews and in documentary films. Her memoirs, published in 2005 and reissued in 2009, have been translated into a number of languages.

Adile, who celebrated her ninety-second birthday in 2012, lives in Sukhumi with her daughter, Leila. Her autobiography, reissued as *My Abkhazia, My Fate*, has made her a local celebrity. The 2008 Russian invasion of Abkhazia and Abkhazia's separatist movement made Adile an unlikely national celebrity. After all, she was a relative of Lakoba who fought against Beria for Abkhazian independence. She remains troubled by the fact that her difficult life traumatized her children, believing that Edik's premature death was the result of his difficult early years.

FEKLA

Fekla took seriously her father's charge to her, to take responsibility for her younger sisters. As the years went by, she also became an advocate for justice, first for her own family members, and then for all of Martyush's innocent victims of repression. The persistence and resilience she needed to survive as the daughter of "an enemy of the people" served her well in her search for the truth about her father's death.

Fekla always remembered her father's last words, spoken hurriedly through the basement window of the Kamensk NKVD prison on September 30, 1938: "Make sure your sisters are educated. You are now the head of the family. They cannot take your education away from you." The next day, Papa was shipped off to Chelyabinsk with the other men of Martyush. Mama and the Andreev sisters continued to hope that Papa was alive.

True to her father's advice, Fekla's excellence in school provided her escape from Martyush. When she was fifteen, the Martyush commandant selected her to study in Kamensk School No. 4 to become a teacher. (She would remember its cafeteria's sweet white buns the rest of her life.) After a year of study, Fekla, age sixteen, was transferred from the Martyush special registry and listed as "studying in advanced classes beyond the boundaries of her special settlement." Her mother, grandfather, and sisters continued to bear the black mark of "special settlers" confined to Martyush. (Fekla learned in 1993 that an NKVD background check at the time concluded that, in the absence of "compromising material" on special settler Fekla Andreeva, she should be "freed from labor exile" but without the right to leave Kamensk and its immediate surroundings.) In 1942, at the age of sixteen, Fekla became a citizen of the country of her birth. As proof, she received an internal passport issued on November 13, 1942.

Fekla suffered two losses in 1944. On March 23, her Martyush sweetheart and classmate, Volodya Kudryashov, was killed at the front. Grandfather died in September of the same year. Fekla graduated from the Kamensk school with the highest marks, but the universities to which she applied did not admit children of kulaks. Instead, Fekla taught in the Martyush school, which had given her refuge after her arrival in Martyush more than a decade earlier. She lived in Martyush with her three sisters and her semi-invalid mother.

In December 1945, sister Katya was sent to a technical school for worker training. After six months, she began work at the Urals Aluminum Factory. Fekla's middle sister, Nina, would eventually also work there. Fekla attributes Nina's early death at the age of forty-seven to the toxic environment of the aluminum factory.

The year 1947 brought major changes. Fekla moved to Grandfather's village of Suvory to teach school. In April, Martyush's special settlers were "freed" from "labor exile," and all except those working on the nearby collective farm were ordered to leave the village which had been their prison-home for sixteen years. The authorities denied those who attempted to stay the ration cards that kept them alive. The expelled Martyush residents scattered. Mama worked in a Kamensk store until January 1948 and then as a building janitor. In June 1948 she moved with Fekla's younger sisters, Nina and Klavdia, to Suvory after her ration card ran out. The four lived on Fekla's meager earnings. Although Fekla was by this time the school's principal, she had to borrow money and work in the fields to feed herself and her family.

In the 1950s, Fekla finally gained admission to the Shadrinsky Pedagogical Institute near Chelyabinsk, subsequently graduated from the Urals State University, and completed her dissertation on Russian dialects as a correspondence student at Krasnoyarsk State Pedagogical Institute in Siberia. Fekla wrote her dissertation under the famed philologist Nikita Tolstoy. Later she taught in Tobolsk in western Siberia and Abakan, in southern Siberia, and served as chairwoman and then dean of faculties of her alma mater, the Shadrinsky Pedagogical Institute. Her work is today cited in encyclopedias of Russian idioms, and she is known as an expert on Pushkin.

In February 1956, party First Secretary Nikita Khrushchev delivered his "secret speech" denouncing Stalin's excesses. Although given to a closed session of the governing Party Congress, the speech was

Fekla Andreeva, 1956.

anything but secret. The text was read to many thousands of people in subsequent weeks, and versions also appeared in the foreign press. In response, Fekla launched a stubborn campaign to learn the fate of her father. On June 26, 1957, Urals authorities sent her a false death certificate, stating that he died in prison of natural causes on July 26, 1944. An attached note from the Urals Military Tribunal certified that her father's case had been closed on December 7, 1956, "because of the absence of criminal activity" and that he was "rehabilitated posthumously."

Although her father had been "rehabilitated," Fekla's search for justice was far from over. After her retirement in 1987, Fekla and her mother returned to Kamensk-Uralsky. Fekla served as a founding member of the Kamensk Memorial Society and of various victims' associations. Her book *Roots and Crowns: Martyush* lists the Martyush victims of political repression and their family histories. Fekla's apartment in Kamensk became a one-woman advocacy center for those seeking rehabilitation and compensation.

Fekla continued to wear down regional authorities as a tireless advocate for family and neighbors. Her files include irritated letters

Trofim Andreev's false death certificate of June 26, 1957, stating that he died in prison of natural causes on July 26, 1944.

from regional and national officials pleading with her to leave them in peace. She had no rights to her father's criminal file, they said. He had already been rehabilitated. Why push the matter further? Undeterred, Fekla pressed on.

Fekla organized a memorial service held on September 9, 1989, in which the remains of Martyush victims of political repression were brought from Golden Mountain in Chelyabinsk for reburial in Kamensk-Uralsky. Nobel Peace Prize laureate Andrei Sakharov, physicist and human rights activist, was present. Mixed among the remains were her father's. Fekla used the new Yeltsin-era laws on victims' rights to finally extract her father's case file, signing her letters as the "granddaughter of a kulak, the daughter of an enemy of the people."

In 1989, Fekla at last received the true death certificate of her father, verifying that he had been shot at the age of thirty-nine in the city of Chelyabinsk under Article 58-2-6-9-11. Under "cause of death," the authorities wrote: "shot as an innocent person during the years of Stalin's repression." The file contained her father's signed confession that he had joined a "counter revolutionary, espionage, diversionary group," but Fekla doubted the authenticity of the signature. Despite torture, he only admitted responsibility for three routine work-related accidents. Her father's file ended with a signed statement by the commanding officer that he was shot at 5:00 p.m. on October 4, 1938.

In 1992, Fekla gained rehabilitation for herself and for all the family, including Klavdia, who had been registered as a "labor exile" at birth so that she could serve as "future unpaid labor," as Fekla would write.

Fekla fought her final battle with authorities for compensation for Grandfather's and Father's Suvory farm. Although legislation in the early 1990s called for restitution payments for victims of political repression, Fekla battled a decade-long runaround by petty bureaucrats who claimed they had no records on the Andreev farm. The January 1993 response of the Commission for the Rehabilitation of Victims of Political Repression did not sit well with Fekla, to say the

СВИДЕТЕЛЬСТВО О СМЕРТИ

Trofim Andreev's true death certificate of November 2, 1989, verifying that on October 4, 1938, he had been shot at the age of thirty-nine in the city of Chelyabinsk under Article 58-2-6-9-11. Under "cause of death," the authorities wrote: "shot as an innocent person during the years of Stalin's repression."

Fekla Andreeva and her sisters Klavdia and Ekaterina, 2011.

least. The commission declared that compensation was envisioned only for victims of camps and prisons where conditions of confinement were more "severe" than in special settlements. Fekla's biting response read, "Citizen Commissioner: You are not able to envision surviving in an unheated earthen dugout, poorly clothed, barefoot, and starving. It seems that no one told you that those repressed in 1937–1938 were either shot or died in prisons and camps."

When the authorities finally handed over a list of expropriated property years later, Mama was able to list the missing items from memory: the red-coated gelding, a foal, two spotted cows, two calves, two oxen, two sheep, thirty chickens, and three ducks. Mama described every item of clothing taken and appended an angry note to those who stole her belongings: "Let God give them health. If we had had these clothes, my mother would not have died of cold, and our children would not have frozen."

Fekla's mother died on April 15, 2000, at the age of one hundred. Sister Katya is married and has children and grandchildren. She is retired and lives in Kamensk-Uralsky. Youngest sister Klavdia is married with children and grandchildren and lives in Yekaterinburg, where she earlier taught math in the Urals Pedagogical Institute.

Fekla Andreeva, 2012.

Fekla Andreeva lives today in her small cottage surrounded by her books, document collections, and files of correspondence. She lives alone but is tended by her sisters, nieces, and nephews. She has completed a memoir of her years as a schoolteacher and activist, which she hopes to see published in her lifetime. When her health permits, she attends memorial events for the Martyush victims of political repression. She celebrated her eighty-sixth birthday in October 2012.

NATASHA

Five-year-old Natasha Ezhova noticed that things were not right. First, Mama disappeared for a long period of time in September 1938. Papa was always at work and no one would tell her where Mama was. On October 29, Mama reappeared in a state of agitation. She told Nanny that she was on her way to a Kremlin hospital. She whispered to Nanny as she departed, "If something happens to me, remember you are the only one she has." Natasha heard everything.

Natasha did not see Mama again, and she got no answer when she asked: "Where is Mama?" Papa no longer played and sang with her. He came home rarely and only in the morning. He would sit and smoke in the study and then would abruptly leave without even seeing Natasha.

On April 9, 1939, Papa came home very early. He asked Nanny to wake Natasha and bring her to him. They drank tea and together they pretended to feed Natasha's pink piglet doll, which they then put in her bed to sleep. Then Papa rushed off to work. The next day and the days after that, men in uniforms searched the apartment, looking through linens, household belongings, books, and papers.

The men in uniform then placed Natasha in a guarded railroad car with "Aunt Nina," an NKVD agent charged with taking the child to Penza, an ancient city of 300,000 people, 388 miles southeast of Moscow. Penza hosted Orphanage No. 1 for children of enemies of the people. On the train, "Aunt Nina" kept repeating to Natasha: "You do not know any Ezhov. You are Khayutina, not Ezhova." To drive the point home, she struck Natasha across the face hard enough to draw blood when the little girl mentioned the name of her father. "Aunt Nina" delivered Natasha to the superintendent of Penza Orphanage No. 1, where she was registered officially as a "child of an enemy of the people."

In her first night in the orphanage, newcomer Natasha entranced the other children with her stories of grandeur: she is not Khautina, but Ezhova. Her Papa—the best father on earth—is a big boss. She spoke of a peacock on the Meshcherino estate where she spent her holidays and weekends. She told her enthralled listeners that not long ago Svetlana Stalina and the daughter of Molotov attended her birthday party.

At the Penza orphanage, Natasha sat at the window waiting for Mama or Papa to come get her. The other children got letters and cards, but Natasha got none.

Natasha was always cold, both in the dorm where they slept and in the class where they studied and sewed uniforms for the soldiers at the front. The teachers were ill-tempered and mean, and the children stole cards, pens, undergarments, and even food ration cards from each other. Some of the boys stole from the local stores.

Like Papa, Natasha had a beautiful singing voice. He had even arranged for her, as a five-year-old, to take piano and singing lessons. One teacher was enchanted by her voice and declared that Natasha should be sent to a music academy. Natasha looked forward to a career in music, and when she was assigned to a technical school, she cried the whole last night of her stay in the orphanage.

At the trade school where she learned watch-making, Natasha placed a portrait of her father in a visible place in her dormitory. When the school director was informed, he rushed in and demanded that she destroy the picture. When Natasha refused, he burned it to ashes with his cigarette lighter.

Natasha hated trade school. She attempted to hang herself, but the cord broke. Her fellow students beat her: "Are you crazy? They'll send us all away!" Natasha could not forget that they worried about being sent away, not about her death. However, Natasha's suicide attempt may have paid off. The authorities decided to let her enter a music school where she studied piano and singing and developed a lifelong love affair with the accordion. Wherever Natasha went, so did the accordion.

After completing music school, Natasha was "allocated" to Magadan province, the remote sub-arctic transit point for forced laborers. During his tenure as head of the NKVD, Papa had sentenced countless tens of thousands of prisoners to work (and die) in the rich gold mines and metal reserves of the remote Soviet northeast.

Natasha knew that many freed prisoners remained in the Gulag zone. If they learned that the daughter of Ezhov lived among them, there was no telling what they would do to her. Despite that, as she moved from one village to another, Natasha hung a portrait of her father on the wall. On each May Day holiday, she celebrated her own and her father's birthday. Papa had been born on May 1.

Natasha did not know her own birthday, so she decided to celebrate hers along with her father's.

In the 1950s, Natasha visited cousin Josef and his mother in Moscow. There she visited her mother's grave and received an accordion as a gift from her Moscow relatives. The accordion would remain her trademark for the rest of her life.

Natasha has spent the rest of her life in the Magadan region, her accordion always by her side. She worked in unheated village clubs, where she taught music, sang her own songs accompanied by her accordion, and wrote poetry. Prior to retirement, Natasha served as the director of a small village cultural center. Natasha never married, but she had a daughter after a brief affair with a married man. Her daughter had six children.

The country learned that the adopted daughter of Nikolai Ezhov was alive in 1998. Natasha had applied to the courts of the Russian Federation to rehabilitate her father. When the courts denied her request, she wrote, "I was the daughter of an enemy of the people, and I remain so until my death." Headlines blared *Ezhov's Daughter Sent to Penza on Stalin's orders*, over articles featuring a photograph of the beaming Natasha and a grandchild.

Journalists, filmmakers, and historians began the long trek to Magadan to satisfy their curiosity about the daughter of the notorious "bloody dwarf," Stalin's loyal executioner. They filmed Natasha playing her own composition, *The Young Communists' Waltz*, on her accordion, and leafing through photos of herself and her father and mother. Films and photographs show her rotund, with bushy, coarse gray hair, dressed simply in a skirt and sweater. Her face is marked by deep wrinkles, and she is chain-smoking.

Natasha realized that her father could never be rehabilitated but she continued to fight for herself. On February 13, 2008, she received what she had waited for: "In the name of the Russian Federation, the court has decided to grant the request of Natalia Nikolaevna Khayutina for rehabilitation." A half-year later she received a letter from the Magadan interior ministry: "You are recognized as a victim of political repression and are rehabilitated."

Today, Natasha lives in Ola, Magadan Oblast, and her daughter and grandchildren live nearby. After a stroke, she moves around her apartment with difficulty. She rarely leaves. Until recently, she remained in contact with her cousin Josef, who resettled in Israel.

Nikolai Ezhov

Nikolai Ezhov had to wait until February 4, 1940, for his execution. At his trial before the military tribunal he declared, "I purged 14,000 Chekists. But my huge mistake is that I purged so few. My life cannot be spared. I plea for one thing: shoot me quietly without torture. I ask that you support my mother in her old age and that you educate my daughter. I ask that you not persecute my relatives who are guilty of nothing. Tell Stalin that I will die with his name on my lips."

Ezhov was shot the day after his death sentence. He was brought to "the place" late at night. When his executioners informed him that his request for mercy had been denied, he became hysterical. He cried and hiccupped. They had to drag him kicking and screaming to the wall. After the execution, his body was cremated and his ashes were spread at nearby Donskoi Cemetery, where his wife lay buried.

Evgenia's brother, Ilya, was executed two days earlier at the age of forty-seven. His remains joined Evgenia's in Moscow's Donskoi cemetery.

Sources

Sources are organized according to character by order of appearance. In the text, material in quotation marks represents directly translated quotations from that character's memoir. Other material is placed in quotation marks, such as phrases in the common vernacular of the period ("no longer among the living") or to denote irony ("enemy of the people"). Citations and page numbers are provided for other direct quotations, for example, from Stalin.

STALIN (Chapters 2, 8, 10, 16)

Grant M. Adibekov and Kirill M. Anderson, eds., *Politbiuro TsK RKP (b) – VKP (b). Povestki Dnia Zasedanii. 1919–1952: Katalog v 3-kh Tomakh*, vol. 2, *1930–39* (Moskva: ROSSPEN, 2001), 828–840.

V. Bogomolova and A. Markov, "Glavnyi Korpus Kremlia. Ot Predsedatelia Sovnarkoma do Prezidenta Rossii," *Rossiiskie Vesti. Federal'nyi Ezhenedel'nik*, no. 16 (April 22–28, 2009), accessed January 5, 2012, http://rosvesty.ru/1957/interes/5668-glavnii-korpus-kremlya.

Bogomolova and Markov, "Po Sosedstvu s Pervymi Litsami. Tamara Soboleva – o Godakh, Provedennykh za Kremlevskoi Stenoi," *Rossiiskie Vesti. Federal'nyi Ezhenedel'nik*, no. 16 (April 22–28, 2009), accessed November 15, 2011, http://rosvesty.ru/1957/interes/?id=1000000835.

Novaia Gazeta, "Chelovek v Kozhanom Fartuke," August 2, 2010, accessed January 4, 2012, http://www.novayagazeta.ru/gulag/2389.html.

Iurii Feklistov, "Leto na Dache u Dedushki Soso," *Ogonek*, no. 34 (August 20, 1996), accessed January 4, 2012, http://www.ogoniok.ru/archive/1996/4465/34-24–26.

Paul R. Gregory, *Politics, Murder, and Love in Stalin's Kremlin: The Story of Nikolai Bukharin and Anna Larina* (Stanford, CA: Hoover Institution Press, 2010), 2, 12, 98, 102, 103, 124.

Gregory, *Terror by Quota: State Security from Lenin to Stalin* (New Haven: Yale University Press, 2009), 173–176, 182.

Gregory, *The Political Economy of Stalinism* (New York: Cambridge University Press, 2004), 71, 176–179, 187–189, 192.

Evgenii N. Gusliarov, *Stalin v Zhizni. Sistematizirovannyi Svod Vospominanii Sovremennikov, Dokumentov Epokhi, Versii Istorikov* (Moskva: OLMA-PRESS, 2003).

"'Iosif Beskonechno Dobr...' Dnevnik Marii Anisimovny Svanidze, Rodstvennitsy I. V. Stalina (Otdel'nye Fragmenty za 1933–1937 gg.)," *Istochnik*, no. 1 (1993), 27–28.

Wikipedia, "Istomina, Valentina Vasil'evna," accessed January 4, 2012, http://ru .wikipedia.org/wiki/Истомина,_Валентина_Васильевна.

Mark Iunge, Gennadii Bordiugov, and Rol'f Binner, *Vertikal' Bol'shogo Terrora* (Moskva: Novyi Khronograf, 2008).

Profi, "Kak Okhraniali Stalina," accessed November 15, 2011, http://www .ohranaprofi.ru/sovet/stalin.htm.

Oleg V. Khlevniuk, *In Stalin's Shadow: The Career of "Sergo" Ordzhonikidze*, ed. Donald J. Raleigh with the assistance of Kathy S. Transchel; trans. David J. Nordlander (Armonk, NY: M.E. Sharpe, 1995).

Tat'iana Khoroshilova, "Priemnyi Syn Stalina Rasskazyvaet o Maloizvestnykh Epizodakh iz Zhizni Ego Sem'i," *Rossiiskaia Gazeta – Nedelia*, November 10, 17, 2006, accessed January 4, 2012, http://www.rg.ru/2006/11/10/sergeev.html; http://www.rg.ru/2006/11/17/sergeev.html.

Sergei Khrushchev, ed., *Memoirs of Nikita Khrushchev, vol. 1, Commissar, 1919–1945* (University Park, PA: Pennsylvania State University, 2004), 188–9.

Anatolii Klepov, "Stalin i Arkhivy," Proza.ru, accessed January 10, 2012, www .proza.ru/2010/04/07/882.

Roi A. Medvedev, "Chto Chital Stalin," *Elitarium*, May 26, 2005, accessed November 15, 2011, http://www.elitarium.ru/2005/05/26/chto_chital_stalin.html.

Medvedev, *Let History Judge: The Origins and Consequences of Stalinism*, eds. David Joravsky and Georges Haupt; trans. Colleen Taylor (New York: Knopf, 1971), 400–405.

"Operational Order of the NKVD no. 00486 'About the Repression of Wives and the Placement of Children of Convicted Traitors of the Motherland'," August 15, 1937, *GARF* (Moscow), Fond R-8131, op. 37, d. 145, ll. 193–197; "Document no. 98," in Iurii N. Afanas'ev et al., *Istoriia Stalinskogo Gulaga: Konets 1920-kh – Pervaia Polovina 1950-kh Godov: Sobranie Dokumentov v Semi Tomakh, vol. 1, Massovye Repressii v SSSR* (Moskva: ROSSPEN, 2004), 363–365.

Osobye Papki, *RGASPI* (Moscow), Fond 3, op. 74, d. 197.

Nikita V. Petrov and Konstantin V. Skorkin, *Kto Rukovodil NKVD, 1934–1941: Spravochnik* (Moskva: Zven'ia, 1999), 335.

Pravda, December 29, 1936.

V. P. Semin, "Knizhnaia Novinka. 'Na Prieme u Stalina'," *Vestnik Arkhivista*, September 18, 2008, accessed January 4, 2012, http://www.vestarchive.ru/component /content/article/188–2010–09–12–12–59–28/37-q-c.html.

Simon Sebag Montefiore, *Stalin: Am Hof des roten Zaren* (Frankfurt: Fischer Verlag, 2006), 25–27, 138–139.

Artem Sergeev and Ekaterina Glushik, *Besedy o Staline* (Moskva: Krymskii Most-9D; Forum, 2006), 39.

Iosif V. Stalin, "O Proekte Konstitutsii Soiuza SSSR: Doklad na Chrezvychainom VIII Vsesoiuznom S"ezde Sovetov 25 Noiabria 1936," in Iosif V. Stalin, *Sochineniia*, vol. 14 (Moskva: Pisatel', 1997), 119–147.

"Stalin Meetings," *Melbourne Gateway to Research on Soviet History – MelGROSH*, accessed January 5, 2012, http://www.melgrosh.unimelb.edu.au/php/pol_meet ing.php.

Aleksei G. Tepliakov, *Mashina Terrora: OGPU-NKVD Sibiri v 1929–1941 gg.* (Moskva: Novyi Khronograf; AIRO-XXI, 2008), 422, 428, 448.

Larisa Vasil'eva, *Deti Kremlia* (Moskva: AST: Izd-vo Atlantida, 1997).

Dmitrii Volkogonov, *Stalin: Politicheskii Portret*, vol. 2 (Moskva: Novosti, 1992), 260–280.

AGNESSA (Chapters 3, 9, 11, 17, 22)

Mira M. Iakovenko, *Agnessa: Ustnye Rasskazy Agnessy Ivanovny Mironovoi-Korol' o Ee Iunosti, o Schast'e i Gorestiakh Trekh Ee Zamuzhestv, ob Ogromnoi Liubvi k Znamenitomu Stalinskomu Chekistu Sergeiu Naumovichu Mironovu, o Shikarnykh Kurortakh, Priemakh v Kremle i... o Tiur'makh, Etapakh, Lageriakh, – o Zhizni, Prozhitoi na Kacheliakh Sovetskoi Istorii* (Moskva: Zven'ia, 1997).

Oleg V. Khlevniuk, *Politbiuro: Mekhanizmy Politicheskoi Vlasti v 1930-e gg.* (Moskva: ROSSPEN, 1996), 214.

Maiia M. Korol', *Odisseia Razvedchika: Pol'sha-SShA-Kitai-GULAG* (Moskva: [Izdatel'stvo Rossiiskogo Obschestva Medikov-Literatorov], 1999).

Sergei A. Papkov, "Statistika Prigovorov Troiki UNKVD Zapadno-Sibirskogo Kraia – Novosibirskoi Oblasti v Massovoi Operatsii 1937–1938 gg.," in Mark Iunge, Bernd Bonvech, and Rol'f Binner, eds., *Stalinizm v Sovetskoi Provintsii: 1937–1938 gg.: Massovaia Operatsiia na Osnove Prikaza 00447* (Moskva: ROSSPEN, 2009), 746–784.

MARIA (Chapters 4, 12, 18, 22)

"Declaration of Former Party Workers of Chita Province to Deriagin, Secretary of the Chita VKP(b) Committee, About the Fabrication of Cases by Officials of the Chita NKVD Directorate, November 21, 1939," "Documemt no. 60," in Afanas'ev et al., *Istoriia stalinskogo Gulaga*, vol. 1, 277–280.

Iurii A. Ignatkin, *Rasskaz iz Tridtsat' Sed'mogo* (Chita: Reklamno-Informatsionnoe Agenstvo "Aziia," 1992).

Ignatkin, "Rasskaz iz 1937 g.," *Malinovskie Vekhi: Sbornik Publikatsii i Vospominanii (ot ALZhIRa do Sovremennoi Malinovki)* (Malinovka; Astana, 2003), 25–45, accessed November 15, 2011, http://www.sakharov-center.ru/asfcd/auth /?t=book&num=1081.

Alena Kozlova, "Russkii Vzgliad v Kharbinskoe Proshloe," *Uroki Istorii: XX Vek*, October 2, 2009, accessed January 5, 2012, http://www.urokiistorii.ru/2009/10 /russkii-vzglyad-v-kharbinskoe-proshloe.

Rebecca Balmas Neary, "Mothering Socialist Society: The Wife-Activists' Movement and the Soviet Culture of Daily Life, 1934–41," *Russian Review* 58, no. 3 (July 1999), 396–412.

Igor' L. Pol', *Oglianis' so Skorb'iu: Istoriia Odnoi Sem'i* (Irkutsk: Sibirskoe Knizhnoe Izdatel'stvo, 1991).

V. I. Vasilevskii and G. M. Liubin, eds., *Zabveniiu Ne Podlezhit: Sbornik Dokumentov* (Chita: Upravlenie Sydebnogo Departamenta v Chitinskoi Oblasti, 2006).

Junius B. Wood, "The Far Eastern Republic," *National Geographic Magazine* 41, no. 6 (June 1922).

EVGENIA (Chapters 5, 13, 19)

Semen Belen'kii, "Narkom Ezhov i Ego Zheny," *Zametki po Evreiskoi Istorii. Internet-Zhurnal Evreiskoi Istorii, Traditsii, Kul'tury*, ed. Evgenii Berkovich, no. 41 (April 18, 2004), accessed January 8, 2012, http://berkovich-zametki.com /Nomer41/SBelenky1.htm.

Patricia Blake, "Researching Babel's Biography: Adventures and Misadventures," in *The Enigma of Isaac Babel: Biography, History, Context*, ed. Gregory Freidin (Stanford, CA: Stanford University Press, 2009).

Valentin Domil', "Shagi Komandarma," *Zametki po Evreiskoi Istorii. Internet-Zhurnal Evreiskoi Istorii, Traditsii, Kul'tury*, ed. Evgenii Berkovich, no. 4 (53) (April 2005), accessed January 8, 2012, http://berkovich-zametki.com/2005 /Zametki/Nomer4/Domil1.htm.

Domil', "Babel' i Budennyi," Bibliotekar'.Ru, accessed January 8, 2012, http:// www.bibliotekar.ru/rus-Babel/29–2.htm.

Yury Dorfman, E-mail correspondence and telephone interview with Natalia Reshetova. Stanford; Chita, 2010.

Tamara Dubinskaia-Dzhalilova and Anatolii Chernev, eds., "Zhmu Vashu Ruku, Dorogoi Tovarishch": Perepiska Maksima Gor'kogo i Iosifa Stalina," *Novyi Mir*, 97 (1997), accessed January 10, 2012, http://magazines.russ.ru/novyi_mi/1997 /9/stalin.html.

Vadim Erlikhman, "Krasavitsa i Chudovishche," *Zhurnal "Kar'era,"* no. 9 (September 2000), accessed January 10, 2012, http://www.kariera.orc.ru/09–00 /Loveko68.html.

Josef Feigenberg, E-mail correspondence and telephone interview with Natalia Reshetova. Stanford; Jerusalem, 2012.

Vasilii S. Grossman, "Mama," in Vasilii S. Grossman, *Neskol'ko Pechal'nykh Dnei* (Moskva: Sovremennik, 1989), accessed September 3, 2012, http://lib.ru/PROZA /GROSSMAN/grossman20.txt.

Igal Halfin, *Stalinist Confessions: Messianism and Terror at the Leningrad Communist University* (Pittsburgh, PA: University of Pittsburgh Press, 2009).

Vladimir Khanelis, "Edinstvennyi moi bratik...," *My zdes'*, no. 311 (June 16–22, 2011), accessed September 12, 2012, http://newswe.com/index.php?go=Pages &in=view&id=3682.

Valerii Lebedev, ed. "Zapredel'nye Protokoly Doprosov. Spetssoobshchenie L.P. Berii I.V. Stalinu s Prilozheniem Zaiavleniia M. P. Frinovskogo, April 13, 1939, no. 1048/b," *Lebed'*, no. 616 (June 20, 2010), accessed January 10, 2012, http:// www.lebed.com/2010/default.htm.

Nikolai Molotok, "Vozobnovili Stroiku," *Izvestiia*, December 20, 2005, accessed January 8, 2012, http://www.izvestia.ru/news/309613.

Iurii I. Mukhin, "Zheny Marshalov," *Duel'*, no. 9 (March 2, 2004), accessed January 10, 2012, http://www.duel.ru/200409/?09_5_1.

Aleksei Pavliukov, *Ezhov: Biografiia* (Moskva: Zakharov, 2007).

Pavliukov, "Neizvestnyi Roman Sholokhova," *Ogonek*, no. 9 (4985) (February 26– March 4, 2007), accessed January 10, 2012, http://www.ogoniok.com/4985/33.

Nikita Petrov and Mark Iansen, *"Stalinskii Pitomets" – Nikolai Ezhov* (Moskva: ROSSPEN: Fond Pervogo Prezidenta Rossii B. N. Eltsina, 2008).

Nikita Petrov and Mark Jansen, *Stalin's Loyal Executioner: People's Commissar Nikolai Ezhov, 1895–1940* (Stanford, CA: Hoover Institution Press, 2002).

Aleksei Polianskii, *Ezhov: Istoriia "Zheleznogo" Stalinskogo Narkoma* (Moskva: Veche, ARIA-AiF, 2001).

Pravda, January 1, 1937.

Vladimir Shakhidzhanian, *Ia + Ia*, 1001.ru, accessed November 15, 2011, http:// 1001.ru/books/I+I/04_04_01.htm.

Erik Shur, "Reabilitiruiut li Ezhova?" *Mezhdunarodnyi Ezhemesiachnik "Sovershenno Sekretno,"* accessed January 3, 2012, http://www.sovsekretno.ru/magazines /article/166.

"Soobshchenie L. P. Berii I. V. Stalinu o N. I. Ezhove s Prilozheniem Protokola Doprosa, April 27, 1939, no. 1268/b," *Stalin: Vremia, Liudi, Imperiia*, accessed January 10, 2012, http://stalinism.ru/Dokumentyi/Soobschenie-L.P.-Berii-I.V. -Stalinu-o-N.I.-Ezhove-s-prilozheniem-protokola-doprosa.html.

USSR na Stroike (Moskva: OGIZ, 1930s).

Feliks Zin'ko, *"Mudryi Rebe": Ocherki* (Odessa: Pechatnyi Dom, 2008).

Aleksandr Taradai, "Semeinye tainy," *Zametki po Evreiskoi Istorii. Internet-Zhurnal Evreiskoi Istorii, Traditsii, Kul'tury*, ed. Evgenii Berkovich, in press (November, 2012), http://berkovich-zametki.com <http://berkovich-zametki.com /Nomer41/SBelenky1.htm>.

Taradai, "Starye fotografii," *Zametki po Evreiskoi Istorii. Internet-Zhurnal Evreiskoi Istorii, Traditsii, Kul'tury*, ed. Evgenii Berkovich, no. 123 (December 2009), accessed September 12, 2012, http://berkovich-zametki.com/2009/Zametki/Nomer20/Taradaj1.php.

Taradai, "Vetvi odnogo dereva," *Mishpoha*, no. 28, accessed September 12, 2012, http://mishpoha.org/n28/28a14.php.

ADILE (Chapters 6, 14, 20, 22)

Adile Abbas-ogly, *Ia Ne Mogu Zabyt'* (Moskva: AST, 2005).

Abbas-ogly, *Moia Abkhaziia ... Moia Sud'ba* (Moskva: AST, 2009).

Sergei Khrushchev, ed., *Memoirs of Nikita Khrushchev, vol. 1, Commissar, 1919–1945* (University Park, PA: Pennsylvania State University, 2004), 188–9.

N.A. (Nestor Apollonovich) Lakoba Papers, 1:1, 3, 7, 8, 10, 12, 15, 34; 2:1, 21, 28, 30, 41, Hoover Institution Archives (Stanford University, CA).

Robert Service, *Stalin: A Biography* (Cambridge, MA: Belknap Press of Harvard University Press, 2005), 296–7.

FEKLA (Chapters 7, 15, 21, 22)

Iurii N. Afanas'ev et al., *Istoriia Stalinskogo Gulaga: Konets 1920-kh – Pervaia Polovina 1950-kh Godov: Sobranie Dokumentov v Semi Tomakh*, vol. 1, *Massovye Repressii v SSSR* (Moskva: ROSSPEN, 2004), 94–95.

Fekla Andreeva, Telephone interview with Natalia Reshetova. Stanford; Kamensk-Ural'skii, 2012.

Fekla T. Andreeva, *Korni i Krony. Martiush,* vypusk 2 (Kamensk-Ural'skii, 2002).

Andreeva, *Spetsposelenie Martiush: Dokumental'naia Povest'* (Kurgan: Chastnoe Izdatel'stvo, 2004).

Andreeva, *Venok Pamiati Martiushovtsam* (Kamensk-Ural'skii, 2005).

Andreeva, *Istoriia Spetsposeleniia Martiush v Dokumentakh (1925–2006 gg.)* (Kamensk-Ural'skii, 2008).

Andreeva, *Istoriia Spetsposeleniia Martiush v Dokumentakh (1930–2007 gg.)* (Kamensk-Ural'skii, 2010).

Nina Chernykh, *Sinarskii GULAG* (Ekaterinburg: Bank Kul'turnoi Informatsii, 2004), 12–22.

Lynne Viola, *The Unknown Gulag: The Lost World of Stalin's Special Settlements* (Oxford: Oxford University Press, 2007), 104–110, 155.

Aleksei G. Tepliakov, *Mashina Terrora: OGPU-NKVD Sibiri v 1929–1941 gg.* (Moskva: Novyi Khronograf; AIRO-XXI, 2008), 274.

About the Author

PAUL R. GREGORY, a Hoover Institution research fellow, holds the Cullen Endowed Professorship in the Department of Economics at the University of Houston, Texas, and is a research professor at the German Institute for Economic Research in Berlin. He is also the chair of the International Advisory Board of the Kiev School of Economics. Gregory is the author of *Politics, Murder, and Love in Stalin's Kremlin: The Story of Nikolai Bukharin and Anna Larina* (2010), *Terror by Quota* (2009), *Lenin's Brain and Other Tales from the Secret Soviet Archives* (2008), and *The Political Economy of Stalinism* (2004), all based on his work in the Hoover Institution Archives. He has also coedited archival publications, such as the prize-winning seven-volume *History of Stalin's Gulag* (2004) and the three-volume *Stenograms of Meetings of the Politburo of the Central Committee* (2007). His publications have been awarded the Hewett Book Prize and the J.M. Montias Prize. Gregory is the coeditor of the Yale-Hoover series on Stalin, Stalinism, and the Cold War. He divides his time between Houston and Palo Alto, CA.

Index

Photo Sources

14: Agnessa S. Korovicheva; Marianna Yarovskaya.

23: Agnessa S. Korovicheva; Marianna Yarovskaya.

26: Agnessa S. Korovicheva; Marianna Yarovskaya.

31: Olga A. Ignatkina; Marianna Yarovskaya.

35: Olga A. Ignatkina; Marianna Yarovskaya.

44: Russian State Archive of Socio-Political History (RGASPI), Moscow; Nikita V. Petrov and Marc Jansen.

50: Adile Abbas-ogly; Marianna Yarovskaya.

52: Adile Abbas-ogly; Marianna Yarovskaya.

53: Adile Abbas-ogly; Marianna Yarovskaya.

54: Memed Dzhikhashvili; N. A. (Nestor Apollonovich) Lakoba Papers, Hoover Institution Archives.

55: Memed Dzhikhashvili; N. A. (Nestor Apollonovich) Lakoba Papers, Hoover Institution Archives.

56: Memed Dzhikhashvili; N. A. (Nestor Apollonovich) Lakoba Papers, Hoover Institution Archives.

62: Fekla T. Andreeva; Marianna Yarovskaya.

109: Previously published in Yury Ignatkin's book, *Rasskaz iz Tridtsat' Sed'mogo* (Chita: Reklamno-Informatsionnoe Agentstvo "Aziia," 1992); Olga A. Ignatkina; Yury V. Dorfman; Marianna Yarovskaya.

124: Adile Abbas-ogly; Marianna Yarovskaya.

127: "Anastasia Zueva, photographs, Soviet actresses," ANO Kino-Teatr, accessed December 5, 2012, http://www.kino-teatr.ru/kino/acter/w/sov/1663/foto/344581.

141: Fekla T. Andreeva; Marianna Yarovskaya.

191: Agnessa S. Korovicheva; Marianna Yarovskaya.

193: Agnessa S. Korovicheva; Marianna Yarovskaya.

197: Olga A. Ignatkina; Natalia P. Belova; Marianna Yarovskaya.

198: Olga A. Ignatkina; Marianna Yarovskaya.

199: Olga A. Ignatkina; Marianna Yarovskaya.

208: Adile Abbas-ogly; Marianna Yarovskaya.

211: Fekla T. Andreeva; Marianna Yarovskaya.

212: Fekla T. Andreeva; Marianna Yarovskaya.

214: Fekla T. Andreeva; Marianna Yarovskaya.

215: Fekla T. Andreeva; Ekaterina T. Karpova; Klavdia T. Poderina; Marianna Yarovskaya.

216: Fekla T. Andreeva; Marianna Yarovskaya.